VIBRATIONAL SHIFT

A GLOBAL AWAKENING TO 5TH DIMENSIONAL CONSCIOUSNESS

BY

DR. KAY VONNE CASON-TURNER

SBPC

SIMMS BOOKS PUBLISHING CORP.

Publishers Since 2012

Published By Simms Books Publishing

Jonesboro, GA

2023924239

Library of Congress Cataloging in Publication Data

Dr. Kay Vonne Cason-Turner

VIBRATIONAL SHIFT

A GLOBAL AWAKENING TO 5TH DIMENSIONAL CONSCIOUSNESS

ISBN: 978-1-949433-57-9

Printed in the United States of America

Book cover and editing by- Emmany_Clair

TABLE OF CONTENTS

CHAPTER 1

WHISPERED WISDOM — SHANIA'S AWAKENING AND THE PROMISE OF TRANSCENDENCE

Shania was born into a family that was critical of her, and her unique qualities were often misunderstood. From a young age, she felt a deep sense of disconnection, as if she didn't quite fit into the mold her family had carved for her. While her parents urged her to conform and embrace a more conventional path, Shania couldn't help but feel drawn to something greater, something beyond the confines of societal expectations.

As a child, she possessed an inherent sensitivity and a profound ability to perceive energies and emotions in those around her. It was as if she could read the very essence of people, discerning their true nature beyond what was visible to the naked eye. But her family, unable to comprehend her gifts, dismissed them as mere imagination or flights of fancy.

In the gentle embrace of solitude, when the world quieted, Shania often found herself immersed in a sacred stillness. During these times, she would talk to The Creator. At other times, she would hear whispers from the ethereal realm beckoning her. Amongst those whispers was the voice of Serena. With her ethereal presence and wise guidance, Serena was none other than the embodiment of Shania's Higher Self, the elevated aspect of her being that transcended time and space, guiding her towards enlightenment and the fulfillment of her soul's purpose. Serena's whispers resonated with familiarity, a guiding force from the realms of expanded consciousness.

One day, burdened by the weight of feeling misunderstood and alone, Shania poured her heart out to Serena, seeking solace in their connection. With a voice tinged with sadness, Shania confided in Serena about her struggles with her family, "They don't understand me."

Serena's response flowed with a river of warmth and understanding, gently enfolding Shania's tender heart in a loving embrace. Each word carried the weight of countless souls who had walked similar paths. "You are not alone, dear one," Serena whispered, her voice a gentle caress. "Throughout time, many have come before you, bearing unique gifts that challenge the limitations of the world. Through your personal journey, you will pave the way for others to follow."

In those sacred moments, Shania felt the weight of her loneliness ease, as if a ray of sunlight had pierced through the darkest clouds. Serena's presence, like a guiding star, reassured her that her struggles were not in vain, but rather an essential part of her purpose. The recognition that she was not the only one to have felt this way, that others had faced similar challenges and emerged triumphant, ignited a flicker of hope within Shania's weary soul.

In the tender sway of night, Serena's ethereal voice whispered, "Shania," carrying a sense of mystique and anticipation. "A time is drawing near, dear one, when the intricacies of 3rd dimensional, 4th dimensional, and 5th dimensional consciousness will unfold before you, revealing the hidden depths of existence." You will understand the barriers that hold humanity back from experiencing the fullness of their divine potential." Serena's words resonated deep within Shania's soul, offering glimpses of a future where humanity could transcend the limitations of 3D consciousness and embrace a more enlightened way of being.

Shania's heart danced with a symphony of excitement, each beat resonating with the exhilaration of what lay ahead. She leaned in, her whole being attuned to Serena's words, eager to immerse herself in the depths of this transformative knowledge. The prospect of unlocking the wisdom necessary to become a beacon of light for others on their path towards 5th-dimensional consciousness ignited a fire within Shania's soul. It was a calling that infused her existence with purpose, a mission that would shape the very fabric of her being.

Serena's whispers persisted, carrying a tantalizing promise in their ethereal tones. "But be patient, dear one," her voice whispered, laced with a hint of enigmatic allure. "As your life's journey unfolds, a tapestry of events will weave together in a symphony of synchronicity. Watch closely for the signs and synchronicities that dance across your path, for they hold the keys to the profound understanding you seek."

Shania's spirit was ablaze with a renewed sense of aliveness, radiating a resolute intention that shimmered in her eyes. She understood that the path that lay before her was veiled in thrilling anticipation and an enigmatic allure. It was a transformative quest that beckoned her to become a catalyst for humanity's liberation, to help others transcend the confines of 3rd-dimensional consciousness and enter into the realm of light and expanded awareness.

Though Shania's understanding of the intricate dimensions of consciousness was limited, she held a profound knowing that embracing 5th-dimensional consciousness would usher in a transformative shift towards a life of serenity and unity, free from the constraints of 3D consciousness that hindered growth, peace, and love.

With Serena as her guide, Shania began to embrace the journey that lay before her, trusting in the synchronicities that would unfold along the way. The mysteries of 3D, 4D, and 5D consciousness summoned her, and she was ready to unveil their secrets and share them with the world.

CHAPTER 2

THE DOUBLE-EDGED SWORD — SHANIA'S VISIONS AND HER CALL TO ACTION

Shania continued her journey of self-discovery and spiritual growth, guided by the whispers of Serena and her connection with The Creator. However, her heightened sensitivity often proved to be a double-edged sword. While she possessed a remarkable ability to perceive energies and emotions, it also meant she absorbed the pain and struggles of those around her.

Yet, there existed another dimension to Shania's spiritual experiences, one that extended beyond the boundaries of her inner world. Shania would often have vivid visions, glimpses into alternate dimensions and the interconnectedness of all things. These visions provided her with a profound understanding of the suffering and struggles of humanity. She witnessed the pain and heaviness that weighed upon people's hearts and yearned to alleviate their burdens.

In the depths of her solitude, Shania often finds herself overwhelmed by the visions. These visions painted a stark picture of destruction, isolation, and the consequences of humanity remaining entrenched in 3D consciousness. She saw cities crumble, forests wither, and hearts shrouded in darkness. She saw marriages and relationships caught in a cycle of trauma and drama. Shania saw visions of children being led astray by a world of hidden agendas. Shania had visions of governments aligned with dark forces, veiling underlying intentions to manipulate and control the masses. The weight of these visions pressed upon her like an unyielding burden.

The visions were not always easy to bear. They showed her the potential for immense destruction and the depths of darkness that humanity could sink into. But they also revealed glimpses of light, the potential for profound transformation and the inherent goodness that resided within each individual. These contrasting visions left Shania with an unshakable belief that a shift in consciousness was necessary, and that humanity had the power to transcend its limitations and create a world of harmony and unity.

One particular vision seared itself into Shania's consciousness, sending her spiraling into a storm of fear and desperation. She saw a world ravaged by unchecked greed, virulent hatred, and profound division. Communities lay fragmented, people entrapped in endless rounds of agonizing anguish, and the very Earth seemed to shudder under the egregious indifference of mankind. The apocalyptic panorama left her breathless, instilling within her an overwhelming sense of obligation to intervene and shift the course of destiny.

As she struggled with the weight of her visions, Shania continued to seek solace in her connection with Serena and The Creator. "Why do I see such destruction and despair?" she asked, her voice tinged with anguish. Serena's response was gentle yet firm. "These visions are not meant to paralyze you, dear one. They are a call to action, a reminder of the urgency to help humanity awaken and embrace the path to 5D consciousness."

The Creator's voice, filled with infinite compassion, echoed in Shania's soul. "You carry the vision of a world transformed, Shania. It is through your understanding and empathy that you will inspire others to transcend their limitations and create a reality rooted in love and harmony."

Though the heaviness of her visions often left her feeling isolated, Shania knew deep within her being that she was not alone.

She was part of a collective journey, interconnected with souls who shared her purpose. With this realization, she resolved to use her gifts to positively impact the world and alleviate the suffering she had witnessed in her visions.

With a fiery resolve burning within her, Shania fully embraced the profound significance of transitioning from 3D to 5D consciousness, recognizing it as a pivotal step on humanity's journey of transformation. She understood that this journey was not solely about her personal growth but about uplifting humanity as a whole. She saw herself as a visionary, a bridge between the realms of higher consciousness and the physical world, a catalyst for transformation.

Armed with this newfound clarity and purpose, Shania took a deep breath, gathering the strength to step forward into the unknown. The path ahead would not be without its challenges, but she was ready to face them head-on. She would become a beacon of light in a world seeking illumination, using her visions to inspire and guide others towards a higher state of being.

CHAPTER 3

AWAKENING THE EMPATH: EMBRACING THE POWER WITHIN

As each day unfolded, Shania's spiritual experiences intensified, her sensitivity heightened, and her empathic nature grew stronger. With each passing moment, she became more attuned to the subtle, energetic currents that flowed around her.

The waves of emotions and energies from others crashed upon Shania like a tumultuous sea, threatening to drown her in their relentless force. Overwhelmed, she sought solace, seeking refuge, in the loving embrace of The Creator. During these sacred interludes, Shania's heart poured forth its deepest longings, and in return, the divine presence enveloped her, offering solace and understanding.

In the solitude of these divine encounters, Shania found sanctuary. Her heart whispered its most profound desires, and The Creator listened, responding with love and guidance. In moments of vulnerability, Shania discovered a profound truth: whenever she sought The Creator, a guiding hand would always be extended to her. The Creator's presence became a steadfast anchor, offering unwavering support as she navigated the currents of her transformational journey.

As the swirling currents of life's energies continued to impact Shania, she found herself standing at a pivotal crossroad, a sacred juncture where the call to master the art of navigating the ebb and flow of emotions and waves of energy became resoundingly clear. The time had arrived, for she had often found herself overwhelmed by the relentless surges of energetic forces. In this profound moment of awakening, Shania's heart now embraced the realization that she needed to learn how to gracefully navigate the tumultuous seas that threatened to engulf her sensitive soul.

Sensing her readiness, Serena materialized in her ethereal form, casting a luminous presence that seemed to radiate wisdom and guidance. It was a pivotal moment in Shania's journey, where the convergence of her own readiness and Serena's celestial intervention set the stage for profound transformation and self-discovery. Serena's voice, soft and gentle, whispered to Shania, conveying the significance of the moment. "Shania, my dear, the time has arrived for you to set forth on the transformative path of self-discovery and understanding of your empathic nature. Together, we shall navigate the depths of your empathic abilities with grace and strength. We will ensure that these gifts do not overwhelm you but become a wellspring of empowerment and healing."

Serena's ethereal voice flowed like a river of guidance and wisdom, enveloping Shania's being with a palpable sense of purpose. "Shania, it is essential for you to delve deep into the depths of your empathic abilities," Serena expressed with a tone of gentle authority. "In this exploration, you will come to comprehend the vast tapestry of emotions and energies that you have the power to perceive and influence. As an empath, you possess a powerful sacred gift that holds within it the potential for profound healing and transformation, not only for yourself but for all those you encounter on your path."

Shania's heart swelled with anticipation, knowing that this knowledge would empower her to navigate the challenging dynamics of absorbing others' energy without being overwhelmed by it. She yearned to discover the ways in which she could maintain her own energetic boundaries and protect her precious auric field.

"Through our journey together, I will teach you the sacred techniques and practices that will allow you to be in the midst of negativity without absorbing the negative energy," Serena continued, her voice enveloping Shania like a comforting embrace. "You will learn how to shield yourself energetically, creating a sacred space within you that remains untouched by external influences."

Shania listened intently, understanding the importance of this lesson in her life. Being an empath had its challenges, but Serena's guidance offered a beacon of hope and a path to inner strength.

"As we explore the depths of your empathic nature, I will show you how to block the energy that does not serve you, how to protect your own auric field, and how to cleanse it when needed," Serena added, her words carrying the weight of profound understanding. "You have been gifted with this ability for a reason, and it is crucial that you learn to harness its power in service of your own well-being and the well-being of others."

Shania's spirit tingled with anticipation, ready to embark on this transformative journey alongside Serena. With her guidance and the sacred teachings that awaited her, she knew that she would grow into her empathic gifts and become a beacon of love and compassion, radiating light in the midst of darkness.

With a renewed sense of purpose and an unwavering trust in Serena's guidance, Shania stood at the threshold of her empathic journey. She felt a burning passion within her, fueled by the knowledge that she was meant to assist others on their spiritual paths. Guided by Serena's gentle whispers and armed with a deep desire to facilitate the collective shift from 3D to 5D consciousness, Shania prepared herself to embark on a sacred mission of transformation and enlightenment. The world awaited her gifts, and she was ready to embrace her role as a catalyst for change.

But as Shania stood on the threshold of this new chapter in her life, she couldn't help but feel a mix of excitement and trepidation. The path ahead was unknown and filled with challenges, but she was determined to follow the whispers of her soul and embrace her calling. Little did she know that this journey would not only transform the lives of others but also lead her to a profound realization of her own inner power and purpose.

As the dawn broke on a new day, Shania took a deep breath, ready to step into the unknown and embrace the extraordinary adventure that lay ahead. With Serena's words echoing in her mind, she whispered, "I am ready."

So, Shania's journey to awaken the world began.

CHAPTER 4

UNVEILING THE SACRED TEACHINGS: HARNESSING THE POWER OF ENERGY

In preparation for the purpose that awaited her, Shania embarked on a sacred journey of learning and growth under the gentle guidance of Serena. With her ethereal presence, Serena unveiled a myriad of transformative practices, equipping Shania with the tools she needed to effectively navigate the intricate dance of emotions and waves of energy that she would encounter. With each step, Shania unraveled the mysteries of her empathic nature, absorbing Serena's wisdom like a thirsty sponge.

Meditation became Shania's refuge, a sacred space where she could ground herself and release the weight of emotions that didn't belong to her. Through breathwork and visualization, she learned to create a protective shield around her energy field, allowing her to maintain her inner balance and peace amidst the chaos. Equally important, during moments of vulnerability, Shania still sought solace in her connection with The Creator, pouring out her heart and finding comfort in the divine presence that enveloped her.

With each passing lesson, Shania's connection with Serena deepened, their energies intertwining in a dance of growth and transformation. Serena's whispers carried the wisdom of ancient realms, nurturing Shania's understanding of her empathic gifts and empowering her to navigate the vast tapestry of energies that surrounded her. As Shania delved deeper into these sacred arts, she would soon emerge as a radiant force, ready to embrace her calling and guide others on their own transformative paths.

Serena imparted to Shania the profound wisdom of nature's healing energy, and, as a healing balm for her sensitive soul, nature, too, became Shania's sanctuary. She would sometimes seek solace in the embrace of ancient trees, allowing their grounded energy to wash away the residue of negativity. The rhythmic sound of flowing water and the gentle touch of the wind on her skin reminded her of the interconnectedness of all things, soothing her spirit and replenishing her energy.

Serena taught Shania about cultivating a deep connection with her intuition, learning to discern which energies were hers to carry and which ones she needed to release. She discovered the power of setting boundaries, both energetically and in her physical interactions, allowing her to protect her own energy and maintain a sense of personal sovereignty.

Through Serena's guidance and the illumination of her spiritual teachings, Shania reached a profound realization that reverberated through the deepest recesses of her being. With each practice embraced and each step taken on her transformative journey, she came more to the realization that her empathic abilities were not a burden to bear, but a radiant gift bestowed upon her by the universe. In this newfound understanding, Shania began to cherish her empathic nature, harnessing its power and ready to use it to uplift others and contribute to the greater good of humanity.

She realized that her sensitivity allowed her to bridge the gap between individuals, fostering understanding, compassion, and healing. As Shania delved deeper into her spiritual journey, she understood that knowledge alone was not enough; she needed to embody the teachings and gain wisdom through direct experience. With unwavering dedication, she devoted herself to diligent practice, immersing herself in the art of sacred knowledge. Shania's desire was not merely to learn, but to master the transformative power that lay within these practices.

With each experience and lesson, Shania grew stronger and more attuned to the subtle energies that danced around her. She embraced her role as a guide and healer, committed to using her gifts to support others on their own path of self-discovery and transformation.

As a result of her teachings guided by Serena, Shania learned how to set energetic boundaries as a means to protect her own energy and maintain a sense of personal sovereignty. She learned that without clear boundaries, she would be susceptible to absorbing the energies and emotions of others, which could lead to emotional exhaustion and a loss of her own sense of self.

To establish these energetic boundaries, Shania was taught to practice visualization techniques that allowed her to create a protective shield around her energy field. During her meditation sessions, she would imagine a radiant bubble of light surrounding her, acting as a filter to prevent the entry of any unwanted energies. This bubble of light served as a sacred boundary, ensuring that only energies aligned with her highest good could enter her space.

Serena also taught Shania how to influence the energy around her. Guided by Serena's ethereal wisdom, Shania delved into the profound art of influencing the energetic currents that coursed

19

through her very being. She learned to visualize a luminous, crystalline channel, shimmering with vibrant hues, gracefully flowing from the crown of her head to the soles of her feet. With focused intention, she could regulate the ebb and flow of this divine energy, consciously adjusting the speed and intensity as needed. Through this sacred practice, Shania discovered the delicate dance of harmonizing her internal energy with external forces, maintaining a dynamic equilibrium that allowed her to navigate the world with grace and empowerment.

Furthermore, as Shania continued her studies, she learned to trust her intuition as a guiding compass in establishing boundaries. She developed a keen sense of discernment, being able to differentiate between energies that were aligned with her growth and those that were draining or disruptive. By listening to her inner voice and honoring her intuitive guidance, she could gracefully step away from situations or individuals that compromised her energetic well-being.

In her interactions with others, Shania practiced assertiveness and clear communication to establish and maintain her boundaries. She became comfortable expressing her needs, setting limits, and graciously declining requests or activities that did not align with her energetic state. By communicating her boundaries with compassion and respect, she fostered healthier relationships and created space for authentic connections based on mutual understanding and respect.

Through these practices, Shania created a harmonious balance between her empathic nature and her need for energetic self-care. She recognized that by setting boundaries, she was not closing herself off from others but rather honoring her own well-being and ensuring that she could continue to serve as a beacon of light and healing for herself and others.

With her energetic boundaries in place, Shania walked her path with a renewed sense of empowerment and inner strength. She knew that she could navigate the world with an open heart and a clear mind, embracing her role as a guide and healer while maintaining a strong connection to her own essence and personal sovereignty.

CHAPTER 5

THE SACRED TEACHINGS CONTINUE: TRANSMUTATION AND CLEANSING

As Shania's divine odyssey further unfolded, Serena imparted deeper knowledge, guiding her to adeptly command the profound potential inherent in energy. Serena unveiled the profound technique of transmuting the dense, negative energies that she absorbed into a radiant force of love and light. With each breath, Shania envisioned herself as a vessel of divine transformation, channeling the stagnant energy through the depths of her being. In her mind's eye, she witnessed the darkness dissolve, replaced by a luminous radiance that emanated from her very core. As she breathed out, a gentle wave of healing energy surged forth, enveloping all in its path with a soothing embrace of compassion and serenity. Through this sacred alchemy, Shania discovered the extraordinary power within her to transmute the shadows of despair into a radiant beacon of love, illuminating the world with its divine essence. She understood that holding onto the negativity would only weigh her down and hinder her own growth, so she made a conscious choice to transform it into something positive and healing.

When Shania felt the weight of negative energy, whether it was from her own experiences or from the emotions of others, she would take a deep breath and center herself in the present moment. Embracing her sacred process, Shania employed the transformative technique of transmuting the dense negative energy within her being.

Shania intended to transmute the darkness into light, the fear into love, and the pain into compassion. Profoundly impacted by the newfound ability she had acquired, Shania experienced a powerful transformation. This sacred practice empowered her to no longer be overcome by the weight of negativity. With every breath, she felt the energetic shift within herself and witnessed the ripple effect of her transmutation spreading outwards.

Even in moments of absorption, Shania would also engage in various energy healing practices to facilitate the transmutation process. She learned how to use visualization, Reiki, and sound healing to channel the transformative power of love and infuse it into the absorbed negativity. Through these modalities, she could release stagnant energy, balance the energetic flow, and bring about a sense of harmony and well-being.

In the realm of Shania's spiritual journey, she delved into the transformative power of sound healing, a sacred practice that allowed her to channel the essence of love and infuse it into the absorbed negativity. Guided by Serena's wisdom, she learned the art of using various resonant sounds and vibrations to create a harmonious symphony within her being.

With sound healing, Shania learned to immerse herself in the healing melodies through the gentle tones of crystal singing bowls, the reverberating sounds of Tibetan singing bowls, or the soothing chants and mantras that carried ancient wisdom. As the ethereal sounds washed over her, they resonated with the deepest layers of her being, dissolving the dense energy and creating a harmonious resonance of love and light.

With each gentle hum or melodic note, Shania felt the vibrations permeate her entire being, reaching every cell and energy center within. The potent frequencies penetrated the absorbed negativity, unraveling its grip and allowing it to be gently released. As the transformative power of love flowed through the sound waves, it transmuted the darkness into a luminous radiance that enveloped Shania's being.

Through the practice of sound healing, Shania discovered that she held within her the ability to transform the energy she absorbed. She understood that when channeled through sound, love could transmute even the densest negativity into a harmonious resonance of healing and restoration. This sacred art became an integral part of her journey, empowering her to navigate the waves of life with grace and imbue every interaction with the transformative power of love.

Furthermore, Shania learned the importance of self-care and replenishing her own energy reserves after transmuting negative energy. She would immerse herself in activities that nourished her soul, such as spending time in nature, journaling, engaging in the practice of meditation or other creative activities. By nurturing herself, she ensured that she remained in a state of energetic alignment and could continue to transmute energy from a place of abundance and strength.

In this way, Shania's empathic nature became a powerful tool for alchemy, where she transformed negativity into love and offered it back to the world. She recognized that transmutation was not only a personal practice but also a way to contribute to the collective consciousness, infusing it with the healing vibrations of love, compassion, and light.

Through her commitment to transmutation, Shania embraced her role as a catalyst for positive change. She saw herself as an emissary of love, weaving her unique, energetic signature into the fabric of the universe. Her ability to transmute negative energy into love became a profound expression of her empathic gifts and a testament to the transformative power of compassion and healing.

Further, as an empath, Shania needed to learn the importance of energetic cleansing to maintain the balance and harmony of her auric field. Under Serena's guidance, Shania learned the art of indulging in sacred baths, immersing herself in the cleansing waters to rejuvenate her mind, body, and spirit... Serena taught her about seeking solace and purification through the ritual of spiritual baths, immersing herself in the transformative power of water and intention.

In the serenity of her sacred space, Shania prepared her spiritual bath with utmost care. She filled the tub with warm water, infused with the essence of her chosen oils—fragrant notes of frankincense and myrrh, known for their purifying and protective properties. The aroma filled the air, creating an atmosphere of tranquility and sacredness.

Before stepping into the water, Shania took a moment to center herself. She closed her eyes, took a deep breath, and recited a protection prayer that invoked the divine energies to surround and shield her. With each word spoken, she felt the presence of higher forces gathering around her, creating a shield of light and love.

As she eased into the water, Shania could feel the subtle energetic currents washing over her, enveloping her in a cocoon of cleansing energy. The oils mingled with the water, caressing her skin and permeating her senses, heightening her connection to the sacred space she had created.

To amplify the energy and frequency of the bath, Shania was taught to occasionally add specific crystals to the water. Crystals like clear quartz, rose quartz or amethyst were carefully chosen to enhance the purifying and healing qualities of the bath. These crystals radiated their unique vibrations, infusing the water with their transformative energy.

As she soaked in the soothing embrace of the bath, Shania surrendered to the healing waters, allowing them to gently wash away any stagnant or negative energies that had accumulated within her auric field. She visualized the water as a purifying river, carrying away all traces of emotional residue and restoring her energetic balance.

With each passing moment, Shania felt a profound sense of release and renewal. The energy of the oils, the power of the protection prayer, and the resonance of the crystals merged into a symphony of healing vibrations, penetrating every layer of her being.

As the spiritual bath came to an end, Shania emerged from the water with a renewed sense of clarity and vitality. She wrapped herself in a soft towel, feeling the echoes of the purifying energies still shimmering within and around her. She knew that this sacred ritual had cleansed not only her physical body but also her auric field, restoring her energetic well-being.

With gratitude in her heart, Shania embraced the power of spiritual baths as a regular practice in her empathic journey. Through these intentional acts of self-care, she found solace, protection, and a deeper connection to her empathic nature. The spiritual bath ritual became a sacred space where she could cleanse, recharge, and fortify her sensitive soul, ready to face the world with strength and compassion once again.

As Shania embraced her true nature as an empath, she carried with her the wisdom and resilience she gained from her early life and spiritual experiences. She knew that her empathic nature was a vital aspect of her being, a beacon of light that would illuminate the way for those seeking solace, understanding, and a deeper connection with their own inner truth. With a deep sense of confidence, Shania embraced her role in guiding humanity towards the transformative shift from 3rd to 5th dimensional consciousness.

CHAPTER 6

AURA VISIONS: A SHIFT IN PERSPECTIVE

As Shania's spiritual journey continued to unfold, the universe orchestrated a symphony of synchronistic events, leading her to a profound discovery that would forever shape her destiny. On that fateful day, Shania found herself walking through the bustling city streets, her mind preoccupied with the thoughts of her day ahead. Just as she was about to turn a corner, she bumped into an old friend she hadn't seen in years, who excitedly shared news of a metaphysical fair happening nearby. Intrigued by this unexpected encounter, Shania felt a tingling sensation, as if the universe was nudging her in a specific direction.

Trusting the guidance, she decided to follow the flow and made her way to the fairgrounds. As she entered the fair, her eyes were immediately drawn to a radiant display of colors and enchanting lights. It was the aura photography booth, glowing with an otherworldly allure. Simultaneously, Shania's cell phone rang, and to her surprise, it was a good friend on the line, telling her about the very same fair. It felt as if the universe was reinforcing its message, urging her to explore the mysteries of unseen energies.

In the midst of the bustling metaphysical fair, as Shania stood there in awe of the vibrant display, a hushed conversation reached her ears. Two strangers nearby shared their tales of profound encounters with aura photography, recounting their experiences amidst the mystical landscapes of Sedona, Arizona. Intrigue filled the air, and as Shania turned her head towards the voices, her gaze met that of one of the women. In that fleeting moment, their eyes locked, and a warm smile passed between them, radiating a profound sense of connection and resonance that stirred something deep within Shania's being. It was as if the universe had orchestrated this encounter, affirming her path towards the transformative power of aura photography.

As Shania gracefully approached the aura photography booth, her eyes were immediately drawn to its mesmerizing display of photographs, captivating her with a tapestry of colors and energies. A profound sense of intrigue and purpose washed over her as if the universe itself had orchestrated this moment, aligning the threads of her destiny. Serena's teachings echoed in her mind, urging her to embrace the signs and synchronicities that gracefully crossed her path. With each event unfolding, Shania knew deep in her soul that these were not mere coincidences, but deliberate guideposts on her transformative journey at the metaphysical fair.

Before her, the aura photography camera beckoned, its presence radiating an otherworldly charm that seemed to whisper directly to Shania's soul. A profound connection was forged in an instant, as if the camera carried within it the power to reveal hidden dimensions of existence. In that exhilarating moment, a surge of excitement coursed through Shania's veins, fueling her anticipation as she lifted the camera. It was a vessel overflowing with infinite possibilities, beckoning her to explore the ethereal realms captured within its lens.

The camera's capabilities were revealed to Shania as she engaged in a conversation with the photographer, Lucas. She was captivated by his descriptions of the camera's extraordinary features, and her excitement grew with each word he spoke. Lucas elucidated to Shania the uniqueness of this particular aura camera, distinguishing it from commonplace models. Crafted by an engineer whose fascination with aura photography spurred him to innovate, the device was a breakthrough, transcending the capabilities of existing equipment. The creator, having made only five such devices, had since pivoted to new ventures. Due to his familial ties with Lucas, two of these specialized cameras had ended up in Lucas's possession — one for personal use and another available for purchase.

"It's truly remarkable, Shania," Lucas exclaimed, his eyes sparkling with enthusiasm. "This camera has the ability to capture the energy fields emanating from every living being in a way that no other models are able to produce. It's like a window into the soul, a visual representation of their inner essence."

Shania's heart raced with anticipation, her mind buzzing with possibilities. The camera held the power to unveil the invisible, to bring to light the subtle energy patterns that flowed within and around each individual. It was a revelation that struck a deep chord within her, resonating with her vision of transformation and awakening.

"How does it work, Lucas?" Shania asked, her voice filled with awe. "How can it capture something as intangible as energy fields?"

Lucas smiled, sensing Shania's curiosity and genuine intrigue. "It's a combination of advanced technology and the understanding that everything in this world is interconnected. The camera is designed to detect and translate the subtle electromagnetic frequencies emitted by living beings. It then translates these frequencies into visual representations that we can perceive."

Shania's eyes widened as she grasped the significance of Lucas' words. The camera was not just a tool for capturing images; It was a portal to a deeper reality, a way to reveal the hidden truths that lay beneath the surface. It held the potential to illuminate the energetic dynamics of relationships, to capture the essence of a person's being in a single frame.

"I can't even begin to imagine the impact this could have," Shania said, her voice filled with wonder. "Imagine being able to visually witness the energetic shifts that occur during moments of healing, during moments of profound transformation. This camera could serve as a catalyst for change, as a means to facilitate deeper understanding and growth."

Lucas nodded, his own excitement mirrored in his eyes. "That's exactly what I believe, Shania. This camera has the potential to empower individuals to help them see the beauty and complexity of their own energy fields. It can provide tangible evidence of the subtle shifts that occur as people embark on their journeys of self-discovery and awakening."

Shania's mind raced with possibilities. She imagined using the camera to capture the radiant auras of individuals as they embraced their true potential, to document the transformational journeys of those who crossed her path. It was a tool that could bridge the gap between the seen and the unseen, offering a tangible visual representation of the profound inner work taking place.

As she held the camera in her hands, Shania felt a surge of inspiration and purpose. She knew that this newfound ability could be the key to unlocking hidden truths and facilitating profound transformation. It was a responsibility she eagerly embraced, fueled by a deep understanding that her sacred work was about to take on a whole new dimension. Ignited by her profound knowing, she took the leap and acquired the camera, embracing the potential it held within its sleek frame. In that pivotal moment, a surge of excitement surged through her veins, propelling her towards a future brimming with untapped magic and transformative encounters.

CHAPTER 7

THE SHUTTER'S SYMPHONY: UNVEILING SOULS THROUGH AURA PHOTOGRAPHY

Filled with a newfound purpose, Shania embarked on a journey to master the art of aura photography. She studied the intricacies of the camera, delving into the depths of its capabilities. With the addition of a tripod and carefully arranged lighting, Shania eagerly captured images. Each click of the shutter unveiled a kaleidoscope of colors, patterns, and vibrations that were invisible to the naked eye but held a profound significance in the realm of energy.

Shania focused on self-portraits, an avenue for honing her skills and discovering the camera's settings that would yield the most captivating results. The camera's unique polaroid-like feature, where the images were developed on special paper, added a sense of wonder to the process. It was an unexpected journey for Shania, who had previously only captured the beauty of nature through her lens. Driven by an unwavering determination, Shania's excitement swelled, propelling her to master the art of photography so that she could skillfully capture the essence of her subjects.

As Shania immersed herself in the study of her photographs, a whole new world unfolded before Shania's discerning eyes. With her empathic ability, she not only saw the colors, patterns, and vibrations captured by the camera, but she could feel them with every fiber of her being. It was as if a symphony of emotions played within her as she intuitively interpreted the meaning behind each shade, each intricate pattern, and each subtle vibration. Awe and amazement filled her as she realized the extent of her newfound ability to unlock the secrets held within the photographs. It was a remarkable journey of self-discovery, where she witnessed the intimate dance between her soul and the visual language of the images.

As Shania studied one of her photographs, a mesmerizing array of colors, patterns, and vibrations unfolded before her perceptive gaze like a swirling symphony of energy. The vivid hues of red and orange revealed the passionate fire that burned within her soul, igniting her creative spirit and fueling her drive for exploration. The calming blues and greens whispered of tranquility and a deep connection to nature, reminding her of the profound healing power of the natural world. Patterns of spirals and waves mirrored the twists and turns of her life's journey, symbolizing growth, transformation, and the constant flow of energy. Through the gentle vibrations captured in each image, Shania could sense the ebb and flow of her emotions, the intensity of her joys and sorrows, and the subtle nuances of her energetic field. It was as if the camera had become a portal to the depths of her being, revealing layers of herself she had yet to fully explore. The photographs became a mirror of her soul, reflecting her essence back to her with remarkable clarity and insight.

Shania started photographing people who were on a spiritual path. These were individuals she had met at various spiritual gatherings. With each photography session, Shania was astounded by the revelations that unfolded. With her intuitive sensitivity, Shania effortlessly perceived the energies and emotions emanating from the aura photographs, skillfully unraveling the revelations they held, much like she had done with her own captivating images. The aura photographs revealed layers of emotions, past experiences, and subconscious patterns. They acted as a mirror, reflecting the innermost truths that individuals often concealed from the world and even themselves.

The impact of the aura photographs was nothing short of extraordinary. As Shania presented the images to her subjects and explained the dynamics that she perceived, Shania witnessed their reactions—awe, surprise, and a profound sense of recognition. It was as if the photographs unveiled a part of themselves that had long been buried or forgotten—a profound insight that shook them to the core.

The aura photographs became a catalyst for deep introspection and self-realization. Shania began to assist individuals with confronting their fears, insecurities, and limiting beliefs. The photographs acted as a roadmap, guiding them toward their true potential and the path to 5D consciousness.

Shania's excitement grew with each transformative experience. She was beginning to realize that her unique gifts really could assist others in their own journey of awakening and self-discovery. The aura photographs became a wonderful tool for healing, empowerment, and spiritual growth—a tangible reminder that the human experience encompasses more than meets the eye.

During a tranquil evening, as Shania immersed herself in a sacred spiritual bath, allowing the warm water to cleanse her auric field after days of intense aura photography sessions, Serena's gentle whispers began to resonate in her mind. With her eyes closed, Shania felt the soothing caress of the water against her skin, a meditative ambiance enveloping her senses.

As Shania luxuriated in the comforting embrace of the spiritual bath, Serena's voice softly permeated her consciousness, carrying a tone of gentle authority. "Shania, dear one, the time has come to manifest a dedicated space for your photography work," Serena whispered. "More people will be drawn to your services, seeking your guidance and assistance. Create a studio infused with sacred energy, a sanctuary that radiates tranquility, love, and healing vibrations. Let the space become a harmonious blend of soft lighting, soothing aromas, and the beauty of nature. As your clients enter, they should feel an immediate sense of serenity and trust, knowing they are in the presence of a compassionate guide. This ambiance will deepen the impact of your work and nurture the transformations that will unfold."

As Serena's words resonated within Shania's being, she felt a surge of excitement and gratitude. With her voice filled with anticipation, Shania replied, "Serena, I am grateful for your guidance. I will find the perfect studio space, one that exudes the sacred ambiance you've described. It will be a sanctuary where people can experience a sense of safety and support as they embark upon their transformative journeys. I will infuse the space with love and intention, incorporating soft lighting, calming scents, and elements of nature to create a harmonious atmosphere. Thank you for showing me the path forward." Shania's heart swelled with determination as she visualized the studio taking shape, knowing that it would serve as a refuge for those seeking inner healing and guidance.

CHAPTER 8

DESTINY'S NUDGE: THE BIRTH OF A SANCTUARY

One day, in a twist of fate, Shania found herself taking a walk through the bustling city streets when a vibrant mural caught her eye. Intrigued, she paused to admire the artwork, completely unaware that destiny was at play. As she continued her journey, a gust of wind suddenly blew a flyer towards her, adorned with the words "Affordable Studio Space Available." She tucked it away, thinking it was a mere coincidence.

Days later, Shania found herself in a lively café, engrossed in conversation with a friend. The topic shifted to photography, and a stranger sitting at the neighboring table couldn't help but overhear. Engaging in the conversation, the stranger shared stories of their own photography journey and mentioned a hidden gem of a studio space that had recently become available.

Curiosity sparked within Shania, and she followed the stranger's lead, embarking on a spontaneous adventure through the city's winding streets. The path seemed to twist and turn, leading her to an old brownstone building with an unassuming "For

Rent" sign. As she stepped inside, she was greeted by an unexpected scene: sunlight streaming through a cracked window, casting a golden glow on the worn wooden floors. Shania could feel the space pulsating with potential.

In that moment, a memory resurfaced in Shania's mind—a whisper from Serena about the significance of synchronistic events. It was then that she realized the magnitude of the path that had led her to this very spot. With renewed excitement and determination, Shania took hold of the opportunity, she rented the space and transformed it into a sacred sanctuary where her aura photography flourished.

As word spread like wildfire about Shania's unique services, seekers of guidance flocked to her door, their paths crossing hers in the most unexpected ways. Despite the growing demand, Shania remained steadfast in her commitment to accessibility, knowing that true value and appreciation went beyond monetary exchanges. With each step forward, Shania couldn't help but feel the subtle nudges from Serena's whispers, guiding her towards the realization that the synchronicity of events had led her to this transformative chapter of her life.

As Shania continued her exploration into the realm of aura photography, she recognized the significance of documenting her discoveries and insights. With every photograph she took, she meticulously observed the nuances of colors, patterns, and vibrations, taking note of their meanings and correlations. Piece by piece, she began compiling a comprehensive manual, a guide that would unravel the mysteries of the auric field and serve as a valuable resource for her future work as an auric field photographer. Shania understood that this manual would become an essential tool, a bridge between the visual realm and the profound understanding of energy and consciousness.

With unwavering determination, Shania resolved to share the gift of aura photography with the world. As the word continued to spread about Shania's work, with more and more people becoming interested, Shania started doing aura photography demonstrations at various venues. This was just the beginning, as she envisioned workshops, retreats, and gatherings where individuals could experience the profound insights and revelations that she had witnessed firsthand. The aura photographs would serve as portals to self-realization, helping others shed the shackles of 3D consciousness and embrace the expansive realm of 5D awareness.

As Shania held the aura photography camera in her hands, she knew that her purpose had been revealed. With every click of the shutter, she captured not just the vibrant hues of the aura but also the potential for transformation and spiritual evolution. The journey had just begun, and Shania was ready to illuminate the path for those seeking their own inner truth.

CHAPTER 9

THE CLASH OF EMPIRICISM AND MYSTICISM

Marcus Wheeler, a renowned scientist of formidable intellect and unwavering dedication, had devoted his entire career to the pursuit of uncovering and understanding the mysteries of the world through the lens of rigorous experimentation and analysis. With his unwavering commitment to empirical evidence and rationality, Marcus had established himself as a pillar of the scientific community.

From the earliest days of his academic journey, Marcus displayed an insatiable curiosity and a relentless pursuit of knowledge. Armed with a razor-sharp intellect and an unyielding work ethic, he immersed himself in the study of physics, chemistry, and biology, seeking to unravel the fundamental laws that governed the universe.

Through countless hours in laboratories and tireless nights of analysis, Marcus sought to bring order to the chaos of the natural world. His mind was a fortress of scientific knowledge, fortified against ideas that could not withstand the scrutiny of empirical evidence. He reveled in the pursuit of truth, guided by the principles of observation, experimentation, and logical reasoning. His meticulous approach and unrelenting pursuit of truth set him apart as a scientist of unparalleled integrity.

While others may have been captivated by esoteric theories or speculative notions, Marcus remained resolute in his dedication to the scientific method. He firmly believed that understanding could only be achieved through rigorous investigation and the accumulation of verifiable evidence. He held firm to the belief that the universe operated according to tangible laws that could be uncovered through meticulous study. His skepticism was not born out of closed-mindedness, but rather from a deep-rooted respect for the power of empirical evidence to unlock the secrets of the natural world.

As fate would have it, Marcus's insatiable curiosity led him to stumble upon an intriguing concept that challenged the boundaries of his scientific understanding. It was during a national conference for scientists that he overheard whispers about Shania and her revolutionary approach to aura photography. Interestingly, these whispers were not just random chatter but came from the esteemed circles of the scientific community he deeply respected.

The name 'Shania', now linked to breakthroughs in energy and consciousness studies, had piqued the interest of several influencers in his field.

Intrigued yet deeply skeptical, Marcus found himself drawn to the allure of the unknown. He couldn't resist the tantalizing possibilities that lay within the realm of aura photography, even as his scientific mind questioned the validity and significance of capturing intangible energies. Driven by a mix of curiosity and skepticism, Marcus made the bold decision to attend one of Shania's aura photography demonstrations. It was a leap into uncharted territory, an opportunity to witness firsthand the claims and marvels of this enigmatic practice. With an open yet critical mind, Marcus embarked on this exploration, ready to challenge his preconceived notions and delve into the depths of the mysterious aura realm.

The long-awaited day of Shania's captivating event had finally dawned. When Marcus arrived, there, in a dimly lit room, hushed anticipation filled the air as the audience gathered for Shania's aura photography demonstration. People from all walks of life sat in a mix of excitement, curiosity, and skepticism. Among them were those who eagerly embraced the possibility of uncovering hidden layers of the human experience, while others were hardened critics, eager to find flaws in what they perceived as a mere illusion.

Freelance writers, their tablets and laptops poised with skepticism, observed the scene, hoping to capture the next intriguing story that would captivate their readers. They remained composed on the edge of their seats, their minds already formulating questions and doubts to challenge the authenticity of Shania's work. Yet, deep down, there lingered a flicker of curiosity, a glimmer of hope that perhaps there was more to this phenomenon than met the eye.

Also, in the audience were those who teetered on the edge of belief, their hearts aching with emotional pain and unresolved issues. They had arrived with a mix of curiosity and skepticism, their souls yearning for answers, for a way to alleviate their burdens and find a path towards healing.

Then, under the soft spotlight, Shania commanded the stage with an otherworldly aura. As her voice, laced with unfeigned confidence, echoed through the hushed room, Marcus found himself ensnared in her captivating presence.

She shared her personal journey of discovery, her encounters with the unseen realms, and her unwavering belief in the power of energy and the human spirit. With each word, she painted a vivid tapestry of possibility, inviting the audience to explore the depths of their own consciousness and embrace the potential for transformation.

Marcus observed the eager yet nervous volunteers stepping up. Under Shania's expert guidance, each one's aura was photographed, unveiling a dazzling spectacle of colors and energy patterns.

The room vibrated with whispers and gasps as Shania revealed the photos - canvases of blue, green, and purple embodying each viewer's essence. Her spot-on interpretations left the audience in awe and emotions palpably stirred. Skeptics squirmed, their belief systems challenged, while those with hope kindled an invigorating mix of excitement and curiosity, glimpsing a broader vista of their existence. Marcus observed as individuals marveled at their own aura photographs and Shania's interpretations. Yet, to him, it seemed like a mere parlor trick—a psychological manipulation at best.

As Marcus stood in the shadows, a sudden surge of unexpected events unfolded before him. Various people, who had initially scoffed at the idea of aura photography, experienced a profound emotional release after seeing their photograph and hearing Shania's explanation of what she perceived. Tears streamed from their eyes as they talked about a weight being lifted, of newfound clarity and purpose.

Marcus's scientific mind reeled at the sight. How could a simple photograph invoke such a visceral reaction? How could Shania know things about a person's life, just from looking at these photographs? He wrestled with his skepticism, torn between dismissing it as coincidence and allowing the possibility of a greater truth to seep into his consciousness.

As the presentation continued, Shania deftly fielded questions, her responses a harmonious blend of scientific explanations and intuitive and spiritual insights. She challenged the skeptics with compelling evidence, inviting them to consider the intricate complexities of human consciousness that lay just beyond the confines of their current understanding.

As the event drew to a close, the room buzzed with energy. Some left with their skepticism reaffirmed, their minds closed to the possibilities that had been presented. Others departed with a newfound curiosity; their hearts nudged towards exploring the mysteries that had unfolded before them.

Among the crowd, a few souls lingered, their faces illuminated with a glimmer of hope. They had witnessed the transformative power of Shania's aura photography demonstrations, and they knew deep within their hearts that this was just the beginning of a remarkable journey towards self-discovery and profound transformation.

As for Marcus, seeds of doubt were planted in his mind, sprouting curiosity and a desire to explore the uncharted territory of the spiritual realm. It was an unexpected turn of events, shaking the foundation of his scientific beliefs. He couldn't deny the impact he had witnessed, even if he couldn't fully comprehend it.

In the depths of the nights that followed, Marcus found himself immersed in research, seeking answers beyond the confines of his scientific textbooks. He delved into the realms of quantum physics, consciousness studies, and metaphysics, hungry for knowledge that might bridge the gap between his skepticism and the mystical experiences he had witnessed.

An internal battle raged within Marcus. His rational mind yearned for tangible evidence, for a logical explanation that could neatly fit into his scientific worldview. Yet, his encounters with aura photography had opened the door to a realm beyond his comprehension—a realm that demanded his attention and investigation.

With each passing day, Marcus's determination grew. He embarked on a journey of exploration, seeking to understand the intricacies of consciousness, energy, and the spiritual dimensions that had eluded his scientific scrutiny. He knew that he could no longer dismiss these experiences as mere illusions. There was something profound and transformative lurking in the shadows, waiting to be revealed.

CHAPTER 10

NATALIA'S ODYSSEY: A JOURNEY BETWEEN TWO REALMS

Natalia nestled into her small, cozy apartment, the air saturated with the soothing scent of vanilla-scented candles. Their flickering flames painted a ballet of light and shadow upon the walls, creating an intimate and ethereal ambiance that enveloped her like a warm embrace. The crackling fireplace, adorned with a vibrant medley of color, radiated a gentle heat, infusing the space with a comforting glow.

In this sacred space, Natalia found solace, a respite from the challenges that dotted her path. Her apartment, a sanctuary from the world's chaos, whispered its secrets of inspiration, stoking the fires of her strength, resilience and unwavering dedication to her quest for truth. This haven of tranquility also served as a sanctuary for her dreams and aspirations, a space where her spirit could soar amidst the comforting embrace of the familiar.

Perched upon a plush sofa, engulfed in a sea of plush pillows, Natalia sank into a haven of serenity. The cushions cradled her weary body, their softness a refuge from the outside world. She wrapped herself in a cozy blanket, its texture a gentle caress against her skin, as she sank deeper into the depths of tranquility.

Surrounded by her cherished books and journals, the room whispered with the wisdom of the ages. The shelves were a mosaic of knowledge, each volume a testament to Natalia's insatiable thirst for understanding. The pages, worn and weathered, held the imprints of her journey—the struggles and triumphs that had shaped her into the resilient soul she had become. As she closed her eyes and took a deep breath, Natalia felt a deep sense of gratitude, ready to face the struggles and triumphs that awaited her on her journey of self-discovery.

Natalia, a quiet observer of the human mind and its complexities, had always felt like an enigma. Born into a world that favored conformity and the pursuit of material success, she had always felt like an outsider. Society's expectations weighed heavily upon her, suffocating her true essence. Deep within her soul, Natalia felt a longing, an innate calling for something greater. She knew there was more to the human psyche than what met the eye. She sought connection, not just on a mental and emotional level, but on a spiritual plane. It had been a long and challenging journey for her, one that had led her to the path of spiritual awakening and guidance.

From a young age, Natalia's insatiable curiosity about the human mind and behavior led her on a dual path of exploration. As she observed people, pondering their motivations and choices, she yearned to unravel the mysteries of the human psyche. This fascination with human nature fueled her desire to delve deeper into the intricacies of the mind.

Simultaneously, Natalia's technological prowess flourished. Surrounded by screens and code, she delved into the realms of artificial intelligence (AI) and virtual reality (VR). With an innate affinity for technology, she honed her skills in coding and system enhancement, creating innovative pathways to explore the intersection of science and consciousness.

As life went on, Natalia's thirst for understanding the mysteries of human nature only intensified. She voraciously devoured books on psychology, philosophy, and spirituality, seeking answers to the questions that burned within her. But the more she learned, the more she realized that true understanding could not be found solely within the pages of a book.

Natalia yearned for a more experiential understanding, a direct connection to the deeper realms of consciousness. She delved into various spiritual practices, exploring meditation, energy healing, and ancient wisdom traditions. Through these practices, Natalia began to tap into a profound sense of interconnectedness, realizing that her journey of self-discovery was intricately linked to the collective human experience.

But Natalia's journey was not without obstacles. As she delved deeper into her spiritual practice, she encountered skepticism and resistance from those closest to her. Friends and family struggled to comprehend her unconventional beliefs, their doubts casting shadows on the validity of her experiences. Natalia often felt like an outsider, a lone seeker traversing a path less traveled.

Amidst conversations filled with raised eyebrows and puzzled expressions, Natalia's unwavering commitment to her spiritual exploration stood firm. She understood that her path diverged from the societal norms and that her quest for deeper understanding and connection set her apart from the familiar. Yet, she couldn't suppress the longing within her, the innate calling to uncover the hidden truths of existence. Despite the misunderstandings and doubts that surrounded her, Natalia remained resolute, embracing her uniqueness and forging ahead on her chosen path.

She was driven by an inner knowing that there was a deeper truth to be discovered, a reality beyond the limited confines of the physical world. She committed herself to a life of exploration, both within and without, determined to uncover the hidden wisdom that lay dormant within each individual.

During her extensive studies, Natalia uncovered a profound revelation: the interconnectedness of psychology and spirituality. She realized that the traditional methods of psychology often neglected the spiritual dimension of human existence, overlooking the profound impact that consciousness and higher states of being had on mental health and well-being.

Driven by her newfound understanding, Natalia pursued further education and training in psychology, eventually earning her doctorate in the field. Armed with her knowledge of psychology and deep spiritual insights, Natalia embarked on a mission to bridge the gap between science and spirituality, to help others navigate the intricate landscape of human consciousness.

Through her studies, Natalia also stumbled upon an intriguing concept: the notion of different levels of consciousness. She delved deeper into the teachings surrounding these levels, understanding that they represented distinct ways of perceiving and experiencing reality.

Intrigued, Natalia explored the depths of 3D, 4D, and 5D consciousness. She recognized that 3D consciousness was characterized by a focus on separation, materialism, and the egoic mind. In contrast, 5D consciousness represented a state of unity, love, and expanded awareness, where individuals operated from a place of deep connection with their higher selves and the greater web of life.

Natalia realized that her own journey of self-discovery aligned with the principles of transitioning from 3D to 5D consciousness. She began to take herself through the process, discerning what level of consciousness she was currently operating from and exploring ways to make the transition to the next level.

Her studies and personal experiences provided her with valuable insights and tools for this transformative journey. Natalia understood the importance of self-awareness, inner healing, and the cultivation of a deep connection with one's intuition and higher guidance. She recognized that the shift from 3D to 5D consciousness required a profound inner transformation, one that involved rewiring the brain (changing habits), releasing limiting beliefs, healing past wounds, and embracing a greater sense of purpose and interconnectedness.

Natalia's journey was one of self-discovery, resilience, and unwavering dedication to her quest for truth. Along her path of self-discovery, she faced formidable obstacles that tested her resolve and resilience. Doubt and uncertainty whispered in her ear, threatening to extinguish her inner flame.

In the depths of her quest, Natalia encountered moments of profound self-doubt. Her footsteps wavered on the treacherous terrain, and she grappled with the fear of failure. The weight of her own insecurities threatened to hold her back, tempting her to retreat to the safety of the familiar. But she pressed on, embracing her vulnerability as a catalyst for growth.

Life's challenges stood tall like mighty mountains in her path. Natalia confronted adversity with unyielding determination. She wrestled with setbacks, stumbling upon the jagged stones of disappointment and frustration. Yet, with every fall, she found the strength to rise again, her spirit unbroken and her resolve unshaken.

Triumph danced amidst the struggles, casting its radiant light upon Natalia's journey. She celebrated the small victories—the breakthroughs and aha moments illuminating her path. Like pearls of wisdom, these moments provided the sustenance she needed to continue forging ahead.

Through her struggles, Natalia discovered the transformative power of perseverance. Each hurdle she overcame became a badge of honor, a testament to her unwavering dedication to her quest for truth. Her battles became stepping stones, guiding her toward a deeper understanding of herself and the world around her.

Natalia's triumphs were not defined by external validation but by an inner knowing that she was living in alignment with her purpose. The joy that radiated from within her soul served as a compass, guiding her toward her highest potential. She reveled in the moments of clarity when everything lined up, revealing the profound interconnectedness of all things.

Her struggles and triumphs became intertwined, forging a resilient spirit that weathered the storms of doubt and uncertainty.

Natalia's journey was a testament to the indomitable human spirit, a reminder that within every struggle lies the potential for growth, and within every triumph, the seeds of inspiration.

With each step forward, Natalia embraced the profound wisdom gleaned from her own experiences. Her struggles became her teachings, her triumphs a beacon of hope for those who embarked on their own quests. Through the tapestry of her journey, she emerged as a guide, a source of inspiration, and a living testament to the transformative power of resilience and unwavering dedication.

The challenges she had faced had not been in vain; they had shaped her into the healer and guide she had become. Natalia knew that her purpose in life was to help others navigate their own journey of awakening and transformation, assisting them in breaking free from the limitations of 3D consciousness and embracing the expansive possibilities of 5D consciousness.

With a renewed sense of purpose and a deep commitment to her calling, Natalia embarked on the next phase of her journey. She knew that there was much work to be done and many souls to guide, and she was ready to step into her role as a catalyst for profound change.

As she closed her eyes and took a deep breath, Natalia whispered a silent prayer, sending her intentions out into the universe. She knew her path would be challenging, but she was prepared to walk it with courage, grace, and unwavering determination.

So, Natalia set forth on her mission, ready to make a difference, one awakened soul at a time.

CHAPTER 11

CONVERGENCE OF DESTINIES: A SHARED VISION EMERGES

Natalia stepped into the bustling café; her senses were immediately greeted by the rich aroma of freshly brewed coffee and the gentle hum of animated conversations. A magnetic pull had drawn her to this place, an intuitive whisper urging her toward a meeting that held profound significance. Little did she know just how deeply intertwined their lives would become.

Navigating through the labyrinth of tables, Natalia's gaze was instinctively drawn to a corner where a woman exuded an aura of serene confidence. Shania, seated with grace, emanated a palpable lightness and peace. Their eyes met, and Natalia couldn't help but be captivated by the depth that shimmered within Shania's gaze.

Curiosity propelled Natalia forward, her heart fluttering with anticipation. With a gentle smile, she introduced herself, "I'm Natalia," her voice tinged with curiosity and a hint of vulnerability.

Shania's eyes mirrored the same sense of recognition and connection. "I'm Shania," she replied, her voice filled with a resonance, an inexplicable familiarity that transcended the boundaries of their brief encounter. In the depths of their souls, they sensed a connection that went beyond mere coincidence—a connection that resonated at a profound level.

As they exchanged words and shared stories, time seemed to stand still. Each conversation, every shared insight, deepened the bond between them. They discovered kindred spirits in each other; their passions and aspirations aligned with an undeniable harmony. It was as if the universe had conspired to bring them together, recognizing the power that would arise from their unity. They found solace in knowing that they were not alone in their spiritual quest, that their paths had converged for a reason beyond mere chance.

Their conversation flowed effortlessly. Shania shared her journey of discovery, recounting how her fascination with aura photography and her natural empathic abilities had led her to explore the depths of human consciousness. Natalia listened intently, captivated by Shania's unique perspective and her unwavering belief in the transformative power of energy and spirituality. Natalia shared her journey of discovery and transformation, and how she was fascinated by different levels of consciousness and how they impacted the human experience. Natalia also spoke about some of her projects with artificial intelligence (AI) and virtual reality (VR).

As Shania delved deeper into conversation with Natalia, a profound sense of synchronicity enveloped them as if a higher force had orchestrated their meeting. Natalia's wisdom and expertise in the realms of 3rd, 4th, and 5th-dimensional consciousness ignited a spark within Shania, resonating with the guidance Serena had imparted. With passionate enthusiasm, Natalia shared the intricacies of each dimension, unveiling the veils that shrouded the path to higher states of awareness. In their exchange of knowledge and shared vision, Shania felt a profound sense of purpose and the birth of a powerful partnership, knowing that together, they would play a pivotal role in guiding others towards the transcendence from the limitations of 3D to the expansiveness of 5D consciousness.

Amid their conversation, Shania retrieved a small, sleek camera bag from her belongings, her eyes shimmering with a hint of excitement and reverence. Natalia watched with intrigue as

Shania delicately opened the bag and revealed a mystical-looking camera nestled within.

"This," Shania said, her voice filled with a sense of wonder, "is the tool that has guided me on this transformative path." "This is the camera that I was telling you about," she said.

Natalia's gaze shifted from the camera to Shania, a rush of anticipation surging through her veins. She leaned forward, captivated by Shania's words, eager to understand the power of this enigmatic device.

With a gentle yet confident tone, Shania shared the camera's extraordinary ability to capture the energetic signatures of individuals. Through the lens, it unveiled the vibrant hues and radiant colors that emanated from their very essence, revealing untold stories and hidden depths.

"I've taken countless photographs," Shania continued, her voice a melodic blend of reverence and conviction, "each one telling a unique story, and I believe your story is waiting to be revealed."

Natalia's heart quickened, its rhythm echoing the pulsating energy that seemed to envelop them both. The camera, with its mystic allure, held the promise of unlocking a profound understanding of her journey—the triumphs, the challenges, and the whispers of her soul.

A mix of curiosity and vulnerability filled Natalia's being as she accepted Shania's invitation. She leaned closer, her hands gently clasped, ready to surrender herself to the camera's lens, to be immortalized in a single frame that would capture the essence of her existence.

With great care, Shania raised the camera, its lens poised to encapsulate the essence of Natalia's being. As the shutter released its soft click, a sense of electric anticipation surged through the air, as if the very fabric of their surroundings held its breath.

In that fleeting moment, Natalia's aura came alive in a vivid display of enchanting hues. A tapestry of colors, each with its own meaning, wove together in a captivating dance of energy. Soft shades of tranquil blues whispered of inner peace and serenity, while radiant greens symbolized growth and healing. Golden threads shimmered with the warmth of wisdom and enlightenment, and gentle lilacs embraced the essence of spiritual connection. Amidst this kaleidoscope of vibrant energy, there were faint traces of unresolved challenges, represented by patches of deep purples and intense reds, reminders of the work that still lay ahead. Yet, overall, Natalia's aura exuded a profound sense of balance and harmony, reflecting her journey of self-discovery and the qualities aligned with 5D consciousness. It was a glimpse into her inner landscape, an exquisite reflection of her journey, and an invitation to join her in the quest for truth.

Natalia's eyes widened in awe. As Shania interpreted the photograph, sharing what it had unveiled, Natalia felt as though her soul had been laid bare, reflecting her inner essence and the depths of her being.

As Natalia continued to gaze upon the photograph, a profound sense of recognition washed over her. The image revealed not only the depth of her being but also the profound interconnectedness that bound her to the vast tapestry of human existence. It was a mirror that reflected her essence back to her—a reminder of her inherent light, her unique contribution to the world.

"This is just the beginning," Shania said, her voice filled with excitement. "Together, we can unlock the hidden potential in others and guide them on their journey of awakening and transformation."

Natalia nodded, her heart filled with a more intense sense of purpose and possibility. She knew deep within her soul that this meeting was no coincidence, but a divine synchronicity that had aligned their paths for a greater purpose.

The encounter with Shania and her camera had become a pivotal moment—a testament to the power of human connection and the unfathomable depths of the human spirit. Together, they would embark on a shared odyssey of exploration, to unravel the mysteries of existence, unlock the hidden truths that lay within, and illuminate the path toward self-discovery and transformation.

With a sense of exhilaration and purpose, Natalia and Shania realized that their individual gifts and insights were not meant to be kept in isolation. They had been brought together for a reason— to combine their unique perspectives and create a transformative experience for others.

Their minds brimmed with ideas, like fireflies in the night sky. Excitement surged through their veins as they envisioned a journey of exploration and illumination, where they would blend the profound wisdom captured by the camera with Natalia's knowledge of the different levels of consciousness and Shania's vision, empathic abilities and spiritual guidance.

They understood that their partnership would catalyze a ripple effect, touching the lives of countless souls who were ready to embark on their own transformative quests. The dynamic interplay of their energies would create a powerful resonance, inviting others to awaken, embrace their highest potential, and step into the radiant light that lay dormant within them.

As they delved deeper into their shared vision, Natalia and Shania's hearts danced with the joy of co-creation. They could already see the transformative ripples expanding outward, gently stirring the souls of those who were ready to embark on a journey of self-discovery and spiritual awakening.

Their alliance was more than just a collaboration—it was a sacred calling, a divine orchestration that had brought them together at this precise moment in time. They knew that the path ahead would be filled with challenges and uncertainties, but they embraced it wholeheartedly, for they understood that through these trials, their spirits would soar and their collective impact would be magnified.

With unwavering determination, Natalia and Shania embarked on this thrilling adventure, their souls intertwined like vines reaching for the sun. Guided by an unseen force, they ventured into uncharted territories, ready to share their insights, wisdom, and love with those who were seeking the path of transformation.

Their hearts brimmed with excitement, their souls ablaze with purpose. Natalia and Shania were not just partners; they became best friends. They were catalysts, weaving threads of light and love into the fabric of humanity. Together, they would create a symphony of awakening, harmonizing their gifts and insights to unlock the limitless potential that lay within every individual who crossed their path.

So, hand in hand, they set forth on their mission, guided by the whispers of the universe and fueled by the boundless love that emanated from their souls. A new chapter had begun—one filled with excitement, adventure, and the promise of touching lives, one awakened soul at a time.

In that extraordinary meeting, Natalia and Shania discovered a kindred spirit—an ally on their respective journeys, united by the vibrations of higher frequencies that resonated between them. They recognized the synergistic power of their shared paths and the remarkable potential that lay before them. United by their unique gifts and shared vision, Shania and Natalia embarked on an astonishing quest.

Guided by Shania's empathic abilities and her skillful aura photography, they will unravel the mysteries of human energy, capturing the essence of souls through vibrant colors and intricate patterns. With Natalia's profound knowledge of the different dimensions of consciousness and her adept use of VR and AI technologies, they will seamlessly merge the realms of perception, creating immersive experiences that open doorways to expanded awareness.

Together, they will become transformative catalysts, guiding others on a profound journey of awakening and assisting them in transcending the limitations of 3D reality. Unbeknownst to them, their combined talents and innovative approach will not only change the lives of those they touch but also ignite a transformative fire within their own beings, forever shaping the intricate tapestry of their intertwined destinies.

So, hand in hand, they set forth on their mission, guided by the whispers of the universe and fueled by the boundless love that emanated from their souls. A new chapter had begun—one filled with excitement, adventure, and the promise of touching lives, one enlightened spirit after another.

As they left the café, the world around them seemed to shimmer with newfound magic and potential. Natalia and Shania embarked on a journey together, united by a shared vision and a deep commitment to facilitating profound shifts in consciousness.

CHAPTER 12

The Journey of Transition: Guiding the Path to 5D Consciousness

As Shania delved deeper into her work, and had conversations with Natalia, she developed a more profound understanding of the intricacies involved in transitioning from 3D to 5D consciousness. She knew that this transformative journey was not a simple overnight process but required diligent inner work and unwavering commitment. It was a voyage of self-discovery and healing, requiring individuals to confront their unresolved issues and illuminate the shadows within.

With a spark of inspiration, Shania conceived a captivating idea that ignited her soul. She yearned to capture the profound stages of personal transformation that individuals experienced on their journey of self-discovery. And so, she embarked on a daring experiment, incorporating her unique aura photography into a sequential format.

Shania was intrigued by the possibility of unraveling the mysteries of the human spirit, by meticulously crafting a series of photographs, each one a snapshot of an individual's energetic imprint. She sought to observe the subtle changes in hues and vibrant colors that danced within the captured images, for they held the key to unlocking the unresolved issues that lay dormant within.

As she embarked on this endeavor, Shania's intuitive abilities as an empath bloomed, enhancing her capacity to read the energetic imprints revealed in the photographs. With phenomenal keen insight and a gentle touch, she deciphered the patterns and symbolism that emerged, gaining profound insights into the areas that called out for healing and transformation.

With each session, Shania's empathic resonance deepened, forging a powerful connection between herself and those who entrusted her with their energetic portraits. She listened attentively to the unspoken stories that unfolded through the hues and colors, recognizing the vulnerabilities, triumphs, and hidden potentials that lay within each soul.

It was a sacred dance, an intimate exploration of the human experience, as Shania guided individuals through the transformative tapestry of their own energies. With compassion and wisdom, she gently illuminated the uncharted territories of their being, bringing awareness to the unresolved aspects that sought resolution and the dormant gifts longing to be awakened.

Through this series of aura photographs, Shania empowered others to embark on their personal odyssey of healing and growth. She became a beacon of light, guiding souls towards the transformation they so deeply desired. With each step taken on this shared path, Shania witnessed the blossoming of countless hearts and the radiance of spirits set free.

The success of her innovative approach was a testament to Shania's unwavering commitment to her craft and her unyielding belief in the power of self-discovery. It was a profound realization that the energetic imprints captured in the photographs held the keys to unlocking the doorways of healing and transformation. With every click of the camera, Shania witnessed the sacred dance of resilience as individuals embraced their innate capacity to heal, grow, and embody their highest potential.

In this sacred union of art and intuition, Shania's work became a catalyst for profound personal revelations and collective awakening. She had tapped into a wellspring of wisdom, becoming a guide and catalyst for those seeking the transformative journey of self-realization.

As the photographs told their stories, Shania's heart swelled with gratitude. She had found her calling, her purpose—a path illuminated by the vibrant hues and colors that revealed the intricate tapestry of the human spirit. With each session, she wove her threads of love and empathy, casting a luminous light upon the path of healing and transformation for all those who crossed her path.

One day, Emma, a respected journalist, and seeker of higher consciousness, stepped into Shania's studio. Their meeting was serendipitous, as Emma's yearning for spiritual growth aligned perfectly with Shania's mission to assist others on their path to enlightenment. They connected instantly, their energies intertwining in a cosmic dance of shared purpose.

In their initial conversation, Shania recognized the layers of unresolved issues that weighed heavily upon Emma's spirit. These unhealed wounds, stemming from past traumas and limiting beliefs, were the very barriers holding her back from embracing the expansive realms of 5D consciousness. Shania understood that the journey ahead would be challenging but transformative.

With compassion and wisdom, Shania explained to Emma that the transition from 3D to 5D consciousness was not a quick fix but a gradual process of inner transformation. It required an unwavering commitment to self-reflection, self-love, and the unraveling of the ego's grip on the mind.

Together, they embarked on this sacred journey. Shania served as Emma's guide, offering insights, tools, and exercises to support her growth. They explored the depths of Emma's unresolved issues, gently peeling away the layers of conditioning and programming that had confined her to the limitations of 3D consciousness.

During Emma's transition, Shania captured her aura in a series of photographs. The images revealed a blend of vibrant hues and murky shadows, representing the spectrum of Emma's experiences and emotions. Shania studied the photographs, analyzing the patterns and colors that danced across the frames.

The aura photography series format was a powerful tool for Shania to guide Emma on her path to 5D consciousness. Together, they delved into the layers of the photographs, deciphering the messages hidden within the energetic imprints. Shania's intuitive gifts, coupled with her empathic nature, allowed her to connect deeply with Emma's experiences, facilitating the process of healing and growth.

Through the interpretation of the aura colors, Shania could discern the areas that required attention and exploration. The vibrant hues of love, compassion, and joy reflected Emma's strengths and aligned with the frequencies of 5D consciousness. However, interwoven among the radiance were subtle shades of fear, anger, and self-doubt, remnants of unresolved traumas that needed to be addressed.

Using her intuitive insights, Shania guided Emma through various healing modalities and practices tailored to her specific needs. They engaged in heart-centered meditations, energy-healing sessions, and transformative self-inquiry exercises. Shania encouraged Emma to embrace her emotions, explore the depths of her pain, and release the patterns that no longer served her.

As Emma's inner landscape began to shift, the aura photographs also transformed. The once-clouded shadows gradually dissipated, replaced by vibrant and harmonious hues that mirrored her newfound clarity and self-empowerment. The photographs became a tangible testament to the progress she was making on her journey to 5D consciousness.

Shania's empathic abilities were instrumental in understanding the nuances of Emma's experiences. Through their deep connection, she intuitively sensed the emotional blocks that hindered Emma's growth. With compassion and gentle guidance, Shania helped Emma navigate the intricate terrain of her emotions, supporting her as she faced her fears and released the grip of past traumas.

Together, Shania and Emma celebrated the small victories along the way—the moments of profound insight, the breakthroughs that shattered long-held beliefs, and the blossoming of newfound self-love and acceptance. Each step forward brought them closer to the radiance of 5D consciousness, a realm where love, harmony, and interconnectedness reign supreme.

The process of transitioning from 3D to 5D consciousness was not without its challenges. Emma experienced moments of resistance and discomfort as she confronted deep-rooted patterns and belief systems. She experienced resistance and doubt as she confronted deep-seated fears and insecurities. The journey demanded vulnerability as she navigated the intricate corridors of her own psyche. But Shania stood by her side, providing a nurturing space for healing and growth. Shania's unwavering support and guidance encouraged Emma to stay the course as she learned to embrace the discomfort as a sign of growth and transformation.

Emma's transition was not a linear process. There were moments of elation and clarity where Emma glimpsed the higher realms of consciousness and felt the interconnectedness of all beings. But there were also periods of intense introspection, where she, again, confronted her shadows and faced her deepest fears.

As they continued to traverse this transformative journey together, Shania marveled at the power of human resilience and the capacity for healing. She witnessed firsthand the profound impact that their work was having on Emma's life, as she shed the layers of conditioning and stepped into her authentic power.

Over time, Emma's dedication and commitment began to bear fruit. Through self-inquiry, meditation, and inner reflection, she unearthed the root causes of her limiting beliefs and patterns. With each breakthrough, her consciousness expanded, revealing new depths of insight and understanding.

The aura photography sessions became a gateway to Emma's soul, allowing her to witness her own evolution. Through the lens of the camera, she saw herself transforming—glimpses of her true essence shining through the layers of conditioning and societal expectations.

Through it all, Shania remained a pillar of support, guiding Emma with unwavering love and compassion. She encouraged her to embrace the process, reminding her that transformation was not about reaching a destination but a continuous journey of self-discovery and growth.

In those sacred moments of self-discovery, Shania realized the profound gift she possessed—the ability to facilitate profound change in others. She felt humbled by the magnitude of her role, knowing that she was not just a guide but a catalyst for the awakening of human potential.

With each session, Shania's purpose crystallized. Through her unique blend of intuition, empathy, and the powerful tool of aura photography, she would continue to assist others on their path to 5D consciousness, one soul at a time.

As the months passed, Emma's progress became evident. The weight of her unresolved issues had been gradually lifting, and she was stepping into the light of 5D consciousness.

The journey continued, with Shania and Emma walking side by side, their connection growing stronger with every step they took. As they ventured into the next phase of Emma's transformation, Shania held onto the unwavering belief that their combined efforts would create ripples that reached far and wide, touching the lives of countless souls who were ready to embrace the radiant truth of their own being.

CHAPTER 13

SKEPTICAL OBSERVATION - THE ALLURE OF THE UNSEEN

Shania's groundbreaking collaboration with Emma was featured in a major magazine article that Emma had written. Emma wanted to share her profound experience with the world. Among the article's readers was the esteemed scientist, Marcus Wheeler. Marcus still found himself irresistibly captivated by Shania's aura photography. The allure of the invisible, so vividly portrayed in her work, continued to challenge his rational mindset. Marcus remembered the time he witnessed Shania's demonstrations, and how the impact of her photography on the volunteers left his scientific intellect in a constant state of marvel and debate. Marcus was still on a journey of seeking to understand the intricacies of consciousness, energy and the spiritual dimensions that elude his scientific scrutiny.

Impassioned by a mix of curiosity and skepticism, Marcus sought out Shania, and they spoke on the phone several times. Then, Marcus organized a rendezvous at her distinctively atmospheric creative sanctuary. As he stepped into the palpable energy of Shania's photography studio, a surge of intrigue and doubt washed over him. Surrounded by mesmerizing visuals of auras, each image a captivating kaleidoscope of dancing colors, he found himself immersed in a world beyond words.

Greeting Marcus with a warm smile, Shania's eyes sparkled with a glimmer of understanding. Sensing his skepticism, she felt a surge of determination to start the demonstration of the profound impact of her work. Prior to the session, Shania had obtained Candice's consent for Marcus to observe, allowing him to witness the transformative power of aura photography.

With graceful precision, Shania guided Candice into position, her hands moving like a conductor orchestrating an invisible symphony. As she adjusted the lighting, a soft glow illuminated Candice's face, accentuating the subtle contours of her being. With every subtle movement, Shania captured the essence of Candice's energy, as if freezing a fleeting moment of her soul's radiance in time. The air crackled with anticipation as Shania prepared to unveil the secrets hidden within the ethereal realm through the lens of her camera.

As the photographs developed before their eyes, Marcus couldn't help but be captivated by the vibrant hues and intricate patterns that emerged. Shania's interpretation of the images resonated deeply with Candice, and her awe-filled expression spoke volumes. Marcus witnessed the raw emotions that coursed through Candice's being, her eyes widening in both wonder and surprise.

At that moment, Candice realized the magnitude of what was being revealed. The photographs became a mirror that reflected the unresolved issues she had carried within, shedding light on the ways in which they had subtly shaped her life. The sight of those unhealed wounds laid bare on the paper, struck a chord deep within her.

As Marcus watched Candice grapple with the emotions stirred by the photographs, he recognized that this was no mere illusion. The images had unveiled profound truths, tangible representations of the challenges she faced and the impact they had on her life. It was a poignant reminder that the photographs held something real, something that resonated with the depths of her being. As Marcus continued to observe, a veil seemed to lift before his eyes, offering him a captivating glimpse into a realm of transformation that had long remained concealed in the shadows.

Once again, Marcus found himself questioning the limits of his understanding. How could something so intangible be captured on film? What scientific principles could explain the enigmatic dance of colors before him? His mind grappled with these questions, still torn between his skepticism and an undeniable fascination with the unexplained.

Shania, sensing Marcus's internal struggle, approached him with a soft-spoken confidence. "Science has its boundaries, Marcus," she said, her voice carrying a hint of reassurance. "There are realms of existence that transcend our current understanding. The aura, the energetic field surrounding every living being, is a glimpse into the deeper dimensions of consciousness."

Marcus leaned in, his scientific curiosity piqued. "But how do you capture it? How do you make the unseen visible?" he inquired, his skepticism still lingering.

Shania smiled knowingly. "This particular aura photography camera is a conduit, a tool that allows us to witness the energetic vibrations that influence our lives. It reads the subtle frequencies of the human energy field and translates them into the colors and patterns you see before you."

Marcus's gaze shifted back to Candice's photographs, and then to some of the other photographs in Shania's studio, apprehensively taking on a newfound appreciation. He observed the variations in color and intensity, each unique to the individual captured in the frame. It was as if the photographs held the stories of their subjects, revealing their emotional states, hidden fears, and untapped potential.

Shania approached Candice, drawn to the profound impact the photographs had on her. With a gentle voice, she continued to interpret the intricate details and hidden messages embedded within the images. Marcus, captivated by Shania's words, found his skepticism gently waver, making space for a sense of awe and curiosity to take hold.

As Shania delved deeper into her interpretation, Marcus began to listen. He felt a stirring within him. The boundaries of his rational mind began to soften, allowing the possibility of a greater, unseen realm to seep into his consciousness. He was on the cusp of being open to the idea that there was more to the human experience than what could be measured and quantified by scientific instruments. There was a vast realm of unseen energies, interconnections, and the potential for profound transformation that lay just beyond the grasp of his rational mind.

Shania, sensing his shifting perspective, approached Marcus once more. "The world is far more intricate and mysterious than we can comprehend with science alone," she whispered. "There is wisdom in embracing the unknown, in exploring the realms beyond what can be explained through empirical evidence."

Marcus contemplated her words, the intense skepticism that once held him captive now slowing beginning to give way to a shockingly newfound sense of wonder. He was beginning to realize that science and spirituality were not mutually exclusive, but rather two facets of a greater truth waiting to be unveiled.

With a sense of purpose and a glimmer of hope, Shania carefully handed Marcus an aura photograph that she had taken of herself during the early days of her journey, capturing the vibrant colors and intricate patterns that danced around her energetic field. Alongside it, she offered a collection of photographs featuring the radiant auras of volunteers who had eagerly participated in her demonstrations. Shania also gave Marcus a copy of her manual of interpretations. In her heart, she believed that these visual glimpses into the unseen realms, along with her manual of interpretations, would serve as a catalyst to ease Marcus' skepticism and possibly gently nudge him to embark on a profound journey of self-discovery and unlock the door to his own transformative potential.

Expressing deep gratitude, Marcus extended his heartfelt appreciation to Shania for the profound experience of being a part of the aura photography session. He acknowledged her generosity in providing him with the treasured photographs and the invaluable manual. As Marcus left the photography studio, he carried with him a lingering curiosity and a newfound openness to the mysteries of the unseen. The allure of Shania's aura photography had ignited a spark within him, propelling him on a journey of discovery that would forever alter his perception of reality.

In the days that followed, Marcus delved deeper into the realms of consciousness and energy, seeking to bridge the gap between science and spirituality. He immersed himself in research, studying ancient texts, engaging with leading experts, and conducting experiments to unravel the mysteries that had captivated his mind and soul.

With each revelation, Marcus's skepticism was in the process of dissolving as an incoming profound appreciation for the interconnectedness of all things emerged. He was beginning to see the world through a different lens, perceiving the subtle energies that permeated every aspect of existence.

The once-renowned skeptic had become an ardent explorer of the unseen, navigating the realms of consciousness with an insatiable thirst for knowledge. Marcus Wheeler was no longer confined by the limitations of his scientific training; he was amid transcending the boundaries of his skepticism, embracing the extraordinary potential that lay within the uncharted territories of the human experience.

Marcus's journey continued, his insatiable curiosity guiding him toward the profound insights and transformative experiences that awaited him in the realm where science and spirituality converged. He was determined to uncover the truths that had eluded him for so long, eager to share his discoveries with a world ready to embrace the power of the unseen.

CHAPTER 14

NAVIGATING DIMENSIONS: NATALIA'S GUIDE TO CONSCIOUS AWAKENING

Natalia stood at the center of the sacred space, radiating a serene and compassionate energy. She was prepared to embark on a profound journey with the participants of her workshop, guiding them through the labyrinth of consciousness. As they gathered around her, eager for transformation, Natalia's gentle voice echoed through the room.

She began by introducing the concept of consciousness and the various dimensions that encompassed it. Natalia explained that consciousness was not limited to the physical realm but extended to ethereal realms as well. She delved into the depths of human existence, guiding the participants to explore the different levels of consciousness.

First, Natalia described 3D consciousness—a state deeply rooted in fear, separation, and materialism. In this dimension, individuals were largely driven by egoic desires and attachments, constantly seeking external validation and defining themselves by material possessions. Natalia emphasized the limiting nature of this consciousness, which hindered spiritual growth and kept individuals trapped in a cycle of suffering.

She then introduced the transitional phase of 4D consciousness. Natalia explained that 4D consciousness represented a pivotal moment of awakening, where individuals began to question their beliefs and explore the inner workings of their minds. This dimension brought heightened awareness of emotions, dreams, and synchronicities. In 4D consciousness, people started to recognize that there was more to life than what meets the eye, leading them on a quest for deeper meaning and spiritual connection.

Finally, Natalia unveiled the pinnacle of their journey—the transformative realm of 5D consciousness. She described 5D consciousness as a state of expanded awareness and unity. In this dimension, individuals operated from a heart-centered space, transcending the limitations of the ego and embracing the interconnectedness of all beings. Love, compassion, and forgiveness were the driving forces, as people recognized their inherent divinity and the power of collective consciousness.

Natalia's teachings went beyond intellectual understanding; she provided practical tools to assist the participants in their transition from 3D to 5D consciousness. She guided them through meditation, visualization exercises, and energy healing techniques, allowing them to tap into their inner wisdom and awaken their dormant spiritual faculties.

Throughout the workshop, Natalia fostered a safe and supportive environment for the participants to explore their consciousness. She encouraged open dialogue, where individuals could share their experiences, ask questions, and receive guidance. Natalia's intuitive abilities allowed her to connect deeply with each participant, tailoring her teachings to their unique needs and challenges.

As the day unfolded, Natalia guided the group through a profound meditation journey. With her soothing voice, she led them on an inner exploration, helping them access deeper layers of their subconscious mind. Through this process, the participants gained insights into their unresolved issues, fears, and limiting beliefs that held them back in 3D consciousness.

Natalia's gentle presence created a space of acceptance and non-judgment, allowing the participants to release emotional baggage and heal old wounds. She facilitated group discussions, encouraging individuals to support and uplift each other on their transformative journeys.

Throughout the workshop, Natalia emphasized the importance of self-reflection and inner work. She guided the participants to explore their shadow aspects, those hidden parts of themselves that were often suppressed or ignored. By acknowledging and integrating these aspects, they could transcend the limitations of 3D consciousness and step into the expansive realms of 5D.

As the day drew to a close, Natalia led the participants in a closing ceremony, where they expressed their gratitude for the profound shifts they had experienced. Tears of joy and relief flowed freely as they shared stories of personal transformation, newfound clarity, and a deep sense of inner peace.

The workshop had served as a catalyst for profound shifts within each participant, planting seeds of awareness and igniting their journey towards 5D consciousness. Natalia's guidance and teachings had facilitated their inner alchemy, empowering them to embrace their true essence and live a life aligned with their soul's purpose.

Natalia's presence illuminated the path of transformation, as she embraced the inherent power of her skills and gifts. The moment was drawing near when Natalia and Shania would embark on a shared journey, their collective energies merging to facilitate profound and transformative experiences. Together, they would guide others to awaken their true potential, embracing the radiant beauty of 5D consciousness. The seeds of collaboration had been planted, and the world eagerly awaited the extraordinary transformation that would unfold as these two remarkable souls joined forces.

CHAPTER 15

MYSTERY IN LIGHT

arcus found himself captivated by the aura photographs Shania had given him. Even though he had the manual of interpretations, as he scrutinized each image, his scientific mind raced to make sense of the colors, lights, and patterns that danced before his eyes. It was as if he had stumbled upon a hidden realm, one where science and spirituality converged in ways he had never imagined.

In his quest for understanding, Marcus turned to his trusted allies: scientific concepts and theories. Quantum physics, electromagnetism, and the study of energy fields became the foundation of his investigation. He dove into the scientific literature, seeking explanations for the ethereal enigma captured in the photographs.

As he delved deeper, Marcus encountered intriguing parallels between scientific discoveries and spiritual teachings. He stumbled upon the concept of entanglement, where particles separated by vast distances could instantaneously influence each other. It mirrored the interconnectedness espoused by ancient wisdom traditions, suggesting that all beings are intricately linked in a vast web of existence.

As Marcus immersed himself in his research, even more, he discovered a wealth of scientific evidence supporting the existence of auras and their potential quantification. He delved into studies conducted by pioneering scientists who had explored the intersection of science and spirituality.

One intriguing line of research focused on bioelectromagnetic fields—the subtle energy fields emitted by living organisms, including humans. Marcus learned that these fields could be measured using sensitive instruments, validating their existence and providing a scientific basis for the concept of auras.

He uncovered studies that revealed correlations between the colors perceived in aura photography and the vibrational frequencies of light energy. Each color corresponded to a specific wavelength, and Marcus began to see how these colors could be linked to the energetic state of an individual.

Colors, as Marcus has known, were not merely arbitrary shades but manifestations of light energy vibrating at different frequencies. The notion of color therapy, which had long been regarded as a purely spiritual or alternative practice, has been gaining a new level of scientific credibility. Marcus found studies exploring how specific colors could affect an individual's mood, emotions, and overall well-being.

All of these revelations sparked a series of "aha" moments for Marcus. He realized that the aura photographs were not simply pretty lights on a screen; they were windows into a realm beyond the physical. The vibrant hues and pulsating energies spoke of unseen dimensions and untapped potential.

Yet, amid these moments of clarity, Marcus couldn't shake a nagging sense of confusion. The scientific data he collected often lacked consistency, leaving gaps in his understanding. Skepticism tugged at his thoughts, urging him to question the validity of what he was witnessing.

He found himself caught in a dualistic struggle between his rational mind and the intangible mysteries that beckoned him. How could he reconcile the concrete principles of science with the ethereal nature of spirituality? Were they irreconcilable or different facets of a greater truth?

As Marcus delved into the scientific literature, he couldn't help but feel a sense of wonder and intrigue. The known scientific principles only scratched the surface of the vast realms of spirituality and consciousness. The quantification of auras and the correlation of colors to energy frequencies were stepping stones, bridging the gap between science and the metaphysical.

In the realm of spirituality, Marcus discovered ancient wisdom traditions and esoteric teachings that had long explored the interconnectedness of light, energy, and consciousness. The concepts of chakras, energy centers within the body, and the flow of life force energy took on new meaning. He saw how these teachings aligned with the scientific understanding of bioelectromagnetic fields and the interconnectedness of all living beings.

This convergence of science and spirituality was like the meeting point of two rivers, merging their waters into a powerful stream of knowledge. Marcus began to see the limitations of viewing the world through a purely scientific lens. Science provided a framework for understanding the physical world but could not fully explain the depths of human experience, the mysteries of consciousness, or the interconnectedness of all things.

With each discovery, Marcus felt a shift within himself. The realm of the unknown, which had once been shrouded in skepticism, now beckoned him with an irresistible allure. He understood that science could offer valuable insights into the mechanics of the universe, but it was through spirituality that he could explore the deeper meaning and purpose of existence.

As Marcus grappled with the convergence of science and spirituality, he realized that the known scientific principles were like guideposts, leading him deeper into the uncharted territories of consciousness. He saw the correlation between the scientific exploration of bioelectromagnetic fields and the metaphysical understanding of auras as a testament to the vastness of human potential.

In the depths of his contemplation, Marcus couldn't help but ponder the question that had haunted philosophers and seekers throughout the ages: What lies beyond the boundaries of scientific understanding? He realized that spirituality offered glimpses into the realm of the unknown, inviting exploration into the mysteries of consciousness, the nature of reality, and the interconnected web of existence.

In his pursuit of answers, Marcus realized that he had been approaching the dilemma from the wrong angle. Science and spirituality were not opposing forces but rather two lenses through which he could explore the multifaceted nature of reality. The scientific method provided a structured approach to unraveling the mechanics of the universe, while spirituality offered insights into the deeper meaning and interconnectedness of existence.

Marcus's skepticism slowly transformed into a deep curiosity, a hunger to bridge the gaps between scientific principles and spiritual insights. He saw the aura photographs as a doorway into a realm that defied easy explanation, an invitation to explore the boundless potential of consciousness.

The more he immersed himself in this exploration, the more he realized that the convergence of science and spirituality held the key to unlocking profound truths. The colors and lights captured in the aura photographs were not just random patterns but symbolic representations of unseen energies and states of being. They hinted at the interconnectedness of all things and the limitless possibilities inherent in each individual.

As Marcus's journey unfolded, he discovered that his role as a scientist was not solely to find definitive answers but also to embrace the beauty of the unknown. Science and spirituality could coexist, enriching each other in the process. The scientific method provided the tools to dissect and understand the physical world, while spirituality allowed him to explore the depths of consciousness and the vast realms beyond.

In the end, Marcus realized that the pursuit of truth required an open mind and a willingness to embrace the mysteries that lay beyond the reach of scientific measurement. Skepticism remained a vital aspect of his approach, as it encouraged critical thinking and discernment. But he also recognized the value of curiosity and wonder, acknowledging that there were truths beyond the grasp of conventional scientific methods.

As Marcus closed his research notes for the day, a sense of awe and reverence washed over him. The aura photographs had unveiled a world that expanded his understanding of reality. He knew that his journey was far from over, and that the convergence of science and spirituality would continue to guide his exploration of the boundless mysteries of existence.

CHAPTER 16

RADIANT BEGINNINGS: THE SACRED RETREAT OF TRANSFORMATION

United by their shared vision, Shania and Natalia decided to host a transformative weekend retreat in the enchanting embrace of Sedona, Arizona. Having deeply immersed themselves in the sacred land of Sedona, Natalia and Shania's intimate connection to its potent spiritual energy guided their decision.

As participants arrive, they will be greeted by the breathtaking beauty of Sedona, its majestic red rock formations whispering ancient wisdom. Natalia will lead the teachings at the onset of the retreat, with Shania taking the helm to guide the teachings during the retreat's final stages.

Each day, the group would gather in sacred spaces, their hearts open to the profound teachings, discussions, and experiences that awaited them. The participants would be in awe of the spiritual energy that permeated the sites they would visit, feeling an electrifying connection to the divine. A palpable sense of anticipation will permeate the air, a prelude to the profound and transformative journey they are about to undertake, guided by the illuminating beacon of 5D consciousness.

As all participants arrived and prior to the commencement of the sacred gatherings, Shania embarked on a distinctive venture, capturing the unique energetic signatures of each individual through her aura photography. With great care and precision, she immortalized their energetic presence in captivating images, providing a tangible reflection of their being. The participants will take another aura photograph on the day of the final gathering.

After the closing ceremony, Shania and Natalia will present each participant with a deeply personal gift: the comparison of their initial and final aura images. By comparing their initial photograph with the final one, the participants will witness the tangible evidence of their transformation, a snapshot of their evolved energy. The contrasting colors, patterns, and energies captured within the photographs will serve as a powerful reminder of their journey and the remarkable shifts they have experienced.

These photographs would become cherished mementos, symbolizing their progress and awakening to the radiant truth of their own being. The visual evidence of their growth would inspire them to embrace their ongoing journey of self-discovery and transformation, forever grateful for the transformative power of their own energetic essence.

On returning home from the Sacred Gatherings Retreat, each participant, drawn by the allure of deep personal revelation, will set a private appointment with Shania. These intimate encounters, a crucial step for those ready to deepen their path of self-discovery, will involve Shania assisting them through their transformation. Utilizing the sequential aura photography as a spiritual tool, she will guide them into the profound insights that lie within the colorful displays of their personal energy. Shania will delve into the deep-rooted revelations that these captivating images hold.

The participants will not only be gifted with aura photographs, but at the beginning of the retreat, they will receive a special journal, carefully designed to capture the essence of their sacred journey. This beautifully crafted journal features a pocket where they could safely keep their aura photographs, with the final one serving as the cover and the initial photograph tucked into an inner pocket at the beginning.

Emblazoned with the title "My Sacred Journey," the journal would beckon the participants to pour their hearts onto its pages, allowing their experiences, insights, and reflections to find expression in the written word. It will become a sacred vessel, holding their stories, growth, and newfound wisdom, encapsulating the transformative essence of their time together.

With each stroke of the pen, the participants would embark on a profound exploration of self-discovery and self-expression. The journal would become a trusted companion, bearing witness to their innermost thoughts, dreams, and aspirations. Within its pages, the vibrant energy of their aura photographs would merge with their heartfelt words, creating a harmonious tapestry of their spiritual evolution.

As they carefully slip their aura photographs into the designated pocket, the cover of the journal becomes a visual reminder of their journey's culmination. Each time they get ready to open its pages, the participants would be greeted by the radiant energy captured in their final aura photograph, igniting a renewed sense of purpose and connection to their higher selves.

"My Sacred Journey" would become more than just a journal; it would become a sacred vessel, holding the transformative essence of their experiences and serving as a tangible testament to their growth and self-discovery. It would serve as a constant reminder of their commitment to embracing the radiant truth of their being, forever guiding them on their path of enlightenment and self-expression.

CHAPTER 17

THE AWAKENING: EMBRACING HIGHER DIMENSIONS OF CONSCIOUSNESS

For the first sacred gathering, the hallway buzzed with an electric energy as individuals eagerly came together, captivated by the prospect of personal growth and the limitless expansion of consciousness. Natalia would take the lead in introducing the retreat. She will begin by teaching the participants about 3D consciousness, 4D consciousness, and 5D consciousness. Her teachings will resonate deeply with the participants, because they are hungry for understanding and eager to embark on this transformative path.

The First Sacred Gathering Begins

As the participants entered the room, ready for the first sacred gathering, their eyes widened with a mix of curiosity and anticipation. They gracefully settled onto plush cushions or comfortable plush chairs, each breath filled with excitement and wonder, ready to embark on a transformative journey of self-discovery. As the first sacred gathering was about to commence, a palpable sense of excitement filled the air, mingling with the anticipation in the participants' hearts. A warm and spirited individual stepped forward, introducing Natalia and Shania with a genuine smile and kind words, inviting them to take their place at the center of the transformative journey. Gratitude resonated in Natalia's voice as she expressed her appreciation for the gathering, followed by Shania's heartfelt words of welcome.

With gentle authority, Shania invited the participants to find a comfortable position, their bodies relaxed, and their minds open. Her soothing voice filled the space, guiding them on a journey of the imagination, a sacred exploration of their inner landscape. "Imagine yourself standing on the edge of a vast, serene lake," she began, painting a vivid picture with her words. "Feel the warmth of the sun kissing your skin, the gentle breeze caressing your face. As you take a deep breath, allow yourself to be fully present in this moment."

As Shania continued to weave her words, the participants embarked on an inner odyssey; their spirits carried away on the currents of her guidance. She led them through lush forests, inviting them to drink from the wellspring of their own wisdom. They encountered radiant beings of light, who whispered ancient secrets of enlightenment and transformation. Each step of the visualization journey deepened their connection to their true essence, igniting a spark of divine inspiration within.

"See yourself bathed in a luminous, golden light," Shania's voice resonated with power and tenderness. "Feel this light infusing every cell of your being, dissolving any remnants of doubt or limitation. You are a vessel of pure potential, a conduit of divine love and wisdom."

As the guided meditation reached its crescendo, the participants' hearts swelled with a profound sense of peace and purpose. They were touched at their core, their spirits awakened to the boundless possibilities that lay before them. The transformative power of Shania's words reverberated through their souls, resonating with a resounding affirmation of their inner light.

Slowly, Shania guided the participants back to the present moment, their hearts aglow with newfound clarity and inspiration. The room filled with a hushed reverence, as if the participants were reluctant to break the sacred stillness that had enveloped them.

As the room embraced a tranquil serenity, Natalia moved forward with graceful poise, emanating an irresistible aura of wisdom and guidance. A collective hush settled upon the space as all eyes were drawn to her, hearts beating with eager anticipation. It was as if time stood still, the participants on the edge of their seats, ready to pioneer a reflective journey of self-discovery and enlightenment.

3rd Dimensional Consciousness

Natalia began by painting a vivid picture of the 3rd Dimensional (3D) consciousness. With each carefully chosen word, she illuminated the limitations and characteristics of this realm of human experience.

"Imagine a world where separation and duality reign supreme," Natalia's voice echoed through the room. "In the realm of 3D consciousness, individuals perceive themselves as separate entities, disconnected from the web of life. They identify primarily with their physical bodies, defining themselves by external markers such as race, gender, and social status."

She paced the room, her gestures conveying the weight of this paradigm. "In 3D consciousness, fear, and survival instincts dominate. People are driven by the need for security, accumulation of material possessions, and the pursuit of power. They believe that

113

life is a competitive game, where success is measured by external achievements and the acquisition of wealth."

Natalia's words hung in the air, causing a ripple of recognition among the participants. They had felt the constriction of this dimension, the limitations it imposed on their understanding of themselves and the world around them.

"With 3D consciousness," Natalia continued, "there is a prevailing belief in scarcity and lack. Individuals operate from a place of separation, perceiving themselves as separate from others and the abundant resources of the universe. This mindset fosters competition, judgment, and the perpetuation of hierarchical structures."

She paused, allowing the significance of her words to sink in. The participants exchanged knowing glances, their collective understanding deepening.

"In the realm of 3D consciousness, the ego reigns supreme," Natalia proclaimed. "Individuals are driven by the need for control, validation, and external approval. They attach their sense of self-worth to achievements, possessions, and societal recognition. The ego maintains a narrow focus, fixated on personal gain and the preservation of its own identity."

As the participants absorbed Natalia's teachings, Shania observed a subtle shift in their energy. It was as if they were peering through a veil, catching a glimpse of the limitations that had confined their perception for so long.

"But," Natalia's voice softened, "the 3D consciousness is not inherently negative or wrong. It serves a purpose in our evolutionary journey. It provides a foundation for individual growth, self-awareness, and the exploration of contrast."

Natalia's words held a note of compassion, acknowledging the necessity of the 3D realm while gently guiding the participants towards a broader perspective.

"As we navigate through life, we may find ourselves moving through various levels of consciousness," Natalia continued. "The key is to become aware of the limitations of 3D consciousness and to transcend them when we are ready. It is an invitation to expand our awareness, to awaken to the interconnectedness of all beings and the vast potential that lies within us."

She looked into the eyes of each participant, a spark of hope and possibility shimmering in her gaze. "By embracing higher dimensions of consciousness, we can access deeper levels of love, compassion, and unity. We can release the grip of fear, scarcity, and separation, and step into a reality where we recognize our intrinsic connection to all of existence."

Shania felt a profound sense of gratitude for Natalia's teachings. The room buzzed with a renewed energy, as the participants contemplated the profound implications of 3D consciousness and the inherent possibilities for growth and transformation that lay ahead.

4th Dimensional Consciousness

Natalia continued as she moved to 4D consciousness. The air was charged with anticipation as Natalia prepared to unveil the intricacies of 4th-dimensional (4D) consciousness. Shania, fully present in the moment, observed the participants leaning forward in their seats, their eyes filled with curiosity and a hunger for knowledge.

Natalia began by creating a palpable atmosphere of expansion and possibility. Her voice, like a gentle breeze, carried the essence of the 4D realm, weaving a tapestry of understanding in the minds of those gathered.

"In the realm of 4D consciousness," Natalia began, "we transcend the limitations of 3D and enter into a state of expanded awareness. It is a dimension of possibilities, where time becomes fluid and perceptions are heightened."

She paused, allowing her words to settle into the collective consciousness of the participants. Shania could sense their receptivity, their eagerness to embark on this new dimension of exploration.

"In 4D consciousness," Natalia continued, her voice rich with vibrancy, "we recognize that there is more to reality than what meets the eye. We become aware of the energetic and spiritual dimensions that coexist with the physical world. We understand that thoughts, emotions, and intentions hold tremendous power in shaping our experiences."

Natalia's words resonated deeply within Shania's being. The participants, too, seemed to be captivated by the prospect of a reality that extended beyond the confines of their senses.

"In 4D consciousness, time is no longer linear," Natalia explained. "We realize that the past, present, and future exist simultaneously, interconnected in a web of experiences. We gain the ability to transcend the constraints of time, accessing wisdom from the past, envisioning the possibilities of the future, and anchoring ourselves in the present moment."

Shania observed the expressions of wonder on the faces of the participants. It was as if a new realm of exploration had opened before them, beckoning them to delve deeper into the mysteries of existence.

"As we embrace 4D consciousness," Natalia continued, "we cultivate a deeper connection to our intuition, our inner knowing. We trust in the wisdom that arises from within and honor the guidance of our higher selves. We recognize the importance of self-reflection, inner healing, and the integration of our shadow aspects."

The room buzzed with a newfound energy, the participants digesting the profound implications of 4D consciousness. Shania felt a gentle stirring in her own soul, a recognition of the expanded possibilities that awaited them all.

"In 4D consciousness," Natalia concluded, her voice infused with a sense of reverence, "we realize that we are co-creators of our reality. We understand that our thoughts, beliefs, and intentions shape the world around us. It is a realm of heightened responsibility, where we become conscious of our impact on ourselves, others, and the planet."

Shania marveled at the transformation unfolding within the sacred gathering. The participants sat in contemplation, their hearts open to the vast potential that 4D consciousness offered.

"As we continue on this journey of exploration," Natalia said, her gaze encompassing the room, "let us embrace the expanded awareness of 4D consciousness. Let us cultivate compassion, understanding, and the courage to step into the realms of possibility that await us."

Shania felt a profound sense of gratitude for Natalia's guidance and the collective energy that filled the room. They were on the threshold of a magnificent voyage, and the exploration of 4D consciousness would be the catalyst for their continued growth and transformation.

CHAPTER 18

AWAKENING TO THE FIFTH DIMENSION: A JOURNEY OF COLLECTIVE CONSCIOUSNESS

As the sacred gathering entered its next phase, the atmosphere continued to buzz with anticipation. Natalia, radiating a sense of serenity and inner knowing, prepared to delve into the wondrous realm of 5th-dimensional (5D) consciousness. Shania, captivated by the energy in the room, could feel the participants leaning forward, their hearts open to the profound insights that awaited them.

Natalia, standing at the center of the sacred space, took a deep breath and began to weave a tapestry of understanding about the joys of 5D consciousness. Her voice, like a gentle melody, carried the essence of the higher dimensions, enveloping the participants in a sense of awe and possibility.

"In the realm of 5D consciousness," Natalia began, her words resonating with a sense of expansiveness, "we transcend the limitations of duality and enter into a state of unity, love, and heightened awareness. It is a dimension where separation dissolves, and we recognize the interconnectedness of all beings and the web of life that unites us."

Shania watched as the participants' eyes sparkled with recognition, their hearts opening to the infinite possibilities that awaited them in the realm of 5D consciousness.

"In 5D consciousness," Natalia continued, her voice brimming with excitement, "we embody love as the foundational energy that permeates every aspect of our being. Love becomes the guiding force in our thoughts, actions, and interactions. We experience a profound sense of unity, compassion, and empathy, where judgment and separation no longer hold sway."

The room seemed to radiate with a warm, golden light as the participants absorbed Natalia's words. Shania, too, felt her heart expand, resonating with the vibrancy of 5D consciousness.

"In 5D consciousness," Natalia emphasized, "we transcend the limitations of the egoic mind and embrace the wisdom of our higher selves. We access higher states of awareness, intuition, and creativity. We live in harmony with the flow of life, surrendering to the divine guidance that flows through us."

Shania observed the participants taking in the profound implications of 5D consciousness. It was as if a veil had been lifted, revealing a world where joy, abundance, and harmony were not only possible but natural states of being.

"In 5D consciousness," Natalia continued, her voice gentle yet resolute, "we awaken to our true essence as spiritual beings having a human experience. We remember our interconnectedness with the universe and tap into the vast well of wisdom, knowledge, and guidance available to us. We co-create a reality aligned with our highest potential, contributing to the collective awakening and evolution of humanity."

The room seemed to shimmer with an ethereal light as the participants absorbed the profound implications of 5D consciousness. Shania felt a sense of awe and gratitude, witnessing the transformation unfolding before her very eyes.

"As we embark on this journey into 5D consciousness," Natalia concluded, her voice filled with reverence, "let us embrace the joy, love, and unity that await us. Let us embody the highest vibrations of the heart and mind, and together, we can create a reality that reflects the beauty, harmony, and peace that reside within us all.

Shania marveled at the transformative energy that filled the sacred gathering. The participants sat in quiet contemplation, their souls resonating with the infinite possibilities that 5D consciousness offered.

"As we continue to explore the wonders of 5D consciousness," Natalia said, her gaze encompassing the room, "let us be guided by love, let us honor our interconnectedness, and let us dance in the joy of co-creating a world where peace, harmony, and unity prevail."

Shania felt a profound sense of gratitude for Natalia's guidance and the collective energy that enveloped the room. Together, they were embarking on a magnificent journey of awakening, embracing the joys of 5D consciousness, and stepping into a reality filled with love, light, and boundless possibilities.

As the sacred gathering progressed, Shania knew that this exploration of consciousness would guide them all towards a greater understanding of themselves and the world they inhabited. So, she eagerly anticipated the next step on their shared journey.

As the soothing melody of meditation music began to fill the room, Shania's voice resonated with serenity and grace, carrying the participants to a place of inner stillness. "Let us now journey within," she gently instructed, "tapping into the wellspring of our intuition, allowing it to guide us in assimilating the wisdom that has been shared."

In the tranquility of the moment, Shania led the group through a 5-minute guided meditation, guiding them to quiet their minds and open their hearts to the whispers of their intuition. As they delved into the depths of their being, visions, and insights began to emerge, like fragments of a mystical puzzle revealing profound truths.

The meditation music continued to play, enveloping the room in a cocoon of serenity for an additional 15 minutes. In this sacred space, participants listened intently to the whispers of their intuition, feeling the gentle guidance of their inner compass. With each passing moment, clarity deepened, and profound revelations unfolded, carrying the participants on a journey of self-discovery and insight.

As the music slowly faded into silence, Shania's voice gently guided them back to the present moment, where they would anchor the golden nuggets of wisdom received from their intuition. "Return now," she whispered, "bringing with you the wisdom bestowed upon you by your intuitive guidance." With gentle guidance, Shania directed the participants to pen their profound experiences in their cherished journals.

With hearts brimming with newfound clarity and inspiration, the participants reached for their journals, capturing the essence of their experience on the pages before them. Each stroke of the pen breathed life into the profound insights that had graced their awareness, creating a tangible record of their sacred journey.

In the stillness of the room, the participants immersed themselves in the act of writing, giving form to the ethereal whispers of their intuition. A sense of reverence filled the air as they poured their experiences onto the pages, knowing that they were etching a lasting imprint of their soul's connection to higher realms.

Shania's voice, like a gentle breeze, encouraged them to honor their unique experiences, assuring them that their insights held immense value. "Embrace the wisdom that has been gifted to you," she softly spoke, "for within the sacred whispers of your intuition lies the keys to your highest self."

So, they wrote, allowing the meditative stillness to linger, savoring the treasures unveiled by their intuitive journey. In the hushed ambiance, the room became a sanctuary, a sacred space of self-discovery, transformation, and inner knowing.

As the enlightening discussions and transformative experiences in the vast realms of consciousness reached their conclusion, a well-deserved lunch break beckoned the eager participants. Natalia, attuned to the vastness of the information shared, reassured the group that she understood the magnitude of the teachings and the need for integration. She unveiled a thoughtful plan for the afternoon session, explaining that upon their return, the group would split into smaller circles, fostering an environment for collective processing and exploration of the profound concepts of 3D, 4D, and 5D consciousness.

As the participants dispersed, their minds buzzing with profound insights, they engaged in animated conversations, walking together towards the hotel's inviting dining area. Finding available tables, they exchanged introductions, forming new connections among like-minded souls who shared their eagerness for spiritual growth. Passionate discussions ensued, as the participants delved into the depths of the teachings on 3D, 4D, and 5D consciousness, marveling at the profound relevance to their own lives. Recognizing the resonance in their shared experiences, many resolved to regroup during the upcoming session, fueling their anticipation for the continued exploration of consciousness.

Amidst the heartfelt conversations that echoed across the tables, a palpable sense of excitement and intrigue permeated the air. As the lunchtime discussions drew to a close, a gentle reminder circulated that the gathering would soon reconvene. With gratitude for the nourishment received, participants tidied their dining areas and returned to the room where the sacred gathering awaited, eager to dive deeper into the transformative journey that lay ahead.

Eager anticipation filled the room as the participants eagerly awaited Natalia's teachings, their hearts open and ready for the transformative experiences that awaited them. Natalia greeted everyone with warmth and enthusiasm, outlining the plan for the remainder of the gathering. Instructing them to form small groups, no larger than five, the participants eagerly engaged in heartfelt conversations, sharing their personal journeys and reflections on 3D, 4D, and 5D consciousness.

Even on this first day of the retreat, profound "aha" moments illuminated their minds, evoking tears of recognition and support from the compassionate group members. The value of this collective experience resonated deeply with the participants, providing a sense of belonging and understanding that they often longed for in their personal lives.

As approximately an hour passed in what felt like mere moments, Natalia guided the group to unite again, fostering a sense of unity and shared growth. Stories of personal breakthroughs intertwined with reflections on the power of the group experience, creating an atmosphere of closeness and connection.

In the final moments of the session, Natalia's words resonated with heartfelt wisdom as she addressed the participants, her voice filled with compassion, saying, "I understand that this information can be overwhelming. Remember, it's not about labeling the levels of consciousness as right or wrong. What matters most is acknowledging where you are on your unique journey." Then, Natalia kindly reminded everyone to continue to chronicle their journey in the pages of their journal. With her concluding words, Shania gracefully stepped forward, guiding the group into a soul-stirring meditation that embraced the very essence of their beings, leaving an indelible imprint on each participant's soul.

With sincere gratitude, Natalia and Shania expressed their appreciation for the participants' presence and unwavering commitment. As the sacred gathering came to a close, the participants departed, some choosing to spend time together, basking in the camaraderie of newfound friendships, while others sought solace in the awe-inspiring vistas of Sedona's majestic red rocks, reflecting on the profound journey that lay before them.

CHAPTER 19

DAY 2: EMBRACING THE POWER OF 5D CONSCIOUSNESS

As the morning sun bathed the majestic red rock formations of Sedona in its golden embrace, a breathtaking display of colors unfolded before the participants. Eager and filled with anticipation, they entered the room for the second day of the Sacred Gathering. The melodic strains of meditation music filled the air, intertwined with the enchanting aroma of burning candles, creating an atmosphere of captivating allure. With eyes closed and hearts open, they settled into their seats, ready to embark on the transformative journey that awaited them.

Natalia and Shania were already seated at the front of the room, their eyes closed, emanating a serene energy that enveloped the space. The ethereal melodies of the meditation music gradually faded away, and Shania's gentle voice resonated, filling the room with tranquility.

"Take a deep breath," Shania began, her voice a soothing melody. "Allow your body to relax, sinking deeper into the support of the chair beneath you. Feel the rhythm of your breath, the gentle rise and fall, as you let go of any tension or thoughts that may arise."

She continued, her words carrying the essence of compassion and guidance. "Now, imagine yourself surrounded by a soft, golden light, wrapping you in a warm embrace. Feel its gentle warmth permeating every cell of your being, soothing and nourishing you."

As the room fell into a profound stillness, Shania gently led them deeper into the meditation. "Now, visualize yourself standing at the edge of a serene lake, its crystal-clear waters reflecting the vibrant colors of the surrounding nature. As you gaze upon this serene landscape, feel a deep sense of peace and connectedness wash over you."

She paused, allowing a moment of stillness to settle before she continued. "In this space of profound tranquility, I invite you to set an intention for today's journey. What is it that you wish to explore, discover, or embrace? Allow this intention to arise naturally within you, anchoring it in your heart with love and clarity."

As Shania concluded her guidance, her voice resonated with a gentle reassurance. "When you are ready, slowly bring your awareness back to the present moment. Open your eyes, carrying the peace and clarity you have cultivated into the sacred space we share."

The room remained in a tranquil silence for a moment, before participants gradually began to open their eyes, their hearts and minds prepared for the transformative experiences that awaited them.

Shania and Natalia greeted the participants with warm smiles, their presence radiating a sense of anticipation and purpose. As the room buzzed with excitement, Natalia stepped forward, capturing everyone's attention.

"Welcome to Day 2 of our Sacred Gathering," Natalia began, her voice carrying a gentle yet invigorating tone. "Today, we delve into the three key aspects of transitioning to 5D consciousness: the Personal, Interpersonal, and Collective Impact."

She gracefully outlined the significance of each aspect, guiding the participants on a journey of self-discovery, deepening connections with others, and embracing the profound impact they can collectively create in the world. The room hummed with attentive energy, each participant eager to explore these transformative realms.

As Natalia concluded her introduction, Shania added her heartfelt words. "We are honored to embark on this journey with all of you. We recognize the hunger within each of you for understanding, growth, and enlightenment. Today, we dive deeper into these realms, uncovering the wisdom that lies within and weaving it into our shared experiences."

The participants leaned in, captivated by the profound possibilities that awaited them. With a renewed sense of purpose, they embraced the day's teachings, ready to embrace the transformative power of 5D consciousness and create a lasting impact in their lives and the world around them.

Natalia took center stage, her presence commanding attention as she began to unveil the profound teachings of transitioning to 5D consciousness. The room grew quiet, the air thick with anticipation and open-mindedness.

CHAPTER 20

EXPLORING THE PERSONAL IMPACT OF 5D CONSCIOUSNESS

She spoke with clarity and conviction, capturing the interest of every participant. "The personal impact of transitioning to 5D consciousness is nothing short of transformative," Natalia began. "As individuals awaken to this higher state of being, they undergo a profound shift in their lives."

She elaborated on the remarkable changes that occur when one embraces 5D consciousness. "Living authentically becomes a guiding principle," Natalia explained, her voice resonating with wisdom and gentle authority. "It is a journey of self-discovery, where individuals align their thoughts, words, and actions with their higher selves."

The room embraced Natalia's words, as participants leaned forward, captivated by the essence of this profound teaching. Natalia took a moment to create a deeper understanding, her eyes scanning the room, ensuring that every soul felt seen and heard.

"What is the higher self?" she continued, her voice carrying a blend of clarity and reverence. "The higher self is the purest essence of our being, the eternal and divine aspect that transcends the limitations of the physical realm. It is the part of us that is connected to the infinite wisdom of the universe, a wellspring of love, compassion, and inner knowing."

As Natalia spoke, the concept of the higher self became tangible, a shimmering light within the participants' hearts. They began to grasp the significance of aligning with this deeper truth, realizing that their higher self held the keys to their purpose, joy, and spiritual growth. It was the aspect of themselves that held an unwavering connection to the divine, guiding them towards their highest potential.

"In the presence of our higher self, we are able to tap into profound wisdom and understanding," Natalia continued, her words weaving a tapestry of enlightenment. "Living in alignment with our higher self allows us to access inner guidance, make choices from a place of clarity, and navigate our journey with grace and purpose."

The room hummed with a shared recognition. Natalia's words had struck a chord within each participant, stirring a deep longing to connect with their higher selves and embark on a transformative journey of self-discovery. They understood that by aligning with their higher self, they would unlock the doors to their true potential, living a life filled with authenticity, love, and profound fulfillment.

Natalia's teaching continued, her words carrying a gentle yet powerful resonance. "As individuals transition to 5D consciousness," she explained, "they embark on a profound journey of healing and transformation. Old wounds, limiting beliefs, and negative patterns that once held them captive are lovingly released, making way for a profound shift towards forgiveness, self-love, and empowerment."

Her voice carried a sense of conviction, compelling each participant to reflect on their own personal journey. They could feel the weight of past hurts and self-imposed limitations being lifted, replaced by a growing sense of self-compassion and empowerment.

"In the realm of 5D consciousness," Natalia continued, her words guiding them deeper into this transformative path, "forgiveness becomes a powerful tool for liberation. It is a sacred act of releasing the burdens of resentment and pain, allowing us to reclaim our inner peace and restore harmony within ourselves and in our relationships."

The participants absorbed these words, contemplating the profound implications of forgiveness as a transformative force. They felt a renewed sense of liberation, as if shackles of resentment were being cast aside, making room for compassion and understanding to flourish.

"As we embrace self-love," Natalia emphasized, her voice brimming with warmth and compassion, "we recognize our inherent worthiness and divine essence. We nurture ourselves with kindness, acceptance, and appreciation, understanding that true empowerment stems from a deep well of self-love."

Her words resonated deeply within each participant, evoking a sense of recognition and the gentle stirring of self-compassion. They began to understand that by cultivating a nourishing relationship with themselves, they could tap into an inner strength that would empower them to navigate life's challenges with grace and resilience.

Natalia's teaching illuminated a path of profound personal growth and transformation. The participants could feel the currents of change stirring within them, as they opened themselves to the possibilities of forgiveness, self-love, and empowerment. It was a powerful reminder that they held the key to unlocking their own liberation, and the journey towards 5D consciousness was one of self-discovery and inner alchemy.

The room seemed to hold its breath, fully immersed in Natalia's guidance. She emphasized the significance of cultivating mindfulness, urging everyone to embrace the present moment fully. "When you learn to experience each moment fully, you will find an inherent peace and joy that is not dependent on external conditions," she explained, her voice carrying a comforting tone.

Natalia's teaching flowed effortlessly, each word carrying the essence of profound wisdom. "In the realm of 5D consciousness," she gently explained, "trusting the flow of life becomes second nature. It is a state of surrendering to the cosmic dance, where challenges are no longer viewed as obstacles but as stepping stones for growth. You begin to recognize that the universe is a benevolent force, always working for your highest good."

Her words resonated deeply within each participant, offering a new perspective on the ebb and flow of life. They could feel the weight of worry and anxiety being lifted, replaced by a growing sense of trust and serenity. The notion of surrendering to the flow of life, with all its twists and turns, brought a profound peace.

"As you cultivate this trust and surrender," Natalia continued, her voice enveloped in soothing warmth, "you tap into a deep well of peace and resilience. Stress and anxiety dissolve, for you understand that you are held and supported by a greater intelligence. This deep sense of peace becomes the foundation from which you navigate life's challenges with grace and clarity."

Her words painted a vivid picture in the minds of the participants, as they imagined themselves immersed in the currents of life, surrendering to its rhythm and finding solace in the knowledge that they were part of a larger, harmonious tapestry. The concept of reducing stress and anxiety through trust and surrender became a beacon of hope, illuminating a path towards inner peace.

"In this heightened state of consciousness," Natalia emphasized, her voice filled with conviction, "you will notice a heightened intuition and synchronicity. The universe communicates with you in subtle ways, guiding you towards your life purpose and aligning you with soul-aligned paths. Signs and synchronicities become the breadcrumbs that lead you towards your deepest desires and dreams."

Her words ignited a sense of wonder within the participants, as they contemplated the profound connection between their inner world and the external manifestations. They began to understand that by attuning themselves to the subtle whispers of the universe, they could navigate their lives with greater clarity and purpose.

Natalia's teaching offered a powerful invitation to embrace trust, surrender, and the innate harmony of the universe. The participants felt a renewed sense of peace and resilience, knowing that they were not alone on their journey. The path to 5D consciousness became clearer, as they embraced the transformative power of trusting the flow of life and surrendering to its divine guidance.

The room seemed to radiate with a newfound understanding. Natalia's teachings resonated with each participant, who recognized the truth in the words being shared. The concept of enhanced intuition and synchronicity stirred excitement, as they began to comprehend the effortless guidance towards their life purpose and soul-aligned paths.

As Natalia concluded her teachings on the personal impact of transitioning to 5D consciousness, the room erupted in a harmonious hum of contemplation. The participants absorbed the wisdom, eager to integrate these principles into their lives. They recognized the immense potential for personal growth and transformation that lay within their grasp, and their hearts brimmed with gratitude for the opportunity to take part in this extraordinary journey of self-discovery.

After a nourishing session of profound insights, Natalia warmly announced a well-deserved break. The participants eagerly embraced the opportunity to stretch their legs and engage in lively conversations, their minds buzzing with the wealth of newfound knowledge. Twenty minutes flew by in a flurry of excitement and anticipation, and with a renewed sense of curiosity, they gradually made their way back to the room.

CHAPTER 21

THE INTERPERSONAL IMPACT OF 5D: COMPASSION AND EMPATHY

As they reentered the space, a palpable energy of anticipation filled the air. Each participant found their seat, settling in with a renewed focus and a heightened sense of curiosity. The room buzzed with an electric atmosphere as if the collective consciousness was on the edge of something extraordinary.

Ready to resume their transformative journey, the participants fixed their attention on Natalia, waiting for her wisdom to once again unfold. They were primed for further insights, their hearts open and receptive, eager to delve deeper into the mysteries of consciousness. Natalia will now teach about the interpersonal impact of transitioning to 5D consciousness.

"My friends," Natalia began, her voice carrying the wisdom of ages, "compassion, empathy, and conscious communication are the keys that unlock the gates of harmonious relationships."

The participants leaned in, their eyes fixed on Natalia, hungry for her guidance.

Compassion

"Compassion," she continued, her voice resonating with deep empathy, "is the gift we offer ourselves and others. It is the understanding that we all experience joys and sorrows, triumphs and struggles. By extending compassion, we create a space for healing, growth, and understanding."

"When we approach relationships with genuine compassion," Natalia continued, "we nurture a sacred space where hearts can truly connect. Compassion is the cornerstone of nurturing healthy connections. It is the ability to extend kindness, empathy, and understanding to ourselves and others, embracing the beauty of our shared human experience."

The room seemed to glow with understanding as participants absorbed Natalia's words. Another nod of agreement followed as she continued, her voice carrying the weight of heartfelt understanding. "When we approach relationships with genuine compassion, we create a safe and nurturing space for vulnerability and growth."

Her words touched upon the fundamental truth that in compassionate relationships, masks can be shed, and souls can be laid bare without fear of judgment or rejection. It is within this safe and nurturing space that profound transformations occur, where individuals can authentically express their needs, fears, and desires, fostering deep understanding and mutual support.

Natalia's gaze moved around the room, locking eyes with each participant as she imparted her insights. "By fostering an atmosphere of compassion, we encourage open and honest communication, enabling us to truly see and hear one another."

Natalia's teachings illuminated the power of compassion to create a harmonious tapestry of interconnected souls, where love, acceptance, and growth thrive. In this space, participants understood that their relationships could become vessels of healing, transformation, and deep connection, enriching their lives and the lives of those around them.

Empathy

Natalia gracefully shifted her focus to the captivating topic of empathy. Initially, Shania had been prepared to share her personal experiences as a naturally empathic individual. However, after an enlightening discussion between Shania and Natalia, they collectively decided that Natalia would take the lead in presenting on empathy during this session. They recognized that empathy held a distinct aspect separate from being an empath, and Shania's unique insights as an empath would be best explored in a special session tailored specifically for participants with empathic tendencies. Shania was eager to support those who faced similar challenges and to provide guidance and understanding in navigating the empathic journey.

In their deep discussion, Shania and Natalia embarked on an exploration of the intricate facets of empathy. They illuminated its nuanced nature, distinguishing it from the empathic experience. While empathy often stirred in response to external stimuli—a phone call, a fleeting expression—an empath's abilities transcended these triggers. An empath possessed a remarkable gift, accessing the energy and emotions of others through intuitive means, without the necessity of physical interaction. It was a profound connection, one that surpassed the confines of the material world.

Recognizing the significance of this distinction, Shania's role in sharing her knowledge with fellow empaths became evident.

Natalia, aware of the importance of this aspect, took a moment to inform the participants about a special session, if needed, during a time after the retreat, designed specifically for those with empathic tendencies. It was a sacred opportunity for Shania to impart her wisdom and provide guidance to individuals who shared similar experiences, a crucial part of their collective journey towards understanding and embracing their empathic nature.

So, Natalia began, her voice carrying a delicate yet resonant tone that effortlessly captivated the room. "Let us embark on a journey to explore the precious gift of empathy," she shared. "It is a divine ability that allows us to step into the sacred shoes of another, to deeply feel and understand their experiences, joys, and challenges. Through the lens of empathy, we cultivate a deep and profound connection that transcends differences and bridges the gaps between us."

Natalia continued, her voice filled with wisdom and compassion, "Empathy is a thread that weaves together the fabric of humanity. It builds bridges, crossing over the barriers that divide us, and embracing the universal truth that we are all interconnected souls on this magnificent journey of life. When we cultivate empathy, we honor the sacredness of each individual's unique experience and open ourselves to a world of profound connection and unwavering support."

She paused for a moment, allowing her words to sink deeply into the hearts of the participants. "To cultivate empathy, we must practice the art of deep listening, setting aside our judgments and preconceived notions. We must be present and fully attentive, creating a safe space for others to express themselves authentically. Through this sincere presence, we can truly hear the unspoken words, perceive the hidden emotions, and understand the unarticulated needs of those around us."

Natalia's words resonated with the room, igniting a spark within each participant's heart. She continued, her voice carrying a sense of inspiration, "When we embrace empathy, we not only enrich the lives of others but also our own. It is through genuine empathy that we can build bridges of connection, fostering a sense of unity and harmony in our relationships."

The room was bathed in a collective silence, as the profound truth of Natalia's teachings settled in the hearts of those present. They recognized that by cultivating empathy, they could transcend differences, heal wounds, and create a more compassionate and interconnected world.

Natalia shared insights on how to nurture empathy, urging the participants to actively listen, observe, and seek to understand others without judgment. Natalia re-emphasized the power of stepping into another person's shoes, immersing ourselves in their experiences, joys, and challenges. By doing so, we transcend our own perspectives and enter a realm of genuine understanding.

"Why is it so vital to cultivate empathy?" Natalia posed the question to the group, her eyes sparkling with an unyielding belief in the transformative potential of empathy. "Because it is through empathy that we create deep connections that nourish and uplift our souls. It is through empathy that we validate the shared human experience, reminding one another that we are not alone on this journey."

Natalia guided the participants on the path towards genuine understanding, encouraging them to embrace vulnerability and open their hearts to the world around them. She re-emphasized the need to listen without judgment, to hold space for others, and to offer unwavering support.

"Through empathy," Natalia continued, her voice infused with a sense of wonder, "we unlock the power of authentic connection. We embrace the beauty of diversity, recognizing that we are all interconnected souls on this intricate tapestry of life. Genuine understanding and unwavering support become the pillars that sustain and uplift our relationships."

The room reverberated with a renewed sense of purpose, as the participants absorbed Natalia's teachings. In their hearts, they carried a profound understanding of the transformative potential that lay within empathy, the key that unlocked doors to profound connections and unwavering support. With each passing moment, their souls embraced the calling to cultivate empathy and contribute to a world brimming with compassion and understanding.

CHAPTER 22

THE INTERPERSONAL IMPACT OF 5D: THE DANCE OF CONSCIOUS COMMUNICATION AND REFLECTION

atalia gracefully transitioned her teachings from empathy to the profound art of conscious communication. As she shifted the focus, the room fell into a hushed reverence, eager to soak in the wisdom that would unfold. Her voice carried a gentle yet commanding tone, filled with grace and clarity.

"Conscious communication," Natalia began, her words woven with wisdom, "is the sacred art of expressing ourselves authentically while being fully present and actively listening to others. It is about speaking from the heart, using words that uplift and empower. It is a dance of the heart, where words become vessels of empowerment, understanding, and love. It is a deliberate choice to honor the sacredness of every interaction, recognizing the power that our words hold to shape our reality."

She paused, allowing her words to settle and permeate the depths of their beings. The participants leaned in, their eyes fixed on Natalia, captivated by the essence of her teachings. Natalia continued, "In conscious communication, we speak from the depths of our being, allowing our words to carry authenticity, vulnerability, and respect. We choose words that uplift, inspire, and bring healing to ourselves and others."

Natalia further illuminated, "In the art of conscious communication, we become skilled navigators of the currents of conversation, gracefully weaving our way through the ebb and flow of words, inviting deep connection and understanding. Like adept sailors on a vast ocean, we steer our conversations with intention, guided by the compass of love and compassion."

Her voice carried a gentle yet profound resonance as she spoke, "With each word we choose, we have the power to paint vivid pictures in the minds of others, evoking emotions and creating spaces of resonance and understanding. We listen attentively, not only to the surface-level words, but also to the unspoken yearnings, the subtle nuances, and the hidden depths. We attune ourselves to the unspoken language of the heart, the vibrations that ripple beneath the surface."

"In our conscious navigation," Natalia acknowledged, "we honor the power of silence, allowing pauses to settle and unfold.

We recognize that within the spaces between words, profound revelations can emerge, deepening our connection and creating bridges of understanding. We hold the space for others to share their truth, creating a safe haven for vulnerability and authenticity."

"Conscious communication requires the art of empathy," Natalia re-emphasized, "the ability to step into another's shoes and truly understand their perspective. We let go of judgment and preconceived notions, embracing curiosity and openness instead. We approach conversations with genuine interest, seeking to learn and grow from the unique perspectives and experiences of others."

"In our conscious navigation, we also practice the art of reflection and clarification," Natalia continued. "We seek to understand before being understood, asking thoughtful questions and genuinely listening to the responses. We offer reflections that show we truly hear and acknowledge the essence of what is being shared, fostering deeper connection and mutual understanding."

"Through conscious communication," Natalia expressed, "we invite others to share their stories, dreams, and aspirations, as we bear witness to their truth with reverence and love. In this sacred space of conscious communication, we build bridges that unite hearts and minds, cultivating a world where understanding, compassion, and deep connection thrive."

"As we navigate the currents of conversation with mindfulness and intention," Natalia further shared, "we embark on a transformative journey of connection and growth. We become the architects of harmonious relationships, co-creating a reality where genuine understanding and unwavering support prevail. With each conscious word we speak, we infuse the world with the transformative power of love, guiding ourselves and others towards a more enlightened and compassionate existence."

Continuing her teachings, Natalia emphasized the importance of active listening, the art of truly hearing and understanding the messages beneath the words. "Through attentive listening, we honor the stories, emotions, and experiences shared by others. We set aside our own judgments and preconceptions, creating a safe and supportive space for them to express themselves fully. Conscious communication goes beyond surface-level interactions; it fosters genuine connection and intimacy."

She continued her words like a gentle breeze that stirred the room, "When we engage in conscious communication, we honor the inherent divinity in every soul. We create an environment where trust and openness flourish, allowing the seeds of love and understanding to blossom. When we engage in conscious communication, we honor the inherent worth and wisdom of each individual, fostering mutual respect and understanding. This deepens our relationships, allowing us to communicate with clarity, authenticity, and love. Through conscious communication, we weave threads of unity, fostering a world where our words become bridges that connect hearts and minds."

The room fell into a hushed reverence as Natalia continued, her words carrying the weight of ancient wisdom. "By embracing compassion, empathy, and conscious communication, we transform our relationships. We create spaces where love flows freely, conflicts dissolve, and understanding and growth thrive."

Natalia's teachings on conscious communication resonated deep within the hearts of the participants, igniting a spark of realization. They understood that through mindful and intentional communication, they had the power to transform relationships, foster harmony, and co-create a reality rooted in love and compassion. It became clear that these teachings were not just concepts but practical tools that could be woven into the fabric of their relationships, enhancing their lives and the lives of those around them.

Natalia's profound insights struck a chord within their hearts, reminding them of their innate capacity for love, empathy, and conscious communication. It was a reminder of the path they were walking, the path of awakening and enlightenment, where relationships blossomed into sacred unions of harmony and unity.

As the session drew to a close, Natalia's final words lingered in the air, "Embrace these teachings, my dear friends, and watch as your relationships flourish with love, understanding, and profound connection."

The participants, filled with gratitude, offered a collective nod of appreciation. Natalia's wisdom had illuminated their path, guiding them towards the transformative power of compassion, empathy, and conscious communication. Natalia's teachings had ignited a desire to embody these principles and create a world where compassion, empathy, and conscious communication were the foundation of every interaction. It was a vision that stirred their souls and propelled them forward on their collective journey of transformation and enlightenment.

The room transformed into a serene sanctuary, enveloped in the gentle melodies of the meditation music. Shania, positioned at the front, prepared to guide the participants on a transformative inner journey.

"Let us now enter the sanctuary of our inner world," Shania's serene voice began, inviting the participants to close their eyes and embrace the stillness within. "Take a deep breath and release any tensions, surrendering to this present moment."

"As you settle into this peaceful state, imagine a soft, radiant light glowing at the center of your being," Shania's voice caressed their senses, painting vivid images in their minds. "Feel this light expanding with each breath, filling your body with warmth, serenity, and a deep connection to your intuition."

"In this sacred space of inner wisdom, let your intuition be your guide," Shania's voice whispered, ushering them through the realms of their inner knowing. Time seemed to suspend as they delved deeper into their own inner wisdom, dwelling in that meditative space for approximately 5 minutes. When the moment was ripe, Shania gently continued, "Slowly open your eyes, and allow the insights and revelations that have surfaced to guide your pen as you bring your thoughts to paper."

Pens poised, shifting their attention to the waiting pages of their journals, they honored the intuitive insights that had graced their awareness.

"Let your intuition speak through your words, honoring the wisdom that has unfolded within you," Shania encouraged, her voice a conduit for divine guidance. "Trust that within you lies the capacity to integrate these teachings into your life, and let your written expressions be a testament to the profound growth and self-discovery within."

Silently, the participants delved into the depths of their intuitive knowing, their pens gliding across the pages, giving voice to the profound insights and "aha" moments that had emerged during their journey.

Completing their journal entries, a sense of empowerment and fulfillment washed over them. They knew they had captured the essence of their transformative experience, carrying within them the seeds of profound growth and self-discovery.

In the peaceful embrace of the room, a palpable sense of unity and shared purpose lingered. The participants acknowledged the profound impact of their journey, not only on their individual paths but on the collective consciousness that was being uplifted by their presence.

With journals clasped gently in their hands, they felt the weight of the wisdom gained, ready to integrate it into their lives and radiate its transformative energy into the world.

The guided meditation had reached its conclusion, but the echoes of its teachings resonated within the hearts and souls of the participants, guiding them on their sacred journey of self-discovery and awakening.

After a refreshing 20-minute break, the participants reconvened, ready to delve deeper into their personal reflections. Natalia instructed them to form pairs, allowing an opportunity to share their individual insights and learnings in relation to their own lives.

Attuned to the principles surrounding compassion, empathy, and conscious communication, the participants engaged in meaningful conversations, supporting and uplifting one another in their exploration. Within the safety of these intimate connections, they shared their experiences, exchanged wisdom, and embraced the transformative power of genuine human connection.

Immersed in these insightful dialogues, the pairs had an hour to explore and discuss their unique perspectives, wisely dividing their time between listening and sharing. As they delved into the essence of their experiences, they found solace in the act of articulating their insights, solidifying their newfound understanding.

After their meaningful exchanges, the participants recorded their reflections in their journals, capturing the essence of their shared conversations. Each word etched onto the page held the power of personal growth and collective wisdom.

As the session continued, the participants reconvened as a whole, their hearts brimming with anticipation and excitement. One by one, various individuals courageously stepped forward, sharing their experiences and insights with the group. Their stories wove a tapestry of inspiration and transformation, igniting a ripple effect of profound understanding and self-discovery.

With each heartfelt sharing, the bonds of unity grew stronger, interweaving the individual journeys into a collective narrative of growth and interconnectedness. The room buzzed with the energy of connection and the power of collective wisdom.

With the conclusion of these enlightening experiences, it was time to break for a well-deserved lunch, nourishing not only their physical bodies but also their souls. Energized by the connections made and the knowledge shared, the participants eagerly engaged in conversations, deepening their understanding and forming lasting bonds.

CHAPTER 23

HARMONIZING THREADS: THE DANCE OF SERVICE, COLLABORATION AND CO-CREATION

After the lunch break, they gathered once again, their hearts open to receive the final teachings on the interpersonal impact of transitioning to 5D consciousness. The air buzzed with anticipation as Natalia prepared to guide them through the culmination of their transformative journey, empowering them to embrace their role in creating a harmonious world filled with love, compassion, and respect for all life.

The stage was set for the conclusion of the teachings, an immersive experience that would imprint an eternal signature on their hearts and minds.

Service to Others

As Natalia was concluding her teachings on the transformative interpersonal impact of transitioning to 5D consciousness, there were a few more essential concepts she wanted to present. Natalia paused, her gaze sweeping across the room, filled with eager faces ready to absorb the wisdom she had to impart. With a gentle smile, she continued, "In the expansive realms of 5D consciousness, the concept of 'service to others' takes on a whole new meaning. It becomes a natural and effortless expression of our essence, a way of being that brings us joy and fulfillment."

She went on to explain how, in 5D consciousness, individuals are driven by a deep-seated desire to contribute positively to the world. It is not borne out of obligation or a sense of duty, but rather a genuine yearning to make a difference. Natalia's voice carried a sense of reverence as she delved into the interconnectedness of all beings and the understanding that when we uplift others, we uplift ourselves and the collective consciousness.

"Service to others is not about self-sacrifice or depletion," Natalia emphasized. "It is about recognizing our inherent interconnectedness and understanding that when we serve others, we serve ourselves and the greater good. It is a dance of giving and receiving, where everyone involved is uplifted."

Collaboration and Co-Creation

She spoke of the transformative power of collaboration and co-creation in the realm of 5D consciousness. Natalia described a vision of people coming together, transcending personal agendas and ego-driven desires, to work harmoniously towards a shared purpose. In this realm, collaboration is not merely a means to an end, but a sacred act of weaving together diverse talents and perspectives, creating something greater than the sum of its parts.

"Collaboration in 5D consciousness is a profound act of co-creation," Natalia shared. "It is a recognition that when we join forces with others, we amplify our impact and unlock limitless possibilities. It is an invitation to release competition and embrace cooperation, recognizing that we are all threads in the beautiful tapestry of life."

As Natalia spoke, the room seemed to come alive with a palpable energy. The participants could feel the power of unity and the potential that lay within collective collaboration. Their hearts swelled with a renewed sense of purpose and a deep longing to contribute to a world where harmony, compassion, and respect for all life forms prevailed.

One participant, Sarah, raised her hand and shared her own experience of embracing service to others in her life. "Ever since I began to align with the principles of 5D consciousness, I have felt a profound calling to serve others," she said with a radiant smile. "Through small acts of kindness and support, I have witnessed the transformative impact it has on both the receiver and myself. It has opened my heart in ways I never thought possible."

Natalia nodded in acknowledgment, her eyes filled with warmth and understanding. "Thank you for sharing your experience, Sarah. Your story beautifully illustrates the power of service to others and how it enriches our own lives as well. When we extend a helping hand or lend a listening ear, we initiate a chain reaction of positivity that can touch the lives of many."

She continued to guide the participants through a series of reflective exercises, encouraging them to explore how they could embody the principles of service, collaboration, and co-creation in their own lives. The room buzzed with excitement as they engaged in deep introspection, envisioning a world where everyone's unique gifts and talents were utilized for the highest good of all.

Natalia concluded her teachings on the interpersonal impact of transitioning to 5D consciousness with a heartfelt reminder. "As we embrace our innate capacity for service to others, collaboration, and co-creation, we become agents of positive change in the world. Each act of kindness, each collaborative endeavor, and each co-creative project has the power to ripple out and inspire others to do the same."

She paused, allowing the words to settle and the energy in the room to deepen. Then, with a serene smile, she added, "It is through our collective efforts that we create a new Earth, a world rooted in love, peace, abundance, and respect for all life forms. In the realm of 5D consciousness, we become the architects of a reality that celebrates unity, diversity, and the interconnectedness of all beings."

CHAPTER 24

EMBRACING THE JOURNEY: PERSONAL BREAKTHROUGHS

As the participants absorbed Natalia's teachings, stories of personal breakthroughs began to emerge. Sarah, who had previously attended a Sacred Retreat, talked about how much she had grown from the first retreat that she attended. Sarah shared how her newfound understanding of service to others had transformed her relationship with her family. "I used to be so focused on my own needs and desires," she explained, her voice filled with gratitude. "But as I started to embrace the principles of 5D consciousness, I realized the immense joy and fulfillment that comes from selflessly serving others. It allowed me to mend strained relationships and create a nurturing environment at home."

Michael, another participant who had also previously attended a Sacred Retreat, shared his experience of collaborating with like-minded individuals on a project aimed at creating sustainable solutions for the local community. "In the past, I used to approach projects with a competitive mindset," he admitted. "But with the teachings of 5D consciousness, I learned to let go of ego-driven desires and embrace the power of collaboration. The result was a project that exceeded our expectations, benefiting not just the community but also fostering deep connections among the team members."

Natalia listened attentively, her eyes sparkling with pride and joy. "Thank you all for sharing your stories of personal breakthroughs," she expressed, her voice infused with warmth. "These examples serve as powerful reminders of the transformative power of service, collaboration, and co-creation. Each of you is contributing to the collective ascension of humanity, one act of kindness, one collaborative effort at a time."

As the gentle notes of meditation music began to fill the room, Shania gracefully stepped forward, bringing the session on the interpersonal impact of the sacred gathering to a serene conclusion with a guided meditation. She invited the participants to anchor the teachings deep within their hearts and envision a world where service, collaboration, and co-creation were the guiding principles. The room embraced a profound stillness as they allowed the visions to unfold, sensing the immense potential that lay before them.

As the meditation reached its peaceful conclusion, Shania's gentle voice resonated, "Carry the essence of these profound teachings within you as you continue on your transformative journey." Let them guide you in your interactions with others, inspire you to serve selflessly, and empower you to collaborate and co-create with love and compassion. Together, we can create a world that reflects the beauty and harmony of 5D consciousness."

With eyes gently opening, the participants embraced a profound sense of purpose and an intensified dedication to embody the transformative principles they had acquired. Eagerly, they retrieved their journals, each page waiting to be filled with the profound experiences and newfound insights that had touched their souls. Concluding this enlightening segment on the interpersonal impact of transitioning to 5D consciousness, the participants were imbued with a deep understanding that the journey towards a harmonious world begins with each individual embracing their innate capacity for service, collaboration, and co-creation.

As the gentle strains of the meditation music continued to serenade the room, gradually fading into the background, a tranquil stillness settled upon the participants. Within this hushed ambiance, a profound sense of unity and shared purpose embraced them all. They were no longer just participants in a gathering; they were agents of change, ambassadors of a new Earth that honored love, peace, abundance, and respect for all life forms. In their actions, in their service, in their collaborations, and in their co-creations, they would continue to ripple out the transformative energy of 5D consciousness, inspiring others to join them on this sacred journey of collective ascension.

CHAPTER 25

THE COLLECTIVE IMPACT

As the day progressed, the focus seamlessly shifted towards the final topic: the profound collective impact of transitioning to 5D consciousness. Natalia's voice, infused with a deep sense of purpose and inspiration, captivated the room, drawing the participants into the realms of possibility and transformation. She shared profound insights about the transformative journey that humanity embarks upon as more individuals embrace 5D consciousness. Natalia painted a vivid picture of the collective ascension, a profound shift that reverberates through the very fabric of existence.

As we bring today's enlightening teachings to a close, I wish to impart upon you a final reflection. "Imagine," Natalia spoke with a deep conviction, "a new earth emerging, where love, peace, abundance, and respect for all life forms become the pillars of our existence. It is a world where social structures and systems built on inequality, exploitation, and destruction are dismantled, replaced by ones that uphold fairness, sustainability, and reverence for all beings."

Natalia delved into the interconnectedness that binds all beings together, emphasizing the immense power of collective intention and action. She spoke of the extraordinary ripple effect that occurs when individuals align with higher frequencies, igniting a wave of positive change that spreads far beyond their immediate surroundings.

"The impact of our personal transformation extends far beyond ourselves," Natalia continued. "It resonates across the globe, inspiring and catalyzing the collective shift in consciousness that we yearn for. As we end today's teachings, I want to leave you with this profound understanding: each step we take towards higher frequencies, towards love, compassion, and unity, holds within it the power to shape the very fabric of our world. Imagine a world where every individual, guided by their inner wisdom, embraces the qualities of love, compassion, and unity in their thoughts, words, and actions. Picture a world where empathy and understanding flow effortlessly, where collaboration and cooperation replace competition and conflict.

In this world, every act of kindness, every gesture of compassion, and every moment of genuine connection creates ripples of transformation that spread far and wide. Each individual's journey towards higher frequencies becomes a beacon of hope, inspiring others to embark on their own paths of growth and self-discovery. The cumulative effect of these collective efforts sets the stage for a profound shift in consciousness, a shift that can elevate humanity as a whole.

Imagine the impact of a world where love and compassion reign supreme. Relationships, both personal and societal, thrive in an environment of deep understanding and acceptance. Through the lens of unity, we begin to recognize the interconnectedness of all beings, acknowledging that we are part of a vast tapestry of life. Our actions, no matter how small, hold the potential to shape the world around us.

By aligning ourselves with these higher frequencies, we become catalysts for change. We become conscious participants in the evolution of our world. Every act of kindness, every choice made with love, every moment of connection becomes a thread that weaves a tapestry of unity and transformation.

So, as we conclude today's teachings, I invite you to reflect on the immense power you hold within. Recognize the impact of your thoughts, words, and actions on the collective consciousness. Embrace the truth that each step you take towards love, compassion, and unity is a powerful contribution to the greater transformation of our world.

May your journey towards higher frequencies be guided by the wisdom within, and may your presence be a beacon of light that illuminates the path for others. Together, let us weave a tapestry of love, compassion, and unity, creating a world that reflects the true essence of our shared humanity."

The participants felt a profound sense of responsibility and empowerment welling up within them. They recognized the pivotal role they played in the grand tapestry of human evolution. Their personal growth and commitment to aligning with higher frequencies became an integral part of the collective journey towards a more enlightened and harmonious existence.

As this Sacred Gathering comes to a close, the atmosphere is filled with the gentle melodies of meditation music, enveloping the space in a soothing embrace. Shania, positioned at the front of the room, prepares to guide the participants on a transformative inner journey through her guided meditation.

Her voice, resonating with a vibrational tone, touches the hearts and stirs the souls of the participants. "Let us now enter the sanctuary of our inner world," she begins, her words carrying a profound resonance that permeates the room. "Align with your intuition to anchor the powerful lessons we have explored today."

Her words carry a reminder that tomorrow marks the final day of the retreat, yet the participants' transformation does not end there. They are encouraged to take these valuable lessons and integrate them into their daily lives, practicing new ways of being that will ultimately ripple out and transform the lives of those around them.

Shania's voice gradually fades, allowing the meditation music to continue playing, creating a serene backdrop for the participants to embark on their own inner journeys. As the music wraps around them, they find themselves immersed in the depths of their own experiences.

After approximately five minutes, Shania's voice gently re-emerges, guiding the participants to slowly open their eyes whenever they feel ready. Their pens find their way to the pages of their journals as they begin to capture the essence of their inner revelations and insights.

The room remains peaceful, with the soft music continuing to play as the participants immerse themselves in their journaling process. One by one, they quietly gather their belongings, each finding a sense of completion in their own unique way. With a quiet reverence, they depart from the room, carrying the transformative energy of the Sacred Gathering within them.

In this serene transition, the collective energy lingers, reassuring that the lessons and experiences shared in this sacred space are not confined to its walls. The participants hold within them the power to radiate their transformed being and touch the lives of others through their way of being.

As the participants quietly leave the room, they carry with them the subtle shifts that have taken place within their hearts and souls. Their journals hold the wisdom and insights gained from the sacred gathering, serving as precious keepsakes of their transformative journey.

Tomorrow may mark the end of the retreat, but it is just the beginning of a new chapter in their lives, where they will continue to embody the lessons learned, creating a ripple effect of transformation in their own lives and the lives of those they encounter.

With hearts filled with gratitude and a deep sense of purpose, the participants quietly depart, knowing that the Sacred Gathering has touched their lives in profound ways that will continue to unfold long after they leave this sacred space.

CHAPTER 26

TRANSCENDENCE AND TRANSFORMATION

As the final day of this transformative retreat dawns, anticipation fills the air as the participants enter the Sacred Gathering. The gentle strains of meditation music envelop the room, creating an atmosphere of tranquility and serenity. At the front of the room, Natalia and Shania, their eyes closed, are in deep meditation, setting the stage for the profound journey that awaits.

With quiet reverence, the participants find their seats, settling into a comfortable position, and closing their eyes as they embark on a shared meditative experience. The room becomes a haven of stillness as the collective consciousness converges and aligns with the higher frequencies of the universe.

After approximately ten minutes of blissful silence, Shania's voice emerges, resonating with a vibrational frequency that permeates the very depths of everyone's being. Her words carry a soothing power, like a gentle wave washing over the souls of the participants, awakening their innermost essence.

In her guided meditation, Shania weaves a tapestry of inspiring and uplifting messages, infusing the space with divine wisdom. She speaks of the transformative journey that the participants have embarked upon during the Sacred Gatherings, reminding them of the profound impact it has had on their lives. Shania emphasizes that moving from 3D to 5D consciousness represents an evolutionary leap from a fear-based existence to a love-based reality. Shania conveyed that this profound shift brings forth a transformation that extends to the personal, interpersonal, and collective realms, ushering in a new reality characterized by love and compassion.

Shania's voice echoed with a mixture of tenderness and strength, "With each step you have taken on this sacred path, you have awakened to a new level of consciousness." "Now, as we approach the final stage of this journey, it is vital to honor your commitment to yourself. The path to 5D consciousness requires unwavering dedication and a willingness to delve deep into your own healing."

Shania emphasizes the importance of self-work, encouraging the participants to embrace the transformative power that lies within. "You are the architects of your own transcendence," she declares. "By embarking on this inner healing journey, you reclaim your power and elevate your existence from fear-based limitations to a reality rooted in love."

The participants listen intently, their hearts and souls attuned to the resonance of Shania's words. They understand that their own healing is an essential part of their journey towards 5D consciousness, and that by diligently doing the inner work, they can create a ripple effect of transformation in their personal lives, relationships, and the world at large.

As the guided meditation continues, Shania guides the participants through moments of introspection and connection with their inner selves. She invites them to cultivate self-compassion, explore the depths of their emotions, and release any lingering fears or limiting beliefs that hinder their growth.

Throughout the meditation, Shania's voice remains a conduit for divine energy, its vibrational frequency harmonizing with the participants' own energetic fields. Her words become a catalyst for profound shifts, gently nudging the participants to expand their consciousness and embrace their limitless potential.

As the meditation draws to a close, Shania imparts her final words of guidance. "As you open your eyes, remember that the transformative journey does not end here," she imparts with a profound sense of purpose. "Carry the wisdom you have gained and integrate it into your daily life. Be diligent in your self-work, for it is through your own healing that you will transcend to the higher realms of consciousness."

Shania's gentle voice permeates the serene space, guiding the participants back from their inner journey to the present moment. With tender encouragement, she invites them to slowly open their eyes, allowing the external world to gently come into focus once again. Their gaze shifts from the depths of their introspection to the room before them, their senses attuned and receptive to the transformative teachings that await.

Rewiring the Brain for the Transition to 5D Consciousness

Natalia gracefully stepped forward, ready to guide the participants on a transformative journey of rewiring their brains for the transition to 5D consciousness. Her words carried wisdom and insight, resonating deeply with each person in the room.

Natalia spoke, her voice filled with gentle authority, "Let us explore the fascinating realm of rewiring our brain, for it is a vital part of our journey to 5D consciousness. You must rewire your brain to transition to 5D consciousness and resonate there." Natalia shared, "Our brains are wired for habits, and throughout the day, we operate on automatic pilot, thinking and behaving in ways consistent with our brain's programs."

She continued, illuminating the influence of caregivers, parents, grandparents, and others who have shaped our thoughts and behaviors since infancy. "From the very beginning, we are taught what to think and how to behave, and these teachings become the programs that govern our lives," Natalia explained. "But it doesn't stop there. Along our life's path, teachers, friends, the media, and social media contribute to the programs that influence our thoughts and actions."

Natalia's words carried a profound truth. She highlighted the presence of unhealthy programs that hinder our growth and keep us from reaching our desired destinations. "Unless we consciously choose to challenge these programs and shift our perspectives, we will continue to operate from the same level of consciousness," she emphasized. "If we want change, we must change our behaviors and thought patterns."

The room was filled with a palpable sense of responsibility and possibility. Natalia stressed the importance of rewiring our brains, hence,reprogramming ourselves to align with our true desires and aspirations. "Others have programmed us, but now it is our responsibility to identify those programs that no longer serve us and embark on the journey of reprogramming ourselves," she urged.

Her teachings echoed through the minds and hearts of the participants. They understood that true transformation required an inner rewiring, a conscious effort to break free from outdated programs and embrace new ones that aligned with their highest potential.

As Natalia continued her teachings, the room was charged with an energy of empowerment and determination. The participants were ready to embark on the profound journey of self-reprogramming, knowing that by doing so, they would shape their own destinies and create a reality aligned with their deepest desires.

Natalia's teachings had struck a chord within their hearts, reminding them of their innate capacity for self-transformation and the power they held to rewire their brains and elevate their consciousness. It was a call to reclaim their autonomy and rewrite the scripts of their lives, ultimately stepping into a new paradigm of awareness and fulfillment.

Shania stepped forward, carrying the torch of wisdom, to delve into the profound topic of triggers and their profound significance in our transformative healing journey. Her voice carried a sense of empathy and understanding as she guided the participants through this transformative exploration.

CHAPTER 27

ILLUMINATING TRIGGERS: A PATH TO HEALING AND HIGHER CONSCIOUSNESS

"Triggers are like signposts, guiding us towards the unhealed parts of ourselves from past experiences," Shania explained, her words flowing with clarity and compassion. "By identifying these triggers, we have an opportunity to heal and resolve the unresolved issues within us."

She emphasized the importance of shifting our perspective when addressing these unresolved issues. "When we resolve an issue, we begin to see the past situation as an obstacle that served as an opportunity for growth," Shania expressed. "We start to view it from a perspective of learning, growth, and the evolution of our consciousness. We do not continue to talk about it as a problem."

Shania delved deeper, shedding light on the impact of unresolved issues and their connection to distressing emotions. "Unresolved issues are composed of perspectives which cause distress in various forms such as frustration, anger, shame, depression, anxiety, and self-loathing," she shared. "While it is natural to experience these emotions as part of the human condition, it is essential to let go of them, to move through them to reach the other side."

Shania's gentle voice resonated with a profound reminder, "In this spiritual journey, we are but visitors on this planet. Our purpose here is to evolve, grow, and awaken by learning from our experiences. It is a gradual process of remembering who we truly are."

She emphasized that at our core, we are infinite awareness, connected to a vast consciousness beyond the physical realm. The journey of self-discovery is a return to this essence, a deep remembrance of our true nature.

As the participants absorbed these words, a sense of reverence filled the room. They were learning that their experiences, challenges, and growth were all integral to the evolution of their souls. Their souls resonated with the profound truth that their journey on this planet was a sacred opportunity to awaken to their inherent divinity and embrace the infinite possibilities that lay within them.

Shania Hits Home

Shania was prepared to delve deep into the depths. Because of her empathic nature, she had already perceived the energy in the room. With compassion and understanding, Shania fearlessly explored the participants' hidden struggles, addressing the unresolved issues that dwelled in the shadows of their beings. Her words resonated with the unspoken pain and hurt that many carried, causing a stirring within the room. Her presence created a safe space for vulnerability and healing to take place.

She spoke with empathy and understanding, "I see the weight you have been carrying, the expectations that have burdened your hearts. The expectations you held for yourselves and for others." Shania's voice was a soothing balm, comforting the wounded souls in the room. She recognized the profound impact these unmet expectations had on their lives, resulting in a clinging to hurt and pain.

Her voice filled with empathy as she touched upon the experiences of women who had longed for fulfilling relationships that didn't unfold as expected, leaving them wounded and carrying the weight of their emotions.

The participants listened intently, their eyes welling up with tears as Shania's words hit home. In her presence, they felt seen and understood, a look of acknowledgment exchanged between them and Shania, a shared recognition that it was time to release the burdens they had carried for far too long.

She addressed the wounds inflicted by familial relationships and the feeling of being cheated out of a fulfilling childhood. Shania's voice, filled with compassion, resonated with the pain and disappointment that had been carried silently within. "It's time to empty your hearts, to let go of the hurt and pain that have taken residence within you." Shania's compassionate voice resonated deeply, validating the participants' experiences.

With heartfelt honesty, she acknowledged the anger that may be harbored towards mothers, fathers, ex-spouses, and others who had played a role in their lives. As her teachings unfolded, Shania urged the participants to cleanse their souls and open themselves up to a higher perspective. "Release the shackles of the past. Embrace healing and self-compassion," she encouraged. Her words created a sacred space for vulnerability and growth.

Shania continued with a profound insight, explaining that the very challenges and experiences that had caused the participants

187

to feel diminished were, in fact, the key to illuminating their lives. She emphasized that the obstacles they had encountered were opportunities for growth and transformation, serving as catalysts to illuminate their inner light.

"What has caused you hurt and pain," Shania revealed, "will ultimately elevate you on this new journey." She encouraged the participants to recognize the valuable lessons and messages embedded within their past and current experiences. While certain aspects of their lives may remain unchanged, it is the shift in perspective that holds the power to release the lingering hurt and pain.

She urged them to embrace a higher perspective, to see their circumstances through the lens of illumination. By viewing their challenges from this elevated vantage point, they would uncover the wisdom and understanding necessary to navigate their path with grace and resilience.

The room held an atmosphere of shared vulnerability as the participants recognized the truth in Shania's words. Shame and guilt were brought into the light, ready to be released and replaced with healing and self-compassion.

At that moment, the participants made a silent commitment to themselves, ready to embark on a journey of letting go. Their eyes locked with Shania's, conveying gratitude for her insight and guidance. They were prepared to release the pain and hurt that had weighed them down to embrace a path of healing and transformation.

Shania's teachings had pierced through the shadows, illuminating the way towards a brighter, more liberated existence. The participants knew that the road ahead would require courage and vulnerability, but they were now empowered with the awareness and determination to release the burdens of their past, allowing their souls to soar freely in the realm of healing and growth.

Their tears, once an expression of pain, now became tears of release and liberation. The room was filled with a sense of collective healing, as the participants were ready to embark on a journey of rewiring their brains, ready to rewrite their narratives and step into a brighter, more empowered future.

Shania continued, emphasizing the connection between unresolved issues and triggers, highlighting how triggers can potentially hinder our transition to 5D consciousness. "Triggers can inhibit our ability to resonate at the higher consciousness levels because they pull us back into the patterns of 3D consciousness," Shania revealed. "While we may have peak experiences of 5D consciousness, if we remain triggered and unable to move past our unresolved issues, we will continue to resonate in the lower frequency."

Shania presented triggers as hidden gifts, bringing to the surface those aspects that keep us stuck in the cycle of 3D experiences. "Triggers serve as a catalyst for growth and self-awareness," she emphasized. "By recognizing and addressing these triggers, we break free from the patterns that keep us cycling in 3D consciousness."

The room was filled with a mixture of contemplation and realization. Shania's teachings illuminated the importance of self-awareness and the need to actively work through our unresolved issues. The participants understood that by embracing and healing their triggers, they could transcend the limitations of the past and pave the way for a higher level of consciousness.

Shania's words lingered in their minds, inspiring them to embark on the journey of rewiring their brain and healing. They recognized that by embracing their triggers as opportunities for growth, they could release the emotional burdens holding them back and step into the expansive realms of 5D consciousness.

It was a profound realization that brought about a sense of liberation and empowerment. The participants felt a renewed commitment to their healing journey, knowing that resolving their unresolved issues would unlock the doors to a reality filled with love, joy, and higher vibrations.

Shania and Natalia's teachings had ignited a spark within each participant, propelling them forward on their path of self-transformation and paving the way for the embodiment of 5D consciousness in their lives.

With a graceful movement, Shania stepped aside, making way for Natalia to step forward and share an eagerly anticipated announcement. Natalia spoke briefly to the participants about the profound process of rewiring the brain, describing it as a retreat within itself. While acknowledging that they wouldn't delve fully into the process during the retreat, she had prepared a valuable resource for them.

Bridging Resources for Transformation

With a warm smile, Natalia shared that she and Shania had purchased books and workbooks to aid them on their personal journey of rewiring the brain. These invaluable resources would serve as a template for reprogramming themselves, providing guidance and support along the way.

"The book is called 'I Rewired My Brain, My Journey to Freedom'," Natalia revealed, the title resonates with the potential for transformation. "Accompanying it is a workbook entitled 'I'm Rewiring My Brain, My Journey to Freedom."

Natalia and Shania's connection with the author, Dr. Kay Vonne Cason-Turner, added a personal touch to the recommendation. Natalia shared that both she and Shania had met the author at a spiritual gathering, and they had been deeply inspired by her work. Natalia stated that they both integrate the book and workbooks' teachings and strategies when they are assisting others on their path.

"For those interested, the book and workbook are available on Amazon," Natalia informed the participants, ensuring they had the opportunity to obtain additional copies or share this transformative duo with others. "Dr. Kay Vonne Cason-Turner's wisdom and insights can continue to support you on your journey."

Natalia further extended her support by informing the participants about Rewire Your Brain groups. These groups would provide a nurturing space where they could connect with like-minded individuals, finding encouragement and guidance as they progressed on their transformative path. Natalia enlightened the participants about the profound impact of group engagement in the transformative mastermind process. She emphasized the collective energy that is harnessed to support each other's paths of transformation.

Natalia shared that within the Rewire Your Brain groups, many members eventually become facilitators themselves, inspired by their own transformative journeys. With the powerful process experienced during the retreat, Natalia believed that the participants had the potential to become exceptional facilitators in the future.

Filled with gratitude, the participants embraced Natalia's words, realizing the immense value of the opportunity before them. The prospect of rewiring their brains and unlocking a profound sense of freedom ignited a spark of excitement and determination within each of them. They eagerly anticipated their involvement in a Rewire Your Brain group, envisioning the day when they would become facilitators, guiding others on their own transformative journeys.

As the session continued, the participants felt a renewed sense of empowerment, knowing that they were not alone on their journey. They had access to knowledge, support, and a community that would uplift and inspire them as they embarked on the profound process of rewiring their brains. Natalia and Shania's thoughtful gesture had set them on a path of more self-discovery and transformation, equipped with the tools and resources necessary to create lasting change.

As the session approached its end, the soothing melodies of the meditation music enveloped the room. Shania's voice resounded with a heightened vibrational frequency, exuding a sense of calm and reassurance.

Shania: "Now, my dear friends, let us prepare ourselves for the upcoming journey of release and healing. Close your eyes and find a place of stillness within."

Her words gently guided the participants, creating a serene atmosphere of anticipation and readiness.

Shania: "In this sacred space, we are on the threshold of a major transformation. As we prepare to release and let go, we must first acknowledge the emotions and experiences that have burdened us."

Her voice carried a compassionate tone, offering support and understanding to those in need.

Shania: "Take a deep breath, inviting the light of awareness to illuminate any pain, hurt, or stagnant energy that resides within you. Feel these emotions as they surface, observing them without judgment."

Her words encouraged the participants to embrace their emotions with an open heart, creating a safe space for self-reflection.

Shania: "This is a time of preparation, of gathering our strength to face what no longer serves us. Together, we shall navigate the depths of our beings and begin the process of healing."

The room was filled with a sense of unity and shared purpose as the participants embraced the upcoming journey.

Shania: "Allow your intuition to guide you to the areas that require healing. Trust the wisdom that resides within and honor the readiness to release, to let go of what holds you back."

Her voice resonated with empowerment, reminding the participants of their innate capacity to embark on this transformative path.

After a serene silence of approximately 10 minutes, Shania broke the stillness with her gentle voice.

Shania: "When you are ready, gently open your eyes and come back to the present moment. Reflect on the insights that have emerged and prepare to capture them in your journals."

Her words signaled the transition from inner exploration to the external world, where the participants would begin to process their experiences.

A profound ambiance filled the room as the participants immersed themselves in writing within the pages of their journals. Emotions stirred within them, evident by the welling of tears in the eyes of some. The cathartic process had already begun as they summoned repressed emotions to the surface, ready to be acknowledged and released.

Shania's voice filled the room, gently guiding the participants through the next phase. "Now, it is time for a well-deserved 30-minute break," she announced, her words infused with warmth and care. "During this time, I encourage you to prioritize self-care and reflection. Nourish your soul by being fully present with the emotions that have surfaced, embracing them with love and compassion. We will reconvene for the next Sacred Gathering, where we will embark on the powerful journey of release and transformation."

The participants, filled with a sense of anticipation and determination, closed their journals and quietly left the room, ready to embrace the upcoming release and healing process that awaited them.

CHAPTER 28

THE SACRED FOREST: ECHOES OF RELEASE

The anticipated moment had finally arrived, marking a pivotal and transformative experience within the retreat. With anticipation in the air, the group stood at the entrance of the Sacred Forest, ready to embark on a cathartic energy release of immense significance. Shania stepped forward, her voice infused with a blend of solemnity and encouragement, as she addressed the participants.

"My dear friends, we have reached a pivotal moment in our journey," Shania spoke with a sense of reverence. "Within the sanctuary of this sacred forest, you are about to embark on a profound journey of letting go. It is here that you will release the heavy burdens of hurt and pain that have weighed upon your souls."

As her words settled into the hearts of the participants, a hushed anticipation filled the air. The rustle of leaves and the gentle whisper of the wind seemed to echo the significance of the moment.

Shania continued, her voice carrying the depth of her guidance, "In this tranquil embrace of nature, you will surrender to the healing power of the forest. You will allow the ancient trees to witness your release as you unburden yourself from the weight that has held you back."

The participants looked at each other with a mix of determination and vulnerability, knowing that within the depths of the Sacred Forest awaited an opportunity for profound transformation.

Shania's voice resonated with reassurance, "As we step into the forest, I invite you to be fully present. Feel the vibrant energy of the majestic trees surrounding you. Take off your shoes and let the earth beneath your feet connect you to the grounding essence of nature. Within this sacred space, it is of utmost importance to surrender to the gentle whispers of the natural world, allowing them to envelop you and serve as your guide in releasing the emotions that have long been carried within your being."

With a collective breath, the group took their first steps into the enchanting realm of the Sacred Forest, ready to embrace the cathartic journey that awaited them. They would soon fully express the repressed energies that have weighed them down.

Immersed in the enchanting energy of the place, the participants instinctively slowed their pace and gathered near one another. They closed their eyes, allowing themselves to be embraced by a gentle breeze that whispered through the air. As moments passed, their eyes gently opened one by one, and they embarked on a slow, mindful walk in different directions as if traversing a sacred labyrinth.

Some gravitated towards the ancient trees, seeking solace in their sturdy presence, while others followed the melodious flow of the nearby stream. Each step carried them deeper into the tranquil embrace of nature's sanctuary.

Time seemed to stand still, and after approximately 15 minutes of immersion in the serenity of the forest, a profound stillness settled upon the group. Then, from the depths of the Sacred Forest, a cathartic release of pent-up emotions began, as if the very essence of the place had ignited a transformative journey of letting go.

The Release

There were primal screams echoing through the trees, mingling with heartfelt cries, passionate yells, and cathartic wails.

Each participant embraced their own unique way of releasing the low vibrational frequencies that have kept them bound.

With every scream, every cry, and every wail, anger was liberated from its shackles. Frustration found its voice and was set free. Sadness, once trapped within, flowed out like a river of tears. The forest became a sanctuary for the release of shame, guilt, and all other distressing emotions that have held them captive.

As some participants ventured deeper into the heart of the Sacred Forest, an array of other powerful experiences unfolded. Each person found themselves drawn to a specific spot, as if guided by an invisible force, tailor-made to facilitate their release.

Near a majestic oak tree, a woman stood with her arms outstretched, her face turned towards the sky. With a primal scream that seemed to emanate from the depths of her soul, her anguish reverberated through the trees. The sound echoed through the forest, carrying with it years of pent-up anger and resentment. As the echoes faded, a profound sense of lightness washed over her, as if a weight she had long carried had been lifted.

In a secluded grove by the stream, a man knelt down, his head bowed in silent surrender. With tears streaming down his face, he released his pain in heartfelt cries that pierced the stillness of the forest. His cries carried the weight of unspoken grief, allowing him to finally mourn the losses he had held within. In that sacred moment, a deep sense of acceptance washed over him like a gentle river soothing his wounded spirit.

A little further down the path, a young woman found herself standing by a cluster of wildflowers. As she unleashed passionate yells into the open space, her voice mingled with the gentle rustle of leaves. With each yell, she felt layers of frustration peel away, leaving her feeling raw and vulnerable. But within that rawness, she discovered a newfound strength, a resilience that had been dormant within her all along.

Amidst the symphony of release, another participant found solace beneath the canopy of a towering cedar tree. With cathartic wails that seemed to merge with the wind's whispers, she let go of the shame and guilt that had plagued her. As her cries subsided, a profound sense of forgiveness and self-compassion enveloped her like a gentle embrace from the ancient tree itself.

Across the expanse of the Sacred Forest, a tapestry of emotions unfolded, interwoven with the sights, sounds, and scents of nature. Each participant, in their own unique way, became a conduit for the release of low vibrational frequencies that had kept them bound. The forest listened, holding space for their healing, as the cathartic symphony of screams, cries, yells, and wails echoed through the trees, carrying their transformative intentions into the universe.

The release was not over yet. A woman found herself drawn to a serene clearing, bathed in the golden glow of sunlight filtering through the leaves. She raised her hands to the sky, and as her voice surged forth, a primal scream erupted from her core. The sound reverberated through the forest, shattering the silence. With each reverberation, she shed the layers of fear that had bound her spirit, a wild and untamed release that echoed her liberation.

Near a majestic waterfall, a young soul stood in awe of nature's power. With trembling hands outstretched, she let out a yell that merged with the thunderous roar of the cascading waters. The sound filled the air, releasing years of repressed frustration and unspoken words. As her voice blended with the rushing current, her entire being vibrated with a newfound sense of empowerment. In that moment, she felt the strength of the waterfall flow through her, cleansing her spirit and igniting a flame of courage within.

In a hidden grove adorned with blossoming flowers, a weary traveler sank to the ground, overwhelmed by the weight of her past. With each wail that escaped her lips, the flowers swayed in harmony, their petals releasing a sweet fragrance into the air. As the traveler released her pain, the flowers absorbed her sorrow, transforming it into vibrant bursts of color and life. In that sacred space, amidst the gentle caress of nature's beauty, she found solace and a renewed sense of hope.

Throughout the forest, a symphony of release echoed in harmony with the rustle of leaves, the whisper of the wind, and the song of birds. Primal screams, heartfelt cries, passionate yells, and cathartic wails intertwined with the very essence of the forest, forming a collective chorus of healing. Each participant, in their own unique way, surrendered to the embrace of nature, shedding layers of pain and emerging lighter, freer, and more alive than ever before.

As the echoes of release faded, a profound stillness settled upon the Sacred Forest, carrying the residue of emotional catharsis. The participants, bathed in the gentle glow of the forest's embrace, stood transformed. They confronted their darkest shadows, allowed their repressed emotions to rise to the surface, and found liberation amidst nature's sanctuary.

In the serenity of the Sacred Forest, they felt a sense of oneness with the world around them, a deep connection to the earth and all living beings. The forest had witnessed their vulnerability, heard their deepest truths, and held them in unconditional acceptance. From that day forward, they carried the forest's wisdom within their hearts, forever guided by the memory of their release and the profound transformation it had brought.

CHAPTER 29

The Waters of Rebirth: Cleansing and Awakening

Shania and Natalia, their voices filled with reverence and anticipation, led the group to the sacred waters of the forest. One by one, each participant was summoned to step into the rejuvenating embrace of the water, a transformative journey of cleansing and rebirth.

As they walked slowly into the glistening waters, a profound sense of liberation washed over them. The labor of letting go had been done, making space for new beginnings. The sacred waters, a symbol of rebirth, will complete the final phase of their cleansing process, leaving them revitalized and ready to embrace the path that awaited them.

As the participants approached Shania and Natalia, who stood immersed in the sacred waters, a palpable sense of the Divine's presence enveloped their very beings. The gentle whispers of liquid purity embraced them, whispering promises of transformation and renewal.

"Are you ready?" Shania and Natalia asked, their voices filled with anticipation and wisdom. Each participant, one by one, their hearts brimming with readiness, answered, "Yes, I am ready." In that moment, a powerful connection formed between the guides and the guided, as Shania and Natalia prepared to lead them through the sacred transformative ritual.

As the participants' bodies were gently dipped back into the tranquil waters, the words of Shania and Natalia carried the weight of profound truth and unwavering guidance. "You have released the old," Shania and Natalia spoke in unison. "You have washed away the burdens of the past. Now, on this threshold of the new, embrace the awakening that awaits you. For it will serve as a guiding light, leading you to the truth of who you are."

As the participants emerged from the water, their souls radiating renewed energy, a large cozy towel was wrapped around them, enveloping them in a warm embrace. They felt cleansed, refreshed, and ready to embark on a new chapter of their journey. The sacred waters had completed the final phase of their cleansing process, leaving them revitalized and ready to embrace the truth that awaited them.

Immersed in a state of mindful presence, the participants make their way towards the glowing campfire, drawn by its radiant warmth. Their eyes fixate upon the dancing flames, mesmerized by their enchanting flickers. In this unified gathering, their hearts aflame with hope; they bask in the profound beauty of the moment. Together, they embrace the boundless possibilities that stretch out before them, ignited by a collective spark of transformative potential.

Having traversed the path of release and renewal, the participants found themselves at this significant juncture, where the radiant light of awakening beckoned them forward. As they embraced the cathartic release of emotions, their awareness remained steadfast on the importance of rewiring their brain. With hearts open and minds receptive, they eagerly looked forward to the transformative work that lay ahead with unwavering enthusiasm and a deep willingness to undergo the necessary changes for their own evolution and enlightenment.

Shania and Natalia, standing at the campfire, witnessed the radiance that emanated from each participant. With smiles of profound joy and pride, they knew that this sacred experience would forever mark a turning point in their lives. From this moment forward, the participants would walk the path of truth, authenticity, and self-discovery, guided by the transformative power of the sacred waters and the wisdom of their own awakened souls.

With utmost tenderness in her voice, Shania shared the enchanting plans that awaited the participants on this final day of the retreat. As her words flowed like a gentle stream, she invited them to embrace the upcoming hours with reverence and solitude. "During the next three hours," she began, "I encourage you to find solace within yourselves. Allow the essence of the transformative experiences we've shared to permeate your being. Immerse yourself in the energy and memories that have unfolded, letting them weave a tapestry of enlightenment in your soul. Also, remember to document your profound experience in your journal, capturing the transformative journey that has unfolded within your soul."

CHAPTER 30

THE ENCHANTED MOUNTAIN

Before leaving the Sacred Forest, Shania's voice, carrying a gentle urgency, continued, "When the time comes, gather at the foothill of the Enchanted Mountain, a sacred realm pulsating with potent spiritual energy. The majestic summit of this enchanted mountain, adorned with its ethereal name, possesses the transformative power to elevate our consciousness to unparalleled heights." The participants listened, their hearts tingling with anticipation.

Immersed in the luminous embrace of 5th-dimensional consciousness, Shania and Natalia emanate an exquisite connection to the sacred energy dwelling atop the mystical summit. With the ethereal resonance of Tibetan singing bowls guiding their meditation, they will embark on a transformative journey through the realms that seamlessly unite the Holy Spirit, celestial angels of love and light, and the wisdom of their ancestors. This transcendent communion will serve as a gateway, not only for Shania and Natalia, but for all participants, to access profound spiritual knowledge and the ancient wisdom that has been lovingly passed down through the ages.

Though the physical manifestation of the Sacred Temple of Ascension may have faded into the tapestry of time, at the mountain's summit, its ethereal remnants continue to reverberate with celestial energy, echoing across the planes of existence. To behold the radiant splendor of this mystical sanctuary, one must attune their very frequency to match the resplendent vibrations that permeate its essence. Alternatively, they may be accompanied by a guide who possesses the ability to harmonize their own frequency with the elevated vibrations of this sacred realm. As the veils between dimensions thin in this sacred space, it is transformed into a sanctuary of spiritual illumination, where profound revelations eagerly await those who approach with open hearts and awakened consciousness.

Once more, Shania's voice gracefully resounded through the air, its cadence akin to a tranquil melody. "Adorned in your sacred white garments, symbolizing the purity and transformative power within, we shall embark on the final stage of our remarkable journey. Together, we will ascend the majestic Enchanted Mountain, guided by the spiritual energy that courses through its very core. A special transportation awaits us, carrying us swiftly and serenely towards our destination. Then, with profound reverence, we shall traverse the remaining path on foot, guided by the ancient wisdom that permeates the mountain's sacred terrain. As we arrive at the hallowed grounds of the Sacred Temple of Ascension, we shall bear witness to the culmination of our collective growth and immerse ourselves in the resplendent radiance of divine wisdom."

The participants embraced Shania's words, their spirits lifted by the promise of this sacred endeavor. With the image of the Enchanted Mountain imprinted in their minds, they allowed anticipation and reverence to fill their hearts. The path ahead held untold treasures of awakening and ascension, a testament to the transformative power of this retreat.

So, they left the Sacred Forest, their spirits cleansed, their souls replenished. The time spent in the forest, engaging in this cathartic energy release became a pivotal moment in their journey of healing and transformation. The forest's echoes of release lingered in their souls, serving as a reminder of the immense power of letting go, and the boundless capacity for healing that resided within them. With a profound sense of release, the participants emerged from the depths of the forest, their souls cleansed and renewed. Their hearts resonated with the higher frequencies of love, joy, and inner peace, as they prepared to embark on a journey of untold mysteries atop the sacred realm of The Enchanted Mountain.

CHAPTER 31

THE CLOSING CEREMONY

As the day's last sunbeam kissed Sedona's red rock formations, it splashed a palette of luminous colors across the expansive sky. Dressed in their Sacred White garb, each participant assembled at the Sacred Mountain's base, a sense of expectant excitement for the approaching closing ceremony pulsing in their hearts. There was a palpable vibration in the air, a charge of pure potential that wove an invisible thread of connection through each individual.

As evening draped its blanket over the land, a gentle wind carried whispered messages of ancient wisdom, causing the fabric of their spiritual garments to flutter and sway. As each moment slipped by, the hues in the sky matured, mirroring the deep internal metamorphosis occurring within each participant. Time seemed to pause, precariously perched between light and dark, as they readied themselves for the ensuing profound spiritual journey.

Nestled within the confines of this revered place, encircled by the grandeur of the Sacred Mountain, they stood united, each engaged in their personal quest for self-realization. The departing light of the sun graced their features, casting an ethereal radiance of expectation and honor over them.

With reverent hush, the participants stepped onto the mountain shuttle, their souls a reservoir of silent anticipation. A profound quietude enveloped them as they began their upward journey, their gazes entranced by the awe-inspiring splendor of the towering peaks. Time appeared to halt its march as they ascended, wrapped in the serene embrace of their surroundings.

Upon reaching the pinnacle, they set foot on hallowed earth, guided by an invisible current of spiritual energy. Soft murmurs of nature steered their path, guiding them ever closer to their destined location. A subtle melody, akin to a serenade for the soul, began to thread itself through the crisp mountain air, seizing their senses. Enveloped in a cocoon of serene allure, they allowed the enchanting music to guide them, pulling them closer to the revered site.

With each intentional stride, the participants sensed a discernible alteration in the surrounding atmosphere, an electrifying wave of energy encircling them as they neared the spiritual site. Their very essences seemed to thrum in harmony with the escalating frequencies emanating from the hallowed grounds of the Sacred Temple of Ascension. The air seemed to shimmer with anticipation, whispering ancient secrets carried on ethereal currents.

As they reached their destination, a breathtaking scene unfolded before their eyes. Eyes glistening with awe and wonder, they beheld a captivating area adorned with an enchanting array of candles, casting a soft, flickering glow upon the sacred space. The air was infused with the intoxicating fragrances of frankincense and myrrh, transporting their senses to a realm beyond the physical.

In this sacred sanctuary, time seemed to stand still. The convergence of heightened energies, flickering candlelight, and divine aromas created an atmosphere of profound reverence. It was as if the veils between worlds had thinned, inviting the participants to embrace the sacredness of the moment. Their spirits stirred, attuned to the ancient wisdom and sacred power that permeated the air. In this mystical tableau, they prepared to embark on the final phase of their transformative journey, guided by the luminous presence of the Sacred Temple of Ascension.

In the tranquil embrace of nature atop the Enchanted Mountain, Shania, and Natalia guided the participants to form a circle, their hands interlocked, symbolizing the unity of their journey. With graceful poise, Natalia settled into the center, nestled upon a soft cushion. Her hands, every so smoothly, tenderly awakened the Tibetan singing bowls to yield ethereal harmonies echoing the soul of the mountain itself.

As the soothing tones reverberated through the sacred space, Shania's voice, infused with serene tranquility, encouraged the group to close their eyes and attune to the whispers of their intuition. The harmonious sounds of the singing bowls soared higher and higher, cascading in a symphony of celestial vibrations.

A palpable surge of energy began to envelop the participants, swirling around them in a graceful dance of heightened awareness. With each passing moment, the intensity grew, weaving a tapestry of profound connection between the earthly and the ethereal.

As the calming tones echoed throughout the hallowed enclave, Shania's voice, imbued with a tranquil calm, guided the assembly to align with the whispers of their inner wisdom. The resonant frequency of the singing bowls ascended, pouring forth a celestial symphony of resonating vibrations. Natalia, embracing a trance-like state, connected deeply with the spiritual realm, while

Shania delved into a meditative practice, harnessing the power of her energy to intensify the collective experience.

A tangible wave of energy began to surround the participants, spiraling around them in an elegant ballet of elevated consciousness. Each passing moment amplified this sensation, creating an intricate weaving of deep bonds between the earthly and the ethereal. As the energy reached its crescendo, Shania's gentle voice resonated, invoking the veil between dimensions to part, granting passage for the Holy Spirit, the angels of love and light, and the benevolent presence of the ancestors to grace the sacred gathering.

A soft breeze, carrying the essence of divine presence, caressed the participants, leaving a gentle kiss upon their skin. The singing bowls, now charged with an even higher frequency, reverberated with the opening of the veil, their ethereal music merging with the mystical currents that coursed through the sacred space. In this transcendental instant, the participants found themselves submerged in an orchestra of energetic currents, interweaving the earthly and the heavenly realms, as the Enchanted Mountain bestowed its profound blessings upon them.

In the gentle cadence of her voice, Shania expressed her gratitude towards the invisible spiritual guides for their presence. She then softly beckoned the group to ease open their eyes, revealing a scene bathed in an ethereal glow. Though the night had descended upon them, a luminescent radiance shrouded their surroundings, unveiling a mystical ambiance that stirred a sense of wonder within each participant. Natalia, already familiar with the enchantment of this sacred place, smiled knowingly, her heart brimming with the anticipation of what lay ahead.

The moment of truth had emerged, the instance wherein the participants were to seal their transformative pilgrimage into the annals of eternity via a final aura photograph. Under the tender stewardship of Shania, the circle gently dissolved, and their joint gaze pivoted towards the right, unveiling an enchanted expanse, vibrating with an air of mystery and captivation. It was upon this sanctified soil they were to make their stand, cradling the imminent surge of mystical energy predestined to harness all that resided in them, including the brilliance of their infinite selves.

In a poised and graceful manner, Shania prepared herself to capture the essence of their evolution - the intricate tapestry of growth, areas still in need of attention, and the radiant spirit within each participant. With deliberate steps, they traversed the sacred ground, their beings aglow with an ethereal luminescence, a testament to their profound metamorphosis. Vibrant auras pulsated with life, embodying the ongoing voyage towards enlightenment. As they found their place before the lens, their eyes spoke volumes of serene tranquility, their hearts pulsating with the embrace and magnificence of their personal transformation.

The photographs capsulated were not just snapshots, but striking reflections of an unprecedented evolution that had taken place within each participant. They stood as tangible evidence of the quantum leaps in growth they had achieved through their attendance at the sacred gatherings. The photographs mirrored a story of transformation - a tale of ordinary individuals evolving, having tremendous breakthroughs, their consciousness reaching unfathomable heights.

Their auras, caught in the static frame, displayed vibrant hues of transformative growth. Each color, each subtle shift in light, was a testament to their awakened consciousness, their newly discovered depths, and the transcendent harmony they had reached within themselves. It was as if the lens had peered deep into their souls, capturing the glow of self-discovery and awareness that now defined them.

Their faces, once laden with the weights of the mundane, now radiated an enlightened serenity. Their eyes sparkled with the wisdom of experiences gleaned, lessons learned, and truths uncovered in the course of their transformative journey. The joy of self-realization, the liberation of casting off old shackles, and the thrill of exploring unchartered territories of the self were all encapsulated within these extraordinary frames.

However, the images also gently suggested the areas that still yearned for growth, the corners of their consciousness that remained untouched. These were not shortcomings, but rather signposts, beckoning them towards their next phase of exploration. They were reminders that the journey of self-evolution is unending, each stage paving the way for the next, each end birthing a new beginning.

In essence, these photographs were not just a testament to the participants' incredible growth but also a compass for their continuous journey towards complete self-realization. Each image held an inspiring narrative of transformation, an enduring testament to the profound evolution that could be achieved through the sacred gatherings and the necessary inner work that lay ahead.

CHAPTER 32

THE 12 UNIVERSAL LAWS OF CREATION

Bathed in the residual radiance of elevated spiritual energies, Shania assumed a prominent position, capturing the attention of the gathered souls atop the majestic Enchanted Mountain. Cocooned in the comfort of plush cushions, the participants were entranced by their profound journey. With a poised presence, Shania stood before them, prepared to deliver the final, pivotal teachings, ensuring they carried with them the invaluable lessons before returning to the world they knew.

Recognizing the significant transformation within the participants, Shania voiced her profound gratitude for their earnest dedication and unwavering commitment to their spiritual retreat experience. With heartfelt sincerity, she emphasized the significance of the final lessons that awaited them, a compass to navigate their path forward as they reentered their normal lives. These last teachings would serve as guiding lights, illuminating their souls and providing invaluable wisdom for the journey ahead.

In the hushed stillness of the sacred gathering, Shania assumed the role of a wise oracle, unveiling the profound wisdom of the 12 Universal Laws of Creation. Her words danced in the air, captivating the participants as they leaned in with rapt attention, eager to delve into the mysteries of existence.

"The 12 Universal Laws," Shania began, her voice carrying the weight of divine revelation, "originates from the very essence of The Creator. They are not mere inventions, but rather profound truths discovered through centuries of human observation and experience." As her gaze met the intrigued eyes of the participants, she continued, "These laws are the irrefutable explanations of how our reality operates, much like the unyielding force of gravity in the physical realm."

With an aura of clarity, Shania emphasized, "The Universal Laws are not subject to creation or destruction. They simply describe the natural order of the Universe, governing every aspect of our existence." Pausing briefly, she imparted a vital insight, "Operating within the parameters of these laws is crucial, for they work incessantly whether we are conscious of them or not. Failing to understand and align with these laws puts us at a disadvantage in life, akin to playing a game without knowing its rules. To truly

224

thrive and flourish, we must first learn to navigate the intricate dance of the Universe by embracing the wisdom of its laws."

As Shania's teachings sank deep into the receptive hearts of the participants, a profound sense of awe and reverence enveloped the gathering. In this moment of divine revelation, they understood that by comprehending and embodying the Universal Laws, they would not only navigate the cosmos with grace but unlock the limitless potential of their own souls.

With serene confidence, Shania delved into the sacred teachings, revealing the profound wisdom encapsulated within the 12 Universal Laws. Each law carried a weighty significance, a divine tapestry intricately woven into the fabric of existence. As her words gently unfurled, she guided the participants on a journey of cosmic understanding.

"Let us begin," Shania spoke with gentle authority, "with the Law of Divine Oneness. This law reveals the interconnectedness of all creation, reminding us that we are inseparable from the very fabric of the Universe. It is the recognition that we are all divine sparks of the same cosmic consciousness, intrinsically linked in an intricate web of unity. It teaches us that we are all part of a unified whole. We are not separate beings."

"As we move forward," she continued, "we encounter the Law of Energy or Vibration. This law teaches us that everything in existence, from the grandest star to the tiniest atom, is in a constant state of vibration. It states that everything in the Universe is made up of energy vibrating at different frequencies. The vibrations we emit through our thoughts, emotions, and actions serve as magnets, drawing in energies of a similar resonance, thus shaping the experiences that manifest in our lives. It is through our vibrational alignment that we shape our reality."

Shania's voice carried a soothing cadence as she illuminated the Law of Correspondence. "This law reminds us that the outer world is a reflection of our inner world, as within, so without. By observing our external circumstances, we gain insight into our beliefs, thoughts, and emotions, enabling us to make conscious shifts in our internal landscape. By seeking alignment within ourselves, we harmonize our external reality, creating a beautiful symphony of resonance and manifestation. "

With a spark of excitement in her eyes, Shania delved into the Law of Attraction. "Ah, the Law of Attraction, a potent force that governs the magnetic pull of like energies. By aligning our thoughts, beliefs, and intentions with our desired outcomes, we magnetize the very circumstances and experiences we wish to manifest. This law is powerful, drawing into our lives experiences, people, and opportunities that resonate with our energetic vibration. Like attracts like, and through conscious intention and alignment, we can manifest our deepest desires."

"The Law of Inspired Action," she continued, "propels us to take intentional steps toward our dreams, guided by our inner wisdom. It is through inspired action that we actively co-create our reality, moving beyond mere wishes and into the realm of tangible manifestation. Inspired Action encourages us to align our thoughts, emotions, and actions with our desires, allowing us to manifest our dreams. "

As the participants hung on Shania's every word, she unraveled the transformative power of the Law of Perpetual Transmutation of Energy. "This law reminds us that energy is ever-flowing and can be transmuted from one form to another. By consciously directing our focus and intention, we can transform lower vibrations into higher frequencies, harnessing the alchemical process of personal growth and expansion. What we learn from The Law of Perpetual Transmutation of Energy is that we can shift negativity into positivity through conscious choice."

Shania recognized the importance of providing tangible examples to deepen the participants' understanding of the Law of Perpetual Transmutation of Energy. With this in mind, she proceeded to delve into further elucidation of the law's principles. Shania's voice carried the wisdom of ages as she expounded on the transformative nature of the Law of Perpetual Transmutation of Energy. "Consider a common occurrence in our lives," she began, "such as encountering a difficult or negative person in your daily interactions. This person may bring about feelings of frustration, annoyance, or anger within you. But remember, you have the power to transmute this energy and shift your experience."

The participants leaned in, eager to absorb Shania's teachings. She continued, "Instead of getting caught in a cycle of negativity, you can consciously choose to transmute the energy by shifting your perspective and response. Imagine the challenging person as a mirror reflecting back to you unresolved aspects of yourself. See them as a catalyst for your own growth and evolution."

Shania's words resonated deeply within the hearts of the participants, who recognized the truth in her teachings. "Now," Shania encouraged, "take a deep breath and release any tension or resistance you may be holding. Inhale love and compassion, and as you exhale, direct those qualities towards the challenging person. Visualize a radiant light surrounding them, enveloping them in warmth and understanding."

As the participants closed their eyes and followed Shania's guidance, a profound shift occurred within them. They could feel the transmutation of energy taking place as their initial feelings of frustration transformed into empathy and compassion. They realized that they held the power to transmute not only their own energy, but also the energy of their interactions and relationships.

Shania's voice gently brought them back to the present moment. "Remember," she emphasized, "transmutation is an ongoing process. By consciously choosing love, forgiveness, and understanding in each moment, you continue to raise your vibration and create a ripple effect of positivity in your own life and in the world around you."

As the participants listened intently, Shania continued, giving more examples on how to transmute energy. While Shania had previously touched upon the transformative power of love in dealing with challenging individuals, she now delved deeper into its profound potential. She enlightened the participants about the awe-inspiring ability of love to transmute even the most formidable negative energies, illuminating the path towards healing, harmony, and profound transformation. Shania stated, "When faced with any challenging situations or circumstances, we have the power to shift our perspective and consciously choose thoughts and emotions that are aligned with love, gratitude, and joy. By consciously directing our focus, we can transmute the lower vibrations of fear, anger, or sadness into higher frequencies of compassion, forgiveness, and peace."

Shania encouraged the participants to actively engage in this process of energy transmutation. "Take a moment now," she urged, "and think of a situation that has been weighing you down, causing you distress or frustration. Close your eyes and imagine surrounding that situation with a vibrant, healing light. As you hold it in this space of light, allow yourself to feel a sense of forgiveness, understanding, and release. See the energy shifting from heaviness to lightness, from tension to ease, as you consciously choose to transmute the energy within and around you."

The participants followed Shania's guidance, immersing themselves in the transformative practice. As they visualized the transmutation of energy, a profound sense of empowerment washed over them. They realized that they possessed the power to alchemize their own experiences, transforming negativity into positivity, and creating a higher vibrational reality for themselves and those around them. It was a pivotal moment of realization, opening the door to infinite possibilities for personal growth and spiritual expansion.

As Shania neared the culmination of this profound teaching, she smoothly transitioned to briefly introducing the remaining Universal Laws of Creation. "The Law of Cause and Effect," Shania continued, "is the recognition that every action we take generates a corresponding consequence. Our choices have ripple effects that shape our experiences. Our thoughts, words, and deeds create a web of consequences, inviting us to exercise conscious awareness and responsibility. "

"With the Law of Compensation," Shania elucidated, "we understand that the Universe operates with a sense of divine balance. Whether positive or negative, the energy we invest into the world returns to us in kind, bringing forth the rewards or lessons that align with our actions. This law ensures that we receive what we give, in abundance and in kind."

Shania's voice took on a compassionate tone as she delved into the Law of Relativity. "This law teaches us that everything in our lives is relative. Our experiences, challenges, and triumphs gain meaning and significance only in relation to other experiences, providing valuable frames of reference for growth. It is through contrast that we gain clarity and perspective."

"The Law of Polarity," she continued, "reveals the dance of duality in the Universe. Light and darkness, joy and sorrow, love and fear—they are all interconnected aspects of the same whole. The Law of Polarity reveals the interconnected duality of the Universe, reminding us that light exists within darkness and joy is born from sorrow. Embracing this law empowers us to find balance and harmony amidst the inherent dualities of life. "

With a rhythmic sway, Shania moved into the Law of Rhythm. "Just as nature ebbs and flows, so does the Universe operate in rhythmic cycles. We witness this rhythm in the changing seasons, the rise and fall of tides, and the breath that sustains us. Understanding this law invites us to navigate life's challenges with grace, knowing that the tides will inevitably turn. The Law of Rhythm illuminates the cyclical nature of life. The tides ebb and flow, and our experiences wax and wane. Embracing the natural rhythms allows us to flow harmoniously with the Universe. "

Finally, with an enigmatic smile, Shania illuminated the Law of Gender. "This law speaks to the fundamental interplay of masculine and feminine energies. It is the recognition that within each of us resides both the nurturing and assertive aspects of creation. Honoring the harmonious union of these energies allows for the fullest expression of our divine potential. The Law of Gender fosters balance and harmony within ourselves and the world."

As the lessons of the 12 Universal Laws unfolded, a sense of awe and reverence filled the gathering. The participants, captivated by the profound wisdom being imparted, felt their souls resonating with the eternal truths of the Universe. With each law unveiled, Shania's teachings ignited a deep sense of reverence within the participants. They were captivated by the interconnectedness of these universal principles, realizing the immense power they held in shaping their own reality.

CHAPTER 33

THE POWER OF LOVE: THE CREATOR'S OMNIPOTENT FORCE

As the final lesson unfolded, Shania's voice resonated with unwavering conviction, drawing the participants closer to the essence of their existence. "Now, my dear ones, let us explore the omnipotent power of The Creator," she began, her words carrying a weight of reverence and profound truth. "The Creator, the divine source from which all life emanates, is pure, boundless Love. It is the very essence of our being, the driving force that permeates every atom of our existence."

With a gentle smile, Shania continued, "Love, my beloveds, is the most powerful force in existence. It transcends all limitations, dissolves all barriers, and transforms even the darkest shadows into radiant light. It is the celestial energy that propels us on our journey of self-discovery and spiritual evolution."

Pausing momentarily, Shania's eyes sparkled with unwavering assurance. "Fear not, for The Creator, in its infinite wisdom and compassion, will always be with you. It will guide you, protect you, and shower you with divine grace. As you walk this sacred path, trust that the divine presence is ever by your side, offering solace, wisdom, and unwavering support."

Basking in the tranquil embrace of the night, Shania began to delve into the metaphysical aspects of love. "Love," she started, her voice enveloped by the soothing hum of the mountain's night song, "is not just an emotion. It is a creative life force, a divine essence that exists in all things. It is as essential to life as the air we breathe."

Shania motioned towards the expansive night sky, awash with countless constellations. "Observe the cosmos above us. Every star, every galaxy, and every cosmic body coexists harmoniously in this vast universe. They are held together by a force greater than gravity, more profound than physics. This force, my dear ones, is Love. It is Love that binds everything, creating a harmonious symphony of existence."

She then softly turned her gaze towards the participants. "Consider your own bodies. Every cell, every organ, and every system works in unison to maintain life. This, too, is Love in action. It is the unseen force that nurtures, sustains, and breathes life into us."

With a serene smile, Shania continued, "Love is a divine canvas, painting our lives with vivid strokes of joy, compassion, and connection. Through Love, we are able to truly appreciate the beauty of creation, the intricacies of life, and our intrinsic connection with all things."

Shania then closed her eyes, absorbing the quiet symphony of the night. "When we open our hearts to Love," she spoke softly, "we begin to experience a profound sense of oneness. We understand that we are not solitary beings, but integral parts of a greater whole, interconnected with all forms of life."

Her voice then rose, resonating with deep conviction, "Through Love, we can feel the pulsating rhythm of existence. Through Love, we can touch the divine essence in every creature. Through Love, we can comprehend the silent whispers of the universe, drawing us towards unity and harmony."

In the silence that followed, Shania opened her eyes, their twinkling depth mirroring the starlit sky. "Through Love," she concluded, "we return to our true nature — a state of unity with all existence. For we are Love, dear ones. We are born of it, we exist in it, and ultimately, we return to it. This is the power of Love."

The hushed gathering absorbed her teachings, the words seeping deep into their hearts. As Shania's profound insights on Love sank in, a palpable wave of understanding washed over the participants. They found themselves closer to a universal truth, touched by the ultimate force of creation and existence — Love.

CHAPTER 34

THE DIVINE DIALOGUE AND JOURNEY BEYOND THE MOUNTAIN

Immersed in a divine radiance that mirrored the gentle luminescence of the moon above, Shania effortlessly captured the undivided attention of every participant. This was their sacred farewell, the pinnacle of their shared pilgrimage atop the Enchanted Mountain. The very air seemed to hum with a potent amalgamation of anticipation and reverence, a testament to the depth of their spiritual journey.

"My dear friends," Shania began, her voice a soothing melody against the still night, "Your journey here may be coming to an end, but your spiritual journey is a continuous path. Now is the time to foster a profound relationship with The Creator, the divine source of love and wisdom that is always available to you."

Her eyes held the gaze of each participant as she continued, "Understand, this connection is not merely a bridge; it is a conduit, an ethereal pathway that allows a continuous flow of celestial wisdom from the Heavenly realm to you. This divine dialogue will illuminate your path, infuse your life with deeper meaning, and guide you towards a higher state of consciousness."

Shania gestured towards the group, her words painting a vivid picture. "Yet, this connection with the Divine, as powerful as it may be, needs to be complemented by a transformation of self. It is essential that we rewire our brains, a process that requires patience, commitment, and shared support. This is why I recommend being part of a rewiring group. It will give you the platform for continuous growth, camaraderie, and the opportunity to utilize the collective energy in the mastermind process."

Her voice dipped lower, carrying a weight of quiet authority, "The more you commit to your self-growth, the more you open yourself up to contain greater love and light. With every step on this path, your vibration raises, aligning you closer to the consciousness of the 5th dimension, a realm of unconditional love, higher wisdom, and expansive freedom."

As Shania's words seeped into the silence, she left a lingering pause before her final impartation. With a tender smile, she said, "Remember, the Creator lives within you. As you step out into the world, know that you are never alone. The Holy Spirit, your angelic

239

guides, and your ancestors are always beside you, supporting and loving you."

Her words hung in the air, the echo of her voice merging with the whisper of the night. The participants, their hearts ignited with Shania's wisdom, embraced the profound truth that they were divinely loved, eternally guided, and never alone. The transformative journey they had embarked upon at the retreat had not only enlightened them but also equipped them with the tools to continue their spiritual evolution beyond the Enchanted Mountain.

Amidst the enchanted gathering, Natalia emerged, sharing her heartfelt thanks and admiration for the participants. She voiced her honor in witnessing their transformation, their leaps of growth, and their courageous journey into self-discovery. "I am overjoyed by your accomplishments, and I have complete faith in your potential to continue soaring to even greater heights," she affirmed, her words brimming with genuine belief in their potential.

Her encouragement resonated powerfully, a beacon of support, urging them to further delve into their paths of self-mastery. She emboldened them to maintain their focus on the ultimate vision of resonating in 5D consciousness, a goal within their reach.

Following Natalia's poignant address, Shania summoned everyone into unity, prompting the formation of a circular assembly, a symbol of their collective journey. As the participants aligned themselves in the circle, Natalia gracefully moved into its heart, positioning herself on a cushion at the center. With serene ease, she began to play the melodious Tibetan singing bowls, their harmonious resonance filling the space.

Amid the soothing lull of the singing bowls, Shania's voice graced the air, softly guiding the participants. "Gently close your eyes," she instructed, marking the commencement of their closing meditation.

Under the luminescent glow of the moon and the ethereal resonance of the singing bowls, Shania began guiding the participants into a deep, transformative meditation. Her voice, a melodious whisper against the harmonious backdrop, invited them to retreat into their inner sanctum, a sacred space where wisdom, knowledge, and clarity resided.

"Anchor your newfound knowledge and the insightful revelations into your core," she gently instructed, "allow it to become a part of you, to guide you as you re-enter your daily lives. Remember, you are never solitary in your journey. The Creator is a constant, a divine presence in your lives."

Her words flowed like a soothing river, carrying the promise of an elevated consciousness awaiting their embrace. "Awaken to the reality of 5D consciousness," she encouraged, her voice imbued with a profound conviction, "It's time to remember the divine essence of your true self."

As Shania guided their introspective journey, the enchanting sounds of the singing bowls filled the space, an ethereal symphony conducted by Natalia, herself absorbed in the spiritual rhythm of the moment.

Once Shania's guiding voice quieted, she offered heartfelt gratitude to the Divine presences who had been integral to their spiritual journey. She thanked the Holy Spirit, the celestial choir of angels, the ancestral guides, and not forgetting the Enchanted Mountain, whose energies had served as a powerful ally in their transformative retreat.

In the ensuing silence, Shania retreated into a profound meditative state. As if on her silent cue, a subtle but palpable shift coursed through the atmosphere. The interdimensional veil that had been lifted for their sacred work began to close, returning the space to its natural order.

Their spiritual mission, the Sacred Retreat on the Enchanted Mountain, was now complete. The sacred silence embraced the night, bearing witness to the transformation they had undergone, the wisdom they had gleaned, and the spiritual heights they had attained.

CHAPTER 35

JOURNEY'S END AND THE DAWN OF NEW BEGINNINGS

Back at their hotel, the participants, each one enveloped in a serene, tranquil aura resonating from their profound journey atop the Enchanted Mountain, engaged in a quiet assembly with both Shania and Natalia. The purpose was to receive their individual aura photographs along with an interpretative booklet, prepared by Shania. Their aura photographs served as a tangible remnant of their transformative journey, a spiritual roadmap of their unique energetic shifts.

Once they returned to their familiar surroundings, each participant could arrange private sessions with Shania for an in-depth interpretation of their aura photographs. In these personal encounters, Shania's spiritual coaching would further nurture their spiritual growth, encouraging them to continue their path of self-discovery and self-mastery.

For those who felt the need for additional psychological support, Natalia, with her therapeutic skills, was available for scheduled sessions. The sacred journey they had embarked upon was an intense experience, profoundly shifting their inner landscapes.

After the evening's affairs were concluded, each participant retreated to their hotel rooms. A sense of finality hung in the air - they were leaving the next day. However, they were not the same individuals who had arrived days earlier. They were now transformed beings, seekers of the Light who had delved into the depth of their souls, braving an intimate encounter with their divine essence.

The Enchanted Mountain had left an indelible mark on their beings, imprinting them with its sacred energy, transforming them from mere seekers into genuine bearers of the Light. Each one now radiated a newfound spiritual vibrance, touched by the divine, and forever changed. They stood on the precipice of a new dawn, ready to carry their luminous wisdom into the world, spreading the light they had discovered within themselves.

As for Shania and Natalia, with hearts brimming with gratitude, they reflected on the sacred retreat they had facilitated. They had willingly become vessels for the divine flow of spiritual energy, and as always, were left astounded by the transformative magic that unfurled. Their roles as guides in the journey of self-discovery and transformation filled them with a deep sense of purpose, and witnessing the participants' metamorphosis was nothing short of an honor.

Together, they shared a prayer of gratitude, their words gently merging with the tranquility of the Sedona air. Their warm embrace symbolized not just a partnership, but a shared spiritual commitment, an alliance of souls dedicated to nurturing enlightenment in others.

Retreating to their hotel room, they found comfort in solitude and reflection. Yet their journey in Sedona was not quite over. For a few more days, they soaked in the spiritual richness of the land, connecting deeper with The Creator, sharing simple meals that transformed into meaningful moments, and visiting friends who had also made Sedona their spiritual haven.

Also, during their brief extended stay, Shania and Natalia found themselves drawn to various sacred sites, each with its unique vibrational signature. These were places that held the potential for future sacred gatherings, sites that could, in time, become crucibles for another wave of spiritual transformation. Their shared vision resonated with the beauty of Sedona, igniting a spark of inspiration for the chapters yet to unfold. Their journey was far from over; it was merely the beginning of another exciting spiritual adventure.

CHAPTER 36

INTO THE UNKNOWN

Months had flowed by since Shania and Natalia graced Sedona with their Sacred Gatherings Retreat. While they continued their spiritual work, Marcus found himself at the precipice of a new expedition in his journey of self-discovery. With a desire to delve deeper, he aimed to chronicle the progressive transformation of an individual as revealed through the sequential series of aura photographs. His sights were set on the loftier goal of crafting a scientific discourse on the subject, an endeavor that sought to bridge the realms of science and spirituality.

Reaching out to Shania, Marcus shared the contours of his idea. An echo of excitement reverberated through her as she perceived the potential his study held, not just for the individual, but for the collective - an opportunity to further illuminate the converging pathways of science and spirituality.

Bringing Natalia into their dialogue, they found themselves in a harmonious agreement. The idea resonated with her own beliefs and interests. There were certain individuals whom Shania and Natalia were jointly assisting, individuals who embodied the spirit of service and were willing to contribute to the broader cause of humanity. From among them, a woman named Janet emerged as a potential subject for Marcus's research. With Janet's journey of transformation at the center, Marcus would begin his explorative documentation.

To bring their plans into focus, Shania arranged a gathering at her studio, bringing together Natalia and Marcus in the same physical space for the first time. Before this gathering, Natalia and Marcus's exchanges had been confined to telephonic dialogues.

Their meeting was charged with anticipation, as they laid out the blueprint for an extraordinary journey that lay ahead. Everything fell into place seamlessly, the meticulous details beautifully aligning with their collective vision. With their strategy set, the trio looked forward to their next assembly, which was scheduled for the day they would embark on the first phase of documenting Janet's transformative journey.

The appointed day dawned. Shania, Natalia, Marcus, and Janet convened at Shania's studio. Janet, previously briefed about the proceedings, knew that both audio and visual records of her sessions would be made. Despite the initial nerves, meeting Marcus infused her with excitement, as she realized the pivotal role she was going to play in helping to merge science with spirituality. Her anticipation for her personal transformational journey was palpable; after all, she had already spent around three months under the guidance of Shania and Natalia. It was time to embark on this new chapter.

In Shania's studio, there was a serene area where they all gathered in comfortable plush seating, preparing to begin. Marcus listened intently as Janet recounted her struggles with anxiety, depression, and the unresolved issues that had plagued her since childhood. Janet shared how her rough upbringing had left her with deep wounds, and as an adult, she had repeatedly found herself in unhealthy relationships that reflected her lack of self-worth.

Marcus was moved by her courage and resilience as she spoke about her decision to embark on the path of self-transformation. Janet acknowledged that her journey had not been easy, but through the guidance and support of Shania and Natalia, she had made remarkable progress in just three months.

With the passing of the months, their regular rendezvous became a weekly rhythm. They would meet for two hours, allowing

Janet's personal exploration to deepen. Marcus, the silent observer, watched with admiration as Shania and Natalia, with their combined wisdom and skills, helped Janet delve into her underlying issues and traverse the maze of her internal landscape. The process was awe-inspiring, to say the least.

Marcus also found himself astounded by Shania's expert guidance as she navigated Janet through each aura photography session. After each one, Shania interpreted the revelations the camera had captured. Then Natalia shared with Janet the metaphysical dance she was performing as her consciousness meandered between the realms of 3D and 4D, even briefly grazing the realm of 5D.

Further, Shania delicately pointed out the regions within Janet that were clamoring for attention, areas in her psyche and energy that called for resolution. Based on the truths revealed in the aura photograph, Shania, with her gentle wisdom, would give Janet a glimpse of the journey they would undertake in their next meeting. This rhythm of reveal, resolve, and advance continued, each session a new chapter in the compelling narrative of Janet's transformation.

As Marcus observed and explored the sequential series of aura photographs that Shania had taken to document Janet's transformation, he was struck by the visible changes in her energy field. The initial photographs had shown a clouded and dim aura, reflecting her struggles and unresolved emotions. But as the woman progressed on her journey, the colors became brighter and more vibrant, symbolizing her newfound clarity and inner peace.

As a full year spun its wheel, Marcus bore witness to a captivating spectacle of Janet's aura. Through this vibrant display of color and light, he began to discern patterns reflecting her journey of transformation. He noted how the hues of her aura shifted, signaling her moments of deep revelations, trials with past afflictions, and periods of anxiety or frustration.

Marcus knew that these colors were not just a beautiful spectacle. They spoke a deeper language, a science of light. Each color was like a different note on a musical scale, a unique frequency of energy that vibrated within the grand symphony of life.

Marcus loved music, and he imagined an orchestra, each musician playing a different instrument at a unique pitch. Together, they create a beautiful melody. Similarly, each color in Janet's aura was like a different musical note, playing in harmony to compose the symphony of her energy field.

When Janet experienced a revelation, a high note was struck and her aura shimmered in bright, luminous hues. When she grappled with her past or felt anxious, the notes were lower, and the colors became more subdued.

Connecting this to the world of science, Marcus was reminded of the principles he studied about energy and light. Just like the colors of a rainbow emerge when sunlight passes through raindrops, Janet's aura colors were born from her unique energy frequencies interacting with light.

This entire process reminded him of the world of quantum physics - where everything, big or small, is connected and constantly interacting, influencing each other's dance of existence. Like a pebble causing ripples in a pond, Janet's inner transformations were causing waves of energetic shifts visible in her aura.

Witnessing this, Marcus felt like he was standing on a bridge where the realms of science and spirituality meet, giving him a glimpse into the fascinating unity of all things. This union fueled his curiosity even more, encouraging him to venture deeper into this enthralling exploration where the seen and unseen, the measurable and mystical, intertwine.

To delve even deeper, Marcus yearned to comprehend Janet's transformation from her perspective, her intimate and personal lens. The wisdom harvested from her experiences would act as the kernel for his future writings, a treasure trove of firsthand insights into the transformative journey.

Before some sessions, as Janet readied herself to do the heavy lifting of emotional exploration, Marcus would venture to ask her questions. Through these dialogues, he uncovered the practices and teachings that were the supporting pillars of Janet's transformation.

As if sharing a well-traveled roadmap, Janet opened up about her journey, speaking of the necessity of self-love, the grace of self-acceptance, and the bravery of internal healing. To her, this transformation was not just a process, it was a commitment—a dedication to her personal growth no matter how challenging the terrain became.

She narrated how this commitment, though fraught with struggles, illuminated her life, profoundly reshaping her relationships into nurturing sanctuaries of love. Even though the work was far from over, the darkness of anxiety and depression that once clouded her days were now a distant memory.

Through the profound teachings of Shania and Natalia, Janet was able to excavate her true self, shedding the layers of societal conditioning and the chains of limiting beliefs that once shackled her spirit. They had served as her guides, lighting up her path towards self-worth, unearthing and healing the deep-seated wounds of her past.

The inner metamorphosis she experienced didn't just heal her heart; it transformed her brain. The journey she undertook rewired her neural pathways, fostering a healthier perspective and nurturing resilience.

Amid Janet's recounting, she also unveiled how prayer and meditation had built a robust bridge between her and The Creator. It was here, she said, in this sacred bond, that she discovered an infinite well of strength to propel her forward. Guided by divine wisdom, her path was ever illuminated, her steps imbued with profound assurance.

She shared that loneliness was now a stranger to her, the companionship of The Creator and the Holy Spirit, a ceaseless presence, a soft echo in every heartbeat.

She spoke of her weekly ritual, her spiritual baths that infused the fragrances of frankincense and myrrh into her soul, cleansing, purifying, and revitalizing her spirit.

Her narrative took a cosmic turn as she relayed the profound realization that her existence was a dance of the spirit in the physical realm. She was a spiritual being on a human journey, her heart beating to the rhythm of universal oneness, the interconnectedness of all things.

Her communion with the spirit realm not only deepened her understanding of this interconnectedness but also accelerated her healing, unraveling the cosmic tapestry of her transformation.

Finally, her voice trembled with gratitude as she acknowledged the benevolence of The Creator, gratitude flowing in her words like a river paying homage to its source. Through the highs and lows, the pain, and the healing, she found herself cradled by the unending love of The Creator, forever imprinted on her heart.

As Janet's transformation unfolded before Marcus, it was as if he was reading a captivating novel, full of struggles, victories, profound insights, and enduring transformations. It was a story that could inspire any reader to embark on their own journey of self-discovery, to embrace the metamorphosis, and ultimately emerge as the truest version of themselves.

Marcus always listened intently, captivated by the profound wisdom shared by Janet. He continued to ask questions, seeking to grasp the intricacies of her journey. As he continued documenting her progress, he found himself experiencing a range of emotions—awe, curiosity, and still a lingering sense of skepticism.

Janet's transformation challenged Marcus's preconceived notions about the limitations of scientific inquiry. He pondered how science, with its focus on measurable data and observable phenomena, could encompass the profound shifts occurring in consciousness. The convergence of science and spirituality appeared both elusive and tantalizing, leaving Marcus with more questions than answers.

In time, Marcus would bear witness to the transformative journeys of a sum total of 15 individuals, all under the guiding hands of Shania and Natalia. Each shared narratives of resilience and revelation, drawing immense strength and guidance from unseen yet undeniably present forces of love—The Creator, the Holy Spirit, and for some, the angels of light and love.

Despite assembling a group of earnest college researchers to help dissect and analyze the data, Marcus found himself sailing in an ocean of profound realization. He was not merely a bystander documenting these transformational stories of individuals transitioning from 3D to 5D consciousness; he was part of an intricate tapestry where his journey was inextricably intertwined with theirs.

Janet's journey particularly resonated with him, acting as a gentle beacon, luring him towards his own path of self-discovery and transformation. He understood that only by journeying through the mysteries of the unknown—both in the realm of science and spirit—could he unearth the profound truths hidden beneath the surface, waiting to be discovered.

CHAPTER 37

REFINED VISION

Shania's dedication to her craft knew no bounds. With each passing day, she tirelessly worked on refining her technique with the camera, seeking to enhance her ability to capture the subtle nuances of the human aura. She understood that by honing her skills, she could reach even greater depths in her mission to help others.

As she delved into her practice, Shania discovered new ways to fine-tune her camera settings, allowing for clearer and more precise aura photography. She experimented with different lighting conditions and angles, aiming to capture even more of the essence of each individual's energy field.

The results were astounding. The aura photographs now possessed a heightened vibrancy and detail, reflecting the unique energy signatures of each person. The hues and shades danced on the prints, revealing a tapestry of emotions, thoughts, and energetic patterns.

With her refined technique, Shania's ability to help others took a significant leap forward. The enhanced clarity in the photographs enabled her to provide deeper insights into the blocks, imbalances, and potential areas of growth for her clients. She could now discern more subtle shifts in energy, indicating the progress individuals were making on their journey from 3D to 5D consciousness.

The news of Shania's improved camera and her remarkable skill spread like wildfire. People flocked to her aura photography demonstrations, eager to catch a glimpse of their own energetic portrait. Some approached with skepticism, their doubts lingering in the back of their minds. Others came with an open heart, ready to embrace the possibilities of transformation.

During the demonstrations, Shania would explain the significance of the colors and their meanings, guiding individuals on a journey of self-discovery. She spoke of the interplay between the energetic and emotional realms, helping participants understand the intricate relationship between their thoughts, feelings, and the vibrational frequencies they emitted.

Through her work, Shania inspired others to delve into their own inner landscapes, encouraging them to explore their unresolved issues, fears, and limiting beliefs. She provided a safe space for individuals to confront the shadows that had held them captive in the 3D realm, guiding them towards the light of 5D consciousness.

With her refined vision and deepened understanding of the energetic realm, Shania became a beacon of hope for those seeking transformation. The photographs she produced served as tangible reminders of the beauty and complexity of the human spirit, instilling a sense of awe and wonder in those who beheld them.

As word of her remarkable ability spread even more, Shania's calendar filled with appointments for personal aura photography sessions. People from all walks of life sought her guidance, yearning to unlock the secrets held within their energy fields. Each session became a sacred exploration, as Shania employed her empathic gifts to interpret the photographs and delve into the heart of the matter.

With each person she helped, Shania felt an indescribable joy, and her passion deepened. Witnessing the breakthroughs, the shedding of old patterns, and the emergence of newfound self-awareness filled her with a sense of purpose and fulfillment. She knew that her mission extended far beyond the boundaries of her camera—it was a mission of transformation, of guiding others towards the realms of love, harmony, and higher consciousness.

As Shania concluded each session, she took a moment to offer gratitude to the Divine, to the Universe, for the opportunity to be of service. She knew that her work was a small but significant piece of the grand tapestry of human evolution. With a heart full of love and compassion, she eagerly embraced the next chapter of her transformative journey.

CHAPTER 38

A LEAP FORWARD

Natalia's journey of assisting others in their transition from 3D to 5D consciousness had taken a significant leap forward. Fueled by her unwavering dedication, she explored new frontiers in her practice, incorporating cutting-edge technologies, which she designed, that would revolutionize the transformational process.

Guided by her intuition and a desire to reach a wider audience, Natalia embraced the power of Artificial Intelligence (AI) and Virtual Reality (VR) in her workshops. These tools became catalysts for profound change, allowing participants to immerse themselves in an experiential journey of self-discovery and growth.

Then, once more, Natalia and Shania joined forces, this time leveraging the power of Artificial Intelligence (AI), Virtual Reality (VR), and aura photography. Natalia had crafted a program, one that was custom-fitted to each individual's distinctive energetic blueprint. The AI algorithms analyzed the person's aura photographs, identifying patterns, imbalances, and areas of potential growth. This data-driven approach provided participants with personalized guidance, helping them navigate the intricacies of their journey towards higher consciousness.

With VR, Natalia created immersive environments where individuals could explore different dimensions of consciousness. Through virtual simulations, participants experienced the vibrational frequencies of 4D and the transformative energies of 5D. This technology allowed for a direct experience of expanded awareness and served as a bridge between the physical and spiritual realms.

The results were nothing short of extraordinary. Participants who went through Natalia and Shania's AI, VR, and aura photographs program experienced rapid progress in their transformational journey. What would have taken years or even decades in the past, now unfolded within a span of the six-month program. The integration of technology accelerated the process, amplifying the effects of the spiritual teachings and energetic work.

As part of the program, Natalia guided participants through immersive VR experiences, leading them into deep states of relaxation and heightened awareness. Then, Shania facilitated soulful meditations, guiding individuals to connect with their inner essence and tap into the infinite well of wisdom within.

Through the AI program, Natalia designed it to provide personalized insights and practices to support each person's unique challenges and goals. It addressed deep-seated issues, hidden patterns, limiting beliefs, and emotional blockages, helping participants navigate their way through the layers of conditioning and societal programming that had kept them anchored in 3D consciousness.

The participants marveled at the rapid shifts they experienced. Anxiety melted away, replaced by a sense of peace and tranquility. Depression lifted, making way for a newfound joy and zest for life. Relationships healed and flourished, as individuals learned to cultivate self-love and attract individuals and partners who honored and valued their authentic selves. They embraced authentic connections based on mutual love and respect.

Whispers of the transformative power of Natalia and Shania's combined program, blending the science of AI and VR with the spiritual aura photography, swept across the globe. From every conceivable corner, individuals were drawn to their weekend introductory workshops as if guided by an unseen force. Yet, the depth of demand, coupled with the program's six-month span, presented a challenge that Natalia and Shania were primed to meet. They realized that the reach and affordability of their program could be enhanced through a synergy of collective effort.

So, they cast a wider net, reaching out to the individuals who had once walked the path of their program, as well as those who had attended any of their Sacred Gatherings Retreats at least three years prior. People from various cultures and continents had experienced these retreats, and some of these seasoned souls were uniquely qualified to spread the transformative teachings in their homelands.

Prompted by this call to service, past attendees of the program and former participants from The Sacred Gatherings Retreats stepped forward, ready to serve in the evolution of humanity. Natalia and Shania, thus, initiated a ripple of transformational energy, training these ready souls to help others tread the path of self-discovery and growth.

The training unfolded seamlessly, cultivating an assembly of new facilitators, each ready to bring this program back to their corner of the world. Natalia had cleverly crafted an application, a digital counterpart to Shania's aura camera, which could turn any computer or smartphone into a portal for capturing aura photographs. She adapted some existing VR gear to match her unique specifications and developed an accompanying AI app to assist the facilitators in their mission.

With the virtual world poised to support them, the facilitators were equipped and ready to carry forward. Shania and Natalia would remain connected with them, conducting weekly video chats and offering their assistance for any technological or supportive needs that emerged. They also had a system to document those who achieved the ascension to 5D consciousness.

Each facilitator returned to their respective regions, their hearts set on creating the necessary environment for the introductory workshops and the six-month programs. Through sheer manifestation power, all the sites were established within a span of three months. Synchronized in spirit and timing, they all launched simultaneously.

Shania and Natalia bestowed upon their program a name that echoed its profound purpose. They called it "Light Evolution," as it was the journey into the light of 5D Consciousness.

The excitement and anticipation were palpable as so many participants embarked on a transformative journey to Light Evolution centers all over the world. Each participant in the program committed themselves wholeheartedly to their own evolution, understanding that the transformation from 3D to 5D required a deep level of self-reflection, dedication, and active participation. Participants were immersed in daily disciplines such as meditation, breathwork, and reflective journaling. These methods fostered a rich landscape of self-awareness, aiding them in shedding restrictive beliefs and unlocking the doors to elevated frequencies of consciousness.

Within the virtual realm of VR, Natalia designed transformative experiences that pushed the boundaries of perception. Participants immersed themselves in vivid landscapes, transcending the limitations of their physical bodies. Under the facilitator's guidance, the participants vibrated at high frequencies and created a bridge to The Creator and energies of love and light. Then, they ventured into sacred spaces, ancient temples, and expansive natural landscapes, connecting with those energies of higher realms.

Through guided meditations within the virtual environment, participants accessed heightened states of consciousness. They experienced profound shifts in their awareness, as more layers of conditioning dissolved, revealing more of the radiant essence that resided within. The boundaries of time and space blurred, allowing them to tap into the interconnectedness of all things.

Through the guidance of Natalia, Shania and the facilitators of the Light Evolution centers, the individuals experienced profound breakthroughs in every aspect of their lives. They tapped into their innate creative abilities, unleashing hidden talents and passions that had long been suppressed. Careers took on new meaning, as they aligned with their soul's purpose, contributing their unique gifts to the world.

The program, focusing on weaving 4D consciousness into the tapestry of their lives, served as the vital bridge from the confines of 3D to the vast expanses of 5D consciousness. Participants explored the realms of expanded perception, intuition, and multidimensionality. They learned to navigate the realm of energy and frequency, harnessing their innate abilities to manifest and co-create their reality.

The facilitators of the centers witnessed the incredible blossoming of each participant, their vibrancy and radiance expanding with each passing day. The deep sense of interconnectedness and unity that emerged within the group fostered a supportive and loving environment for growth and transformation.

Natalia and Shania stood at the forefront of a new paradigm, merging spirituality, science, and technology. Their dedication and tireless exploration birthed a groundbreaking approach to personal growth and conscious evolution. The synergy between ancient wisdom and modern innovation proved to be a potent catalyst for profound change.

With each successful transition, Natalia and Shania felt a deep sense of fulfillment. The testimonials poured in, sharing stories of personal empowerment, spiritual awakening, and the reclamation of one's true essence. The impact of their work rippled through communities, inspiring individuals to step into their highest potential and embrace the limitless possibilities of 5D consciousness.

As they looked back on their journey, Natalia and Shania felt immense gratitude for the gifts that had guided their path. The synergy with Shania's aura photography, the integration of Natalia's AI and VR technology, and the unwavering support of their spiritual guidance had propelled them forward. They knew that their mission was far from complete, and with each leap forward, the world was being transformed one consciousness at a time.

CHAPTER 39

A Skeptic's Dilemma

Marcus found himself at a crossroads, torn between the rigid beliefs of his logical mind and the compelling evidence that lay before him. The aura photographs and now the AI and VR technology, in addition to the stories of transformation he had witnessed, challenged his worldview, forcing him to confront the limitations of his scientific perspective.

Deep within, Marcus knew that he could no longer ignore the stirring of curiosity and wonder within his heart. The time had come for him to embark on his own path of self-discovery and transformation, even if it meant venturing into uncharted territories of the unknown.

Determined to keep his exploration private, Marcus refrained from reaching out to Natalia or Shania for guidance. He felt the need to maintain a sense of independence, making sure to shield his journey from the possibility of scrutiny from the scientific community. Instead, he turned to the wealth of information he had gathered through his observations and the articles written about

Shania and Natalia's work. While Marcus was fully aware that his quest would lack not only the visual guidance of Shania's aura photography, but also Natalia's AI and VR devices, he harbored no reservations. His desire was to journey into the uncharted territories of the intangible - the sphere of spirituality.

Marcus leaned into the methodologies and practices gleaned from his intensive study of the transformative journeys of the fifteen individuals, meticulously documenting his personal experiences into confidential notes. He was careful to apply scientific principles wherever possible, seeking to quantify his journey and analyze the data he collected along the way.

With a fervor fueled by both skepticism and a desire for deeper understanding, Marcus delved into various disciplines that bridged the gap between science and spirituality. He explored the realms of quantum physics, consciousness studies, and the merging field of neuro-spirituality, seeking to find correlations and patterns that could shed light on the phenomenon he had witnessed, as well as his own experiences.

Drawing from his scientific background, Marcus attempted to replicate certain practices, using the college lab after hours to measure his brainwave patterns, and physiological responses during moments of heightened awareness. The college also had a SQUID magnetometer that Marcus used to measure his bio-magnetic field. He sought to validate his experiences through empirical evidence, meticulously scrutinizing each finding and analyzing the data with an unwavering commitment to objectivity.

As Marcus delved deeper into his exploration, he encountered synchronicities and coincidences that seemed to guide him along his path. Chance encounters with like-minded individuals led him to hidden pockets of knowledge and insights that he had not anticipated. Each new revelation nudged him further towards a profound understanding of the interconnectedness of science and spirituality.

Yet, amidst the excitement and discoveries, Marcus also experienced moments of doubt and confusion. The data he collected often seemed elusive, resistant to traditional scientific methods of analysis. The mysteries of consciousness, energy, and the realms beyond the visible world proved to be formidable challenges, demanding a level of open-mindedness that went against the grain of his skeptical nature.

In the depths of his uncertainty, Marcus found solace in the wisdom of renowned scientists who had also embarked on similar journeys. Their writings and research provided him with a sense of validation and a broader perspective that extended beyond his own limited experiences. They offered him the reassurance that he was not alone in his quest to bridge the gap between the known and the unknown. This reassurance and Marcus's unwavering tenacity propelled him forward to continue his exploration.

Marcus delved deeper into the captivating realm of quantum physics, its intricate dance with the fabric of reality, and its implications for the convergence of science and spirituality. He immersed himself in the works of renowned physicists, exploring the mind-bending theories that shattered the conventional understanding of the physical world.

He learned about the fundamental principle of quantum superposition, where particles exist in multiple states simultaneously until observed or measured. The very act of observation collapses the wave function, determining the particle's definitive state. This concept challenged Marcus's perception of reality, raising profound questions about the interconnectedness of consciousness and the material world.

Marcus marveled at the entanglement phenomenon, where particles separated by vast distances remained inexplicably connected. This interconnectedness defied the limitations of space and time, hinting at a universal web that bound all things together. It resonated with the spiritual concept of oneness, where every being and every particle shared an underlying unity.

As Marcus delved even deeper, he encountered the pioneering work of consciousness studies. This emerging field explored the nature of consciousness, its origins, and its far-reaching implications. He discovered that consciousness was not confined to the realm of the individual mind but permeated the fabric of the universe itself.

Consciousness studies highlighted the profound interplay between the observer and the observed, mirroring the insights of quantum physics. It suggested that our perceptions and intentions could shape the very reality we experienced, a concept rooted in ancient spiritual teachings across different cultures.

The emerging field of neuro-spirituality further captivated Marcus's attention. It examined the intersection of neuroscience and spirituality, seeking to unravel the neural mechanisms behind transcendent experiences and states of heightened awareness. Marcus discovered that certain brain regions, specifically the prefrontal cortex and the anterior cingulate cortex, show a significant increase in activity during prayer, meditation and other spiritual practices.

The heightened activity in these areas can lead to an enhanced sense of self-awareness, emotional regulation, and empathic understanding, which are key facets of personal transformation. From a scientific standpoint, these physiological changes, which can be measured with fMRI scans, constitute tangible evidence of the transformative power of such practices.

Neuro-spirituality offered a profound window into the convergence of science and spirituality. It bridged the gap between objective measurement and subjective experience, offering insights into the physiological changes that occurred as individuals delved deeper into their spiritual journeys.

Marcus marveled at the intricate dance between the firing neurons and the expansion of consciousness. The brain's neural pathways reshaped themselves, forming new connections and pathways that facilitated the transcendence of limited perspectives. He realized that science was beginning to unlock the door to understanding the mysterious terrain of the mind, confirming the age-old wisdom passed down through spiritual traditions.

In his exploration, Marcus encountered accounts of near-death experiences and mystical encounters that defied conventional explanation. These personal testimonies, combined with scientific research, painted a compelling picture of a reality far grander than the narrow confines of the material world.

As Marcus wove together the threads of quantum physics, consciousness studies, and neuro-spirituality, he discovered a profound truth—the convergence of science and spirituality. The once unrelated realms were revealing themselves to be intricately intertwined, offering glimpses into the underlying unity that permeated all of existence.

He marveled at the idea that the very fabric of reality might be composed of conscious energy, interwoven in an intricate tapestry of vibration and frequency. The exploration of spirituality was not a retreat from reason but a journey into the heart of reality, where scientific inquiry and the mysteries of the soul met in a dance of profound discovery.

Marcus continued to walk his unique path, embracing both the scientific and spiritual aspects of his exploration. He knew that the answers he sought were not confined to a single discipline but resided in the convergence of seemingly differing realms of understanding.

As he delved deeper into the mysteries of consciousness, Marcus began to catch glimpses of profound truths that lay just beyond the reach of his logical mind. He marveled at the intricate dance between science and spirituality, really realizing that they were not separate entities but rather two facets of a greater whole.

Though Marcus had not yet fully grasped the concept of 5D consciousness, he felt a profound shift within himself. The rigid boundaries of his skepticism began to soften, and a sense of wonder and awe enveloped his being. He understood that his journey was far from over, and that the answers he sought would continue to reveal themselves in their own time.

In the silence of his private reflections, Marcus remained steadfast in his commitment to bridging the gap between science and spirituality. He knew that one day, he would synthesize his findings, his own personal notes, and the collective wisdom of those who had embarked on similar paths. He would contribute to the growing body of knowledge that aimed to unite the realms of the seen and the unseen, empowering humanity to embrace a more expansive understanding of reality.

Driven by a relentless thirst for knowledge and a burning desire to uncover the profound mysteries that lay just beyond the veil of the known, Marcus pressed forward. With each step, he moved closer to his ultimate goal of unraveling the enigma of consciousness and illuminating the path towards a harmonious integration of science and spirituality.

In his private moments, Marcus contemplated the significance of his findings. He knew that his journey of exploration was not merely a personal pursuit but a quest to expand the collective understanding of the nature of existence. One day, he would meld his wisdom and insights, sharing his findings with the world to inspire others to embark on their own journeys of transformation.

So, Marcus continued to walk the path of a skeptic turned seeker, driven by an insatiable curiosity and an unyielding commitment to discovering the extraordinary within the ordinary. With every step, he moved closer to unraveling the enigma that had captivated his mind and heart—a quest that would forever change the trajectory of his life and contribute to the ever-growing tapestry of human understanding.

CHAPTER 40

UNDER FIRE

As Shania and Natalia's program gained more momentum, a significant backlash began to stir. Their efforts to help people transition from 3D to 5D consciousness faced staunch opposition from those who sought to maintain the status quo, perpetuating a world steeped in fear and control.

Shania and Natalia's legitimacy was called into question by powerful forces that thrived on the manipulation and subjugation of the masses. These individuals, driven by their own agenda, aimed to keep people trapped in the confines of 3D consciousness, where fear reigned supreme, and the Elite Ruling Class held power over the disempowered underclass.

The "Powers that be" recognized the transformative potential of Shania and Natalia's work. They understood that when individuals awakened to their inherent power and connectedness, they became more difficult to manipulate and control. It threatened the carefully crafted systems of dominance and exploitation that had kept humanity divided and enslaved.

The backlash manifested in various forms. Criticism and skepticism were hurled at Shania and Natalia, questioning the validity of their methods and the authenticity of their intentions. They were accused of peddling false hope, preying on the vulnerabilities of those seeking solace and transformation.

Media outlets controlled by the same powers that resisted change launched smear campaigns, attempting to discredit Shania and Natalia's work. Articles were published, quoting self-proclaimed experts who dismissed the concept of transitioning to higher states of consciousness as mere fantasy or delusion.

As media coverage persisted, additional voices joined the growing chorus of critics. Condemnation arose from diverse sectors of society, each voicing their unique objections. Secular factions, who denied the existence of a divine entity by any name, stood in opposition, as did those deeply ingrained in specific religious ideologies. The latter held steadfast to the conviction that their doctrines were the solitary vessels of truth, looking upon Shania and Natalia's work with a cynical eye.

These devout adherents claimed they had no faith in the concepts of 3D, 4D, or 5D consciousness. However, a deeper, more introspective study of their own scriptures would have revealed reflections of these very principles. Just as a river's flow remains concealed beneath a frozen surface, so too did the wisdom of their teachings remain veiled beneath rigid religious interpretations.

Despite the onslaught of opposition, Shania remained steadfast in her mission. She knew that the path of transformation was not always easy, and it often attracted resistance from those who sought to maintain the status quo. She understood that true change required courage and perseverance, even in the face of adversity.

Shania found solace in the unwavering support of the individuals whose lives had been profoundly transformed through their work. The stories of personal growth and empowerment served as a testament to the authenticity of their approach. Their testimonials spoke louder than any criticism, igniting a spark of hope in the hearts of those who yearned for a different way of being.

Natalia, too, stood firm in her conviction. She recognized that the resistance they faced was a clear indication of the importance and power of their work. She understood that the path of awakening could be met with resistance and skepticism, but she remained resolute in her commitment to guide others toward a higher consciousness.

As the resistance against Shania and Natalia's transformative work intensified, a beautiful support network began to emerge. They were a growing community of like-minded individuals, united in their desire to transcend the limitations of 3D consciousness.

This community became a haven, a refuge where individuals who resonated with their teachings and vision could come together. In this community, they found solace, understanding, and encouragement as they embarked on their own journeys of growth and evolution.

Recognizing the hurdles that Shania and Natalia were navigating, the spiritual community rallied in unity to assist. Delving into intercessory prayer, they released a cascade of love, healing energy, and positive intentions, aiming to buoy Shania and Natalia along their spiritual trajectory.

The community's collective impact was felt. Shania recognized that she had been absorbing the undercurrents of negativity and knew that it was time for her to retreat into her spiritual practices. She summoned Serena's guidance during her meditation, and indeed, Serena appeared, offering much-needed support.

Shania embarked on a journey of energetic cleansing, converting dormant, negative energy into a flow of pure positivity and liberation. She alchemically transformed dark shadows into beams of radiant light and morphed lurking fear into expansive love. As part of her process, she visualized a radiant corridor of crystalline light, sparkling and streaming from the crown of her head, cascading down to discharge through the soles of her feet.

To complete her cleansing process, Shania initiated the ritual of taking a spiritual bath infused with frankincense and myrrh. To safeguard her aura, she crafted a protective energy shield through her potent visualizations.

These practices, her spiritual lifelines, facilitated the re-establishment of balance and harmony within her. In her spiritual sanctuary, she reclaimed her equilibrium, demonstrating the strength of her inner light in the face of adversity.

As Shania cleansed and revitalized her energy field, she felt her intuitive abilities and spiritual gifts intensify. Downloads of information, divine in origin, started to flow into her consciousness, like streams of wisdom from the Holy Spirit. Each revelation filled her with a profound sense of alignment, an affirmation of her purpose.

With the amplification of her intuitive abilities came an enhanced perception of the energetic imprints of others. This newfound clarity assisted her in traversing the challenging times of skepticism and adversity, shielding her from those who aimed to manipulate and control.

Natalia, in turn, sought solace and guidance within the spiritual depths of her being. As she embarked on a journey of meditation and prayer, and engaged in her profound inner work, she faced an unresolved issue that surfaced in the face of criticism. Yet, in dealing with this, she found herself on the receiving end of profound guidance from The Creator.

Soft whispers of wisdom and clarity resonated within Natalia, lighting her path amid the criticism and condemnation. Each whisper was a beacon of light, guiding her steps with steadfast resolve as she continued her journey, now untouched by the cacophony of negativity surrounding her.

Both Shania and Natalia placed their faith and trust in the spiritual guidance they received. They tapped into the wellspring of divine wisdom, following the whispers of The Creator, their souls, and the nudges of the universe.

Together, Shania and Natalia stood as beacons of light, their spirits ignited by the collective prayers, energy, and love of the spiritual community. With each step they took, they moved closer to their shared vision, guided by the wisdom and grace of the spiritual realm. They found comfort in the unwavering belief in their mission and the knowledge that they were part of a greater tapestry of change sweeping across the world.

Amidst the challenges and resistance, they forged ahead, buoyed by the support of their community, and their unwavering connection to the divine. They knew that the journey ahead would not be easy, but they remained steadfast in their commitment to serve as catalysts for transformation, knowing that their work was integral to the unfolding of a new paradigm.

With hearts aflame and unwavering determination, Shania and Natalia continued their work, fueled by the knowledge that even in the face of adversity, the spark of transformation could never be extinguished.

CHAPTER 41

BREAKING BARRIERS

The unfolding plight of Shania and Natalia came to Marcus's attention amid the swirl of the negative campaign against their initiative. His heart stirred, he reached out to them both, extending his deep, heartfelt support while maintaining the shield of privacy over his personal journey into the realm of spirit— a journey he felt must remain an intimate, solitary expedition.

Marcus, having been directly involved in the exploration of Shania and Natalia's endeavor, held no doubt about its authenticity. His scientific mind, once bound by skepticism, had been untethered by the discoveries made within their program. However, he also understood the human tendency to close the gates of comprehension and acceptance when faced with unfamiliar concepts, perhaps a mirror reflecting his past self. He pondered on the possibility that those who sought to tarnish the program's reputation were merely grappling with their own reluctance to open their minds to the unfamiliar landscape of beliefs that stretched beyond their well-trodden paths.

As the events unfolded, Marcus was consumed with a sense of urgency to culminate his research—his scientific testimony to Shania and Natalia's mission. He held firm in his belief that his work, carefully threading the link between the perceived chasm separating science and spirituality, could cast a beam of validation upon their endeavor. Yet, Marcus realized the gravity of the task and the necessity for broadened research. In order to instill greater credibility, he understood the need to include more participants, each adding a unique thread to the intricate tapestry of shared experiences.

Simultaneously, Marcus recognized that his own exploration, his personal metamorphosis towards 5D consciousness, was as vital as his scientific pursuits. He understood that a mere study of the data was akin to understanding a symphony by only reading the musical notes. Some experiences transcended the boundaries of empirical measurements and brought into focus the limitations of his scientific methodologies. The spiritual nuances entwined in the transition to 5D consciousness evaded quantification, which presented challenges in his research. Yet, instead of being deterred, Marcus saw this as an invitation to delve deeper into his own personal journey, an inner expedition that would, in turn, enrich his understanding and bring him closer to bridging the divide between the realms of science and spirituality.

With more fervor, Marcus delved deeper into his exploration of 5D consciousness, his understanding began to evolve. The barriers he had built around his skepticism started to crumble, making way for a newfound acceptance and curiosity.

Marcus continued to seek out various resources, including books, research papers, and personal accounts, to expand his knowledge of 5D consciousness. He discovered that the concept went beyond mere spirituality; it encompassed a higher state of awareness and interconnectedness with all aspects of existence.

As his studies continued, Marcus's perception of reality shifted. He began to see the interconnectedness of all things and how consciousness played a fundamental role in shaping our experiences. He started to comprehend the significance of energy and vibration on a deeper level, understanding that our thoughts and emotions had a direct influence on our reality.

With each revelation, Marcus felt a sense of liberation. He recognized that the rigid boundaries between science and spirituality were artificial constructs. Marcus's excitement grew as he grasped the implications of his findings. He understood that the exploration of consciousness was not separate from scientific inquiry but an integral part of it.

With each passing day, Marcus dove deeper into his inner world, embracing meditation, visualization, and other spiritual practices. These tools allowed him to transcend the confines of his logical mind and tap into higher realms of awareness.

In moments of stillness, Marcus experienced glimpses of the interconnectedness of all things. He felt the subtle energies that permeated his surroundings and sensed the presence of something greater than himself. These moments of revelation stirred within him a deep longing for something more, beyond the confines of the material world.

Every advancement Marcus made on his personal journey sparked not just an intellectual epiphany but ignited an intense transformation within his very core. The once seemingly distant realms of science and spirituality began to merge in his understanding, their interconnectedness unveiling before him like a long-awaited secret. He started to perceive and experience them not as individual entities but as intertwined threads of a universal tapestry. His journey into the understanding of 5D consciousness stirred up feelings of astonishment and deep reverence within him. His eyes, mind, and soul were opening to a magnificent reality he had only begun to fathom.

As Marcus's journey continued to unfold, he found himself increasingly engaged with spiritual practices. This sacred immersion drew him into an intimate dance with the Universe's subtlest whispers. One meditative evening, an unequivocal cosmic impulse surged through him, urging him to bring his pioneering research to completion. Guided by this celestial push, he delved into the rich experiences gathered from his fifteen subjects and began finalizing his study.

While he was acutely aware of the vast expanse of the unexplored terrain before him, Marcus listened to his intuition's gentle coaxing and wrapped up his work. With a hopeful heart, he submitted his research paper to a peer-reviewed scientific journal. Much to his surprise and delight, the journal deemed his work of merit and accepted it for publication.

His research findings found a place among an emerging corpus of scientific work that was breaking down the barriers between the once-separate realms of science and spirituality. Yet, his contribution held its own unique significance. Marcus was the pioneer who had ventured into uncharted territory, exploring the transition from 3D consciousness to 5D consciousness. The innovative use of an aura camera added another dimension to his groundbreaking study.

Intertwining his extensive scientific knowledge with the experiential wisdom he had gathered along his journey, Marcus's research paper emerged as a holistic tapestry of science and spirituality. His personal insights played a crucial role in connecting the dots, resulting in a seamless and enlightening exploration of this transformative journey.

CHAPTER 42

IN THE COURTROOM

The legal challenge that Shania and Natalia faced was not to be taken lightly. The dark forces opposing their transformative work were relentless in their pursuit to maintain control over the masses, and they would stop at nothing to discredit and undermine the validity of their practices. But amidst the storm, a glimmer of hope emerged—a lawyer who had been undergoing his own journey from 3D to 5D consciousness, and who believed wholeheartedly in Shania and Natalia's work.

The lawyer, named Daniel, had come across their story through a synchronistic twist of fate. Intrigued by their mission, he had been following their progress with keen interest. Having experienced his own personal awakening, Daniel felt a deep resonance with their teachings and the potential for transformation they offered. When he learned of the legal challenges they were facing, he felt compelled to step forward and offer his support.

With Daniel by their side, Shania and Natalia began the arduous process of preparing their defense. The first step was to gather and organize the evidence that would substantiate the effectiveness of their transformative practices. They meticulously compiled case studies, testimonials, and documented the before-and-after experiences of those who had undergone the 5D transition.

The discovery process was both enlightening and disheartening. As they delved deeper into the opposition's evidence, they discovered a web of lies, misinformation, and false witnesses. It became evident that the powers that be were determined to discredit their work and maintain their grip on power and control.

Interrogatories and depositions became battlegrounds of conflicting narratives. Shania and Natalia's legal team worked tirelessly to expose the truth and dismantle the false claims made against them. They sought to uncover the hidden agendas behind the opposition's efforts and reveal the vested interests that sought to suppress the awakening of humanity.

Through it all, Shania and Natalia remained resilient. Their faith in their work and their unwavering commitment to the greater good fueled their determination. They drew strength from the spiritual community that stood firmly in their corner, sending waves of love, light, and intercessory prayers to support their cause.

Amidst the chaos, Shania's mind wandered to Marcus. She wondered about his research and if he had discovered any scientific evidence that could support their case. With a flicker of hope, she decided to reach out to him, recognizing the potential value of his research in validating their transformative practices.

As the legal battle waged on, Shania and Natalia tirelessly prepared for the courtroom showdown. They reviewed their evidence, refined their arguments, and sought solace and guidance through meditation and prayer. They tapped into their heightened intuition, trusting the divine wisdom that flowed through them, guiding their every step.

Despite the uncertainty that loomed over them, they remained undeterred. Their journey had never been about personal gain or fame—it was about awakening the masses and empowering individuals to embrace their full potential. The courtroom battle was just another opportunity to spread their message of transformation and illuminate the path to 5D consciousness.

As the chapter came to a close, Shania sent her message to Marcus, filled with anticipation and curiosity. She hoped that he had made progress in his own research and that his findings could shed light on the scientific underpinnings of their work. Perhaps his insights would provide the missing piece of the puzzle, solidifying their case and bridging the gap between science and spirituality.

CHAPTER 43

TRIAL BY FIRE

As the trial drew near, Shania and Natalia faced a torrent of personal threats and public defamation that tested their resilience. The forces opposing their transformative work had escalated their efforts, seeking to dismantle their credibility and cast doubt on their mission. The darkness they encountered challenged their resolve, bringing moments of anxiety and concern.

In the face of these daunting challenges, Shania and Natalia found strength in each other. Their deep bond served as an anchor in the storm, providing unwavering support and reminding them of their shared purpose. When one faltered, the other offered words of encouragement and upliftment, reminding them to stay focused and centered.

Their personal journey towards transformation had not reached its conclusion. They were still learning life's lessons, and this trial by fire was one of the greatest challenges they had ever faced. But amidst the shadows, they discovered that their support system extended far beyond themselves.

Their spiritual community rallied together, uniting in a powerful display of solidarity. Friends, family, and even strangers who had been touched by their work, sent them love, positive energy, and prayers. Meditation groups sprouted in various corners of the world, dedicating their collective practice to the success of Shania and Natalia's trial.

These groups came together with a shared intention: to raise their own vibrations and send waves of love and support to Shania and Natalia. Through focused meditation, they visualized the courtroom filled with light, love, and positive energy. They sent these vibrations across time and space, knowing that energy knows no bounds.

As Shania and Natalia prepared for the trial, they felt the love and support pouring in from every corner of the globe. The positive energy uplifted their spirits, reinforcing their belief in the power of collective consciousness. They knew that they were not alone in this battle; they had an army of lightworkers standing by their side.

In moments of doubt or anxiety, Shania and Natalia turned inward, seeking solace and guidance from their spiritual connection. They immersed themselves in meditation, allowing the stillness to calm their racing minds and anchor them in the present moment. Through this practice, they tapped into the wellspring of strength within themselves, accessing the wisdom that resided in the depths of their souls.

Divine whispers continued to guide them through the turbulent times. Serena's presence was palpable, offering gentle reassurance and reminding Shania of the profound purpose behind their work. With every breath, they surrendered to the flow of divine guidance, trusting that they were being led on the path of their highest good.

As the trial approached, Shania and Natalia found themselves embracing a renewed sense of empowerment. The outpouring of love and support had become a lifeline, fueling their determination and infusing their beings with the unwavering belief that they were on the side of truth and justice.

The courtroom would become the battleground, where the light of truth would shine, dispelling the shadows of deceit and manipulation. Shania and Natalia were ready to present their case with clarity, conviction, and unwavering faith. They knew that they were not fighting alone, but rather as conduits of a greater force— a force that sought to bring about transformation and awakening on a global scale.

As the chapter drew to a close, the trial loomed on the horizon, and Shania and Natalia stood tall, embodying the resilience and determination that had carried them thus far. Their journey had led them to this pivotal moment—a moment where they would reclaim their power and demonstrate the strength of their convictions. Their spirits were ablaze with the fire of justice, and they were prepared to face whatever lay ahead.

CHAPTER 44

UNEXPECTED ALLY

In the midst of the ongoing trial, Marcus, having published his research and buoyed by his newfound understanding of the 5D consciousness transition, felt compelled to support Shania and Natalia. Resonating deeply with their work and fully grasping the transformative potential it held, Marcus was keenly aware of the trial's grave consequences. Thus, he readily made his way to the court, ready to offer moral support and willing to bear witness to their authenticity.

Amidst the electrifying atmosphere of the courtroom, the final chapter of the trial commenced. Positioned directly behind Shania and Natalia, Marcus held his breath as each moment unfolded with growing intensity. Shania and Natalia, backed by their impassioned legal team, confronted the relentless assault of deceptions from the opposition. Their commitment and determination were palpable, inspiring Marcus as he witnessed the battle for their credibility play out before his eyes.

The opposition painted a narrative laced with deceit and shadowed intentions, suggesting Natalia had crafted her unique AI with ulterior motives. They brazenly proclaimed that Natalia's algorithm was not an unbiased tool of science, but rather a cunningly constructed instrument, fine-tuned to corroborate her own theories regarding the transition to 5D. In their portrayal, Natalia's AI was not an objective analyzer, but a puppet echoing her views, a technological ventriloquist bent on broadcasting her theories without offering a fair examination.

Under the banner of "Unregulated Tech", the opposition wove a narrative suggesting that the AI and VR tools Natalia employed were unproven and potentially dangerous. They insinuated that her cutting-edge technology bordered on pseudoscience, asserting that there was a conspicuous lack of scientific evidence to substantiate the devices' effectiveness in the transition from 3D to 5D consciousness. In their accusations, they painted Natalia not as a pioneer but as a risk-taker, carelessly wielding powerful technologies in an irresponsible manner.

The opposition took this narrative a step further with the "Lack of Standardization" claim. They focused on the absence of set guidelines or standards within the field of psychological or spiritual practices that could regulate Natalia's particular AI and VR designs. They suggested that she was operating in a nebulous gray area outside of any recognized oversight, thus potentially endangering the mental and spiritual wellbeing of her program's participants.

With a cunning twist, they highlighted Natalia's credentials, stating that as a holder of a doctorate in psychology, she was knowingly venturing beyond the parameters established by the American Psychological Association (APA). They subtly suggested that Natalia's actions were not only professionally questionable, but that she had deliberately chosen to operate outside recognized boundaries, further enhancing the shadow they sought to cast over her pioneering work.

Drawing on the "Insufficient Scientific Backing" claim, the opposition intensified their campaign against Natalia. They underscored the supposed lack of rigorous, peer-reviewed studies to substantiate Natalia's AI and VR applications for 3D to 5D consciousness transitions. They framed her methods as speculative and under-researched, implying a reckless disregard for the scientific method. With cunning precision, they depicted Natalia as a maverick operating on the fringes of science, painting her groundbreaking work as reckless experimentation rather than pioneering innovation.

Witness after witness took the stand, their testimony carefully crafted to cast doubt on the legitimacy of the transformation from 3D to 5D consciousness. Marcus watched in awe as the opposing side presented a seemingly ironclad case, weaving a web of deceit and misinformation. It was a masterclass in manipulation, leaving the jury and spectators captivated.

One witness, a former participant of the program, testified that he was promised immediate and profound changes in his life. He claimed that when these changes didn't materialize, Shania and Natalia brushed off his concerns and insisted that he wasn't trying hard enough. However, the truth was that the program clearly outlined that personal growth and transformation are individual journeys that require consistent effort and self-reflection. He had only attended a few sessions and showed little dedication to the process, expecting a quick fix rather than a deep, meaningful change.

Another witness, a disgruntled parent, told a story of her young adult daughter, who supposedly fell into a deep depression as she was going through the program. She claimed her daughter became isolated, losing interest in social activities and her usual hobbies. This mother said that she went through a lot of stress herself as she was trying to support her daughter emotionally. Well, the actual truth was that her daughter was going through an introspective period, often common during profound shifts in consciousness, allowing her to reassess her life priorities. This process was mistaken for depression, fueling the parent's concern and misconstrued perception of the program.

Yet another witness, a local psychologist, expressed his professional opinion, stating that Shania and Natalia were exploiting vulnerable individuals with pseudo-scientific claims. He described their program as a hotbed for generating psychological dependence. In reality, this psychologist had a long-standing rivalry with Natalia and had not taken the time to fully understand the program, instead choosing to cast defamation based on his own biases.

Each narrative was intricately crafted and spun into a seemingly solid testimony. Yet, beneath the surface of each tale was a labyrinth of misunderstanding, personal grievances, and unfounded fears, warping the actual truth of Shania and Natalia's program.

As each witness delivered their carefully rehearsed statements, Marcus felt a mix of frustration and anger. Lies and half-truths danced through the air, threatening to overshadow the profound impact Shania and Natalia had made on countless lives. The courtroom became a battlefield of words, where the truth struggled to emerge from the shadows.

Throughout the proceedings, Marcus observed the meticulous cross-examinations and the relentless attempts to dismantle the foundation of Shania and Natalia's work. The opposing side cunningly exploited any inconsistencies, using them as weapons to undermine the authenticity of their claims. The air was thick with tension, uncertainty looming over the courtroom like a dark cloud.

Witnesses were grilled under intense scrutiny, and their testimonies were dissected and analyzed. The opposing counsel, with calculated precision, aimed to shake the very core of Shania and Natalia's mission. The courtroom had become a theater of manipulation, where the lines between truth and deception blurred.

In response, Shania and Natalia's legal team fought back, countering with unwavering determination. Their lawyer, a fierce advocate for their cause, skillfully exposed the fallacies in the opposing arguments. He artfully presented evidence, scientific studies, and testimonials from individuals whose lives had been transformed by Shania and Natalia's guidance.

One pivotal moment occurred when the lawyer dissected the testimony of the participant who had claimed he was promised immediate changes. He pointed out that the program material provided to each participant clearly stated that transformation was a gradual process that required active involvement and commitment. The lawyer even produced the exact workbook given to participants that emphasized the journey over the destination. The participant's impatience and misunderstanding were laid bare for the court to see.

Then, when the distressed parent took the stand, Shania and Natalia's lawyer showcased her daughter's written testimonials before and after the program. Her words echoed the positive growth she experienced, highlighting her newfound sense of peace and personal understanding, a stark contrast to her mother's claims of depression and isolation. The court heard the daughter's voice directly, triumphant evidence against the misconstrued narratives.

The lawyer did not stop there. He confronted the professional criticism from the opposing psychologist with a slew of peer-reviewed studies supporting the integrative approach Shania and Natalia were taking. He outlined how their methods were rooted in a blend of conventional psychology and spiritual practices. This not only debunked the accusations of pseudoscience but also elevated the credibility of Shania and Natalia's program.

Through these strategic maneuvers, the lawyer cast a new light on the evidence, allowing the court to witness the transformational power of Shania and Natalia's work despite the opposing side's misleading narratives.

CHAPTER 45

MARCUS TESTIFIES

Taking a moment to peruse through his meticulously organized case files, Shania and Natalia's attorney readied himself before the next important move. With a strategic glance exchanged between him and his clients, he beckoned Marcus to the witness stand.

In an atmosphere charged with anticipation, Marcus promptly began to weave his compelling testimony with remarkable brilliance. He elucidated his published research in a reputable peer-reviewed scientific journal, detailing the transition from 3D to 5D consciousness facilitated through the utilization of aura photography. His findings offered tangible, scientific evidence that directly supported the principles and practices used by Shania and Natalia in their transformative work.

Marcus carefully explained the methodology and process of his research, ensuring that the jury could understand its significance. He shared the key insights that he had gained from his participants, underscoring their individual growth and transformation. His testimony was delivered with such clarity and conviction that it offered a stark contrast to the preceding misinformation.

The presentation of his well-respected and peer-reviewed research lent undeniable credibility to Shania and Natalia's program. It created a strong counter-narrative to the unfounded accusations previously presented. His testimony was a beacon of veracity in a trial beset by dubious claims, painting a compelling picture of Shania and Natalia's work as grounded in genuine, transformative processes.

Both the lawyer and Shania and Natalia were immensely satisfied with Marcus's testimony. It added substantial weight to their defense, showcasing the scientific underpinnings of their work and the authentic transformation they facilitated. It was a turning point in the trial, shifting the tide in their favor.

As the trial progressed, Marcus felt the weight of the courtroom drama bearing down upon him. The magnitude of the stakes became clear—the outcome of this trial would not only determine the future of Shania and Natalia's work but also shape the broader landscape of consciousness and spirituality.

With each passing day, Marcus's admiration for Shania and Natalia grew. They exhibited unwavering strength and resilience, remaining calm in the face of relentless attacks. They leaned on each other for support, offering words of encouragement and finding solace in the unshakeable belief they shared.

As the trial approached its climax, the tension reached its peak. Marcus watched as the final witnesses were called, the opposing side desperately attempting to deliver a fatal blow to Shania and Natalia's credibility. The courtroom was a battlefield of words, where truth fought against manipulation, and justice hung in the balance.

In a climactic twist, the opposition summoned a former participant of Shania and Natalia's program. This individual, amidst the stifling courtroom silence, spun a tale of alleged mental manipulation.

The former participant narrated how the program's teachings seemed orchestrated to challenge and disassemble long-held beliefs, which she claimed was an insidious strategy to weaken participants' mental resilience. She suggested that this allowed Shania and Natalia to substitute these dissolved beliefs with their teachings on 5D consciousness.

The accuser also highlighted instances where she felt coerced to abandon personal relationships, ostensibly to liberate herself from past constraints and fully immerse in the program's teachings. She expressed a growing feeling of lost individuality, her personality reshaped to fit the mold dictated by the program.

In a masterful theatrical display, the individual likened Shania and Natalia's program to a cult exercising mind control, casting a cloud of suspicion over the program's methods and purpose.

Behind the seemingly distressing testimony of the former participant, there was a story that deviated sharply from the accusations hurled in court. The truth was far removed from the sinister cult narrative that had been woven.

In reality, this participant had approached Shania and Natalia's program burdened with deeply rooted beliefs and fears. The program's focus on introspection and self-growth did indeed challenge these beliefs, but not with the intention of manipulation. Rather, it was to encourage the individual to examine their conditioned thought patterns, liberate herself from the mental shackles that held her back, and embark on a journey towards her own spiritual awakening.

The allegations about being coerced to sever personal ties were a skewed representation of the program's teachings about toxicity and the importance of maintaining healthy relationships. The teachings encouraged participants to let go of harmful relationships, not to isolate them, but to help them foster a supportive and positive environment conducive to personal growth.

The person had chosen to misinterpret these aspects of the program as mind control, primarily due to her struggle with the transformative changes it required. Overwhelmed, she distanced herself from the program, ultimately deciding to paint her experience as a victim of a cultish program in a misguided attempt to justify her reluctance to confront her own inner barriers.

Moving Forward

The day arrived when the courtroom would adjourn, leaving the fate of Shania and Natalia's work in the hands of the jury. The judge's voice echoed through the room, announcing the adjournment and instructing the jury to reconvene on a later date to deliver their verdict.

As the courtroom emptied, Marcus felt a mix of emotions washing over him. Hope and anxiety intertwined, leaving him on edge. The trial had presented a labyrinth of challenges, unexpected twists, and relentless attacks. The suspenseful nature of the proceedings had held the audience captive, their hearts yearning for justice.

Shania, Natalia, and Marcus gathered their belongings, their minds reeling from the intensity of the courtroom battle. Yet, despite the uncertainty that loomed overhead, a glimmer of hope remained. The support of their allies, the unwavering faith within their hearts, and the unexpected ally that Marcus had become—all provided a beacon of light amidst the darkness.

As they exited the courtroom, Marcus turned to Shania. "We will see this through," he said, his voice filled with determination. "No matter the outcome, we have made a difference. We have touched lives, and that in itself is a victory."

Shania nodded, a mixture of weariness and resolve etched on her face. "You're right," she said, a flicker of a smile crossing her lips. "No matter what happens, we have already succeeded in opening minds and hearts, and with your scientific research, we have the missing piece of the puzzle."

The trio walked out of the courthouse, their steps heavy with anticipation and the weight of their collective journey. The trial had tested their resolve, pushing them to the limits of their strength. But as they faced the uncertainty that lay ahead, their spirits remained unbroken, ready to face whatever challenges awaited them.

As the doors of the courthouse closed behind them, a glimmer of hope lingered in the air. The trial may have adjourned for the day, but the battle for truth and transformation had only just begun. With each passing moment, the anticipation grew—the jury's decision would shape the destiny of Shania, Natalia, and the countless lives touched by their work.

To be continued...

CHAPTER 46

NAVIGATING THE STORM

The echoes of the court proceedings reverberated through the fabric of society, sparking a whirlwind of societal turmoil. The televised trial had become a spectacle, drawing attention from around the world. As the news spread, skeptics and believers clashed in a battle of ideologies, each side fiercely defending their stance.

The court proceedings had thrust Shania and Natalia into the public eye, making them the subject of intense scrutiny. Their work, once confined to the realm of personal transformation, now faced the harsh glare of the spotlight. Supporters hailed them as catalysts for change, while critics dismissed their teachings as mere illusions.

The televised trial had become a dividing line, separating those who were open to the possibility of a higher consciousness from those who clung to the comfort of their 3D existence. Even social media became a battleground, with skeptics and believers engaging in heated debates and online confrontations.

For Natalia, the weight of the public's judgment was both a burden and an opportunity. She understood that the skeptics' criticism stemmed from their own fears and limitations. The journey from 3D to 5D consciousness was an unfamiliar path, challenging the very foundations of their beliefs. But Natalia also recognized that the societal turmoil was an indication of the magnitude of their work. The very fact that it had stirred such controversy meant that they were onto something significant.

As the news of the trial spread internationally, support and criticism came from all corners of the globe. People shared their stories of personal transformation, inspired by the teachings of Shania and Natalia. They celebrated the profound shifts they had experienced, testifying to the authenticity of their journey. But there were also those who remained skeptical, dismissing the concept of 5D consciousness as a mere illusion.

Natalia witnessed the polarization with a mix of concern and determination. She knew that their work was not about convincing the skeptics or winning debates. It was about offering a different perspective, a possibility for those who were ready to embrace it. She held onto the belief that their teachings had the power to awaken minds and hearts, even in the face of opposition.

In the midst of the societal turmoil, Natalia and her companions found solace in their support network. Friends, family, and followers continued to rally around them, providing a shield of love and understanding. Meditation groups continued to emerge, uniting in their collective intention to send positive energy and support to Shania and Natalia.

As the storm of criticism and doubt raged on, Natalia turned inward, seeking guidance from The Creator. She found comfort in the whispers of divine wisdom, assuring her that the path they were on was purposeful and necessary. She drew strength from the unseen realms, knowing that their mission went far beyond the confines of the courtroom.

Natalia also discovered unexpected allies within the scientific community. Researchers and scholars, intrigued by the convergence of science and spirituality, began to examine the evidence presented by Shania, Natalia, and Marcus. They recognized the gaps in their own understanding and embarked on their own journeys of exploration. The scientific community became a platform for open dialogue, bridging the gap between the known and the unknown.

Despite the challenges they faced, Natalia's determination remained unyielding. She knew that navigating the storm required staying grounded in their purpose and remaining true to themselves. They would continue to share their teachings, even in the face of criticism and skepticism. The storm may have tested their resolve, but it also revealed the depth of their commitment.

But in the midst of uncertainty, Natalia held onto hope. She looked at Shania and Marcus, their eyes reflecting the strength and resilience that had carried them thus far. They had faced adversity together and would face whatever lay ahead with unwavering faith.

CHAPTER 47

THE TURNING POINT

The air in the courtroom crackled with anticipation as Shania and Natalia stood together, waiting for the final ruling on their case. The tension was palpable, their hearts pounding with hope and trepidation. The fate of their work and their mission hung in the balance.

"All rise," the bailiff called out, signaling the judge's entrance. The courtroom fell into silence as the judge made his way to the bench, his gaze stern and focused. The time had come for the verdict to be delivered, the moment that would determine their future.

But just as the judge was about to begin, the courtroom doors swung open with a burst of energy. The attorney's assistant hurriedly made his way towards Shania and Natalia's table, holding a manila envelope in his hand. Their attorney's eyes widened with surprise and urgency as he took hold of the envelope and swiftly opened it.

Sensing the gravity of the situation, the attorney requested permission to approach the bench. The judge nodded, granting him the opportunity. With determined steps, the attorney approached the bench, holding the contents of the envelope for the judge to review. The courtroom held its breath, awaiting the outcome of this unexpected turn of events.

The judge's eyes scanned the documents, his expression shifting from neutrality to intrigue. He wasted no time and immediately called for a meeting in his chambers with both the defense and prosecuting attorneys. The courtroom buzzed with speculation and curiosity as the judge and the attorneys disappeared behind the doors, leaving everyone in suspense.

Shania and Natalia exchanged glances, their hearts pounding with a mixture of hope and uncertainty. What had just transpired could change the entire course of the trial. The evidence held within the mysterious envelope held the potential to reveal the truth and vindicate their work.

As the courtroom waited, whispers filled the space. Speculations swirled, rumors danced through the minds of onlookers, and the tension continued to mount. Shania felt a mix of anticipation and nerves, the weight of the trial's outcome resting heavily on her shoulders. She knew that the evidence contained within the envelope had the power to shatter the lies and expose the truth.

In the judge's chambers, a heated discussion ensued. The defense attorney presented the evidence, meticulously outlining its relevance to the case. The prosecuting attorney, caught off guard by this unexpected development, found himself grappling with the weight of the revelations. The truth was a formidable adversary, and the walls of deception began to crumble.

The evidence presented was no ordinary piece of information. It unveiled the dark underbelly of the prosecuting attorney's law firm, revealing their involvement in unscrupulous activities orchestrated by the Elite, the hidden forces that sought to maintain their power and control. The private investigator hired by the defense had uncovered a web of corruption, manipulation, and even attempts to eliminate key witnesses.

The mysterious person at the center of this revelation turned out to be the CEO's wife, who had been living in the shadows, concealing herself in Australia for her own safety. She had known the truth, aware of her husband's corrupt activities and his controlling and abusive behavior. In her search for purpose and escape from her unhappy marriage, she embarked on her own journey from 3D to 5D consciousness.

Attending Shania and Natalia's workshop years ago, she had become enlightened about the possibility of a higher consciousness and the transformation it could bring. As she witnessed the unfolding of the trial, she made the courageous decision to gather evidence, documenting the incriminating documents and photographs that would expose her husband's wrongdoings.

After considerable deliberation and careful examination of all the evidence presented in the trial, the presiding judge passed down the ruling. He announced that the jury's verdict was in favor of the defendants, Shania and Natalia, indicating they were free from all allegations.

However, his gavel fell with certain stipulations concerning their program. He expressed particular concern regarding the use of AI and VR technology in their spiritual practice, identifying the following key areas: 'The Unregulated Tech', 'Insufficient Scientific Backing', and 'Lack of Standardization'.

Addressing the courtroom, he stipulated, "Although Shania and Natalia have been operating with good intentions, the AI and

VR technology used in their practice remains unregulated and lacks standardized usage protocols, specifically within the field of psychology and spiritual practice. As such, their application poses potential risks that we cannot overlook."

He further elaborated, "The lack of sufficient scientific backing in the field of transitioning consciousness from 3D to 5D through AI and VR technology adds to the complexity of the matter. While some studies point towards possible positive outcomes, the overall body of research is still insufficient to conclusively substantiate its widespread application."

Concluding his ruling, the judge declared, "Therefore, until such time that comprehensive regulations and guidelines are established and there is sufficient scientific evidence supporting the use of such technologies in the spiritual and psychological realms, Shania and Natalia are prohibited from using AI and VR devices within their program." The finality of his gavel echoed in the silent courtroom, underscoring the gravity of his decision.

As the judge's gavel struck the sound block, the courtroom rippled with a wave of surprised gasps and whispers, the implications of the ruling spreading like a shockwave throughout the room. In the eye of this storm sat Natalia, Shania, and Marcus.

A surge of hope and relief coursed through their veins, their hearts beating in unison with the palpable rhythm of change in the air.

The court's decision was not exactly what they had hoped for, but it brought with it a spark of optimism. The ruling meant that their journey would continue, albeit in a different way. The trio, in their intertwined destinies, took a moment to share a quiet understanding, acknowledging the path that lay ahead.

Yes, they would have to adapt and revert to the earlier ways of aiding those in transition from 3D to 5D consciousness. But this was a process they knew well, a rhythm they had danced to before the advent of AI and VR technology. People seeking this shift would have to stay committed to their transformative process, ready to delve deep within themselves and patiently embrace the time it would take to make the transition. As part of their process, in order to maintain a resonance at 5D consciousness, people would have to rewire their brains.

Shania and Natalia, ever the pillars of faith and resilience, knew in their hearts that everything was unfolding as it should. They deeply believed that everything was in Divine Order, a guiding principle that had steered them through the tumultuous waters of the trial and would continue to light their way on this challenging yet rewarding path.

As they left the courtroom, a sense of victory washed over them. The storm they had weathered had tested their resilience and unwavering belief in their mission. They had overcome seemingly insurmountable obstacles and emerged stronger than ever. The truth had prevailed, and now they could continue their transformative work with renewed purpose and determination.

Outside the courthouse, their support system gathered; their presence a testament to the power of unity and belief. Meditation groups from around the world had sent energy and prayers, their collective intentions fueling the fight for truth and justice. Shania, Natalia, and Marcus were embraced by a wave of love and support, reminding them that they were not alone in this journey.

With each step they took, they were reminded of the significance of their work. The path they had chosen was not easy, but it was necessary. They were agents of change, catalysts for a collective awakening to 5D consciousness. As they moved forward, they carried within them the strength and determination to navigate the storms that lay ahead.

CHAPTER 48

RIDING THE WAVE

The courtroom ruling had ignited a fire that spread like wildfire, catapulting Natalia, Shania, and Marcus into the heart of a global movement. The resonance of their message reached far and wide, captivating the masses and igniting a sense of hope and inspiration in their hearts. They were no longer just individuals on a mission; they were catalysts for transformation, riding the wave of a profound shift in consciousness.

As news of Shania and Natalia's triumph echoed across the globe, their following grew exponentially. Social media platforms buzzed with excitement as people shared their stories of personal transformation and the impact their work had on their lives. The outpouring of gratitude and support fueled their passion, reminding Shania and Natalia of the magnitude of the journey they had embarked upon.

Communities flourished around their teachings, including the process of rewiring the brain. They were both online and offline, creating a vibrant tapestry of like-minded individuals hungry for spiritual growth and a deeper connection to their true selves. Workshops, retreats, and gatherings sprung up in cities around the world, serving as portals for seekers to explore the depths of their own consciousness. The energy within these spaces was electric, pulsating with the anticipation of profound change.

Natalia, Shania, and Marcus were now revered figures in the movement, sought after by scientists, artists, healers, and visionaries who recognized the power of bridging science and spirituality. The converging forces of their expertise offered a new lens through which the world could understand the profound mysteries of existence. Together, they became the driving force behind a paradigm shift that would redefine humanity's relationship with the universe.

But amidst the rising tide of support and adoration, there were still pockets of resistance. Skeptics and critics emerged from the shadows, seeking to undermine Shania and Natalia's work and discredit the truth that they unveiled. They accused them of peddling illusions and exploiting vulnerable souls in pursuit of personal gain. Their words stung, but Natalia and Shania stood firm in the knowledge of their authenticity and the genuine transformations they had witnessed.

Despite the challenges and opposition, they were not deterred. Their resilience grew stronger with each passing day, fueled by the unwavering belief in the power of 5D consciousness. Shania and Natalia had witnessed the magic it wrought, the profound healing it brought, and the unity it fostered among diverse individuals. Their journey was not just about personal growth; it was a collective endeavor to uplift humanity.

Throughout the entire ordeal, Shania's bond with Serena, as well as the spiritual kinship both she and Natalia shared with The Creator, remained an unshakable pillar of strength. The whispers from the spirit realm, suffused with wisdom and inspiration, persisted in guiding them, reiterating the profound interconnectedness of all life. Amid fleeting moments of concern, The Creator's reassuring presence served as a beacon of clarity, affirming their path was right and true, despite the apparent uncertainty and challenge that lay ahead.

As the movement gained momentum, Shania and Natalia dedicated themselves to providing guidance and resources to those who sought a deeper understanding. Shania honed her aura photography technique, capturing the essence of energy and consciousness in vivid, captivating images. Each photograph was a testament to the invisible realms of existence and a reminder that there was more to this world than what met the eye.

Natalia delved deeper into her spiritual teachings, developing immersive experiences that allowed participants to tap into the limitless power of their own divine essence. She skillfully guided them through the realms of 3D to 5D consciousness, helping them shed limiting beliefs, rewire their brain, and embrace their true potential. The workshops and retreats became transformational journeys, where many individuals discovered their innate wisdom and the interconnectedness of all beings.

Their movement resonated with people from all corners of the globe, transcending cultural boundaries and bridging divides. Meditation groups formed in remote villages and bustling cities alike, united in their intention to uplift humanity. Through collective intention and focused energy, they sent waves of positive vibrations and unwavering support to them, acting as an energetic shield against the onslaught of resistance.

Amidst the challenges, Shania and Natalia celebrated every milestone and every life touched by their work. They were no longer just a duo of pioneers; they were truly beacons of hope, lighting the way for others to step into their own power and embrace the fullness of their being. The swell of support grew stronger with each passing day, carrying them forward with a renewed sense of purpose and determination.

As the waves of change crashed around them, they held steadfast to their vision. Shania and Natalia knew that their journey had only just begun, and there were still countless souls waiting to awaken to the possibilities of 5D consciousness. With hearts ablaze and a shared conviction, they rode the wave of transformation, guided by the knowledge that they were co-creators of a new world, a world where love, harmony, and expanded consciousness prevailed.

Together, Shania and Natalia would continue to ride the wave, empowering others to embrace their inner light and ushering in a new era of profound connection and limitless potential. The movement had just begun, and its momentum showed no signs of slowing. The world was awakening, and they were at the forefront, ready to shape the course of history with the power of love and consciousness.

CHAPTER 49

TRANSFORMATIONS

Marcus found himself immersed in a world of profound transformation. As he witnessed the power of 5D consciousness unfolding before his eyes, he couldn't help but be captivated by the beauty and potential of the human spirit.

With his scientific mind and open heart, Marcus delved deep into documenting the experiences of individuals transitioning to 5D consciousness. Armed with his camera and journal, he embarked on a journey of exploration, capturing the essence of their remarkable metamorphosis.

Each story unfolded like a tapestry, weaving together the threads of personal growth, inner healing, and expanded awareness. Marcus witnessed individuals rewire their brains, shedding layers of fear and limitation, embracing their true essence, and stepping into a reality where love, compassion, and interconnectedness reigned supreme.

The individuals he documented were diverse in their backgrounds and experiences, yet they all shared a common thread - a deep yearning for a more meaningful existence. Through their encounters with Shania, Natalia, 5D facilitators, and the teachings of 5D consciousness, they discovered the keys to unlock their full potential.

Marcus meticulously recorded their journeys, capturing the radiance and the newfound joy that emanated from within. He marveled at the profound shifts he witnessed, as individuals transcended the limitations of their past and embraced the limitless possibilities of the present moment.

Each description he penned was infused with a sense of awe and wonder. He vividly painted portraits of individuals breaking free from the chains of self-doubt and stepping into their authentic power. Their stories became testaments to the human capacity for growth, resilience, and spiritual evolution.

In his conversations with those who had transitioned to 5D consciousness, Marcus was humbled by their wisdom and depth of understanding. They spoke of a profound shift in perception, where the world appeared vibrant and alive, infused with a sense of interconnectedness that transcended previous boundaries.

He listened as they shared their experiences of heightened intuition, synchronicities, and profound connections with others. They spoke of a deep sense of purpose and alignment with their true calling, guided by the wisdom of their higher selves. It was as if a veil had been lifted, revealing the truth and beauty that had always been present but previously unnoticed.

As Marcus continued his documentation, he noticed a common theme among those who had transitioned to 5D consciousness - a deep sense of inner peace and joy. They radiated a magnetic presence, drawing others towards them with their genuine love and compassion.

These stories of transformation served as a beacon of hope for humanity, inspiring others to embark on their own journey of self-discovery and spiritual awakening. Marcus realized the immense power of his work, not just in documenting the process but in illuminating a path for others to follow.

The more he immersed himself in the stories of transformation, the more Marcus himself experienced a profound shift in consciousness. He shed the remnants of skepticism and fully embraced the reality of 5D consciousness. The knowledge he had gained through his scientific pursuits now merged seamlessly with his expanding spiritual awareness. Marcus discovered that certain truths cannot be imparted through teaching, but rather must emerge from inner knowing.

In the depths of his soul, Marcus understood that this was not just a personal journey; it was a collective awakening. He had become an advocate for the convergence of science and spirituality, shining a light on the extraordinary potential that lay dormant within each individual.

As he concluded each interview and took his final snapshots, Marcus couldn't help but be overwhelmed by a sense of gratitude. He had been privileged to witness the beauty of the human spirit in its most radiant form, and he knew that his work would serve as a catalyst for further transformation.

With renewed purpose and a heart full of inspiration, Marcus committed himself to sharing these stories with the world. He envisioned a future where the barriers between science and spirituality dissolved, and a unified understanding of consciousness emerged.

He knew that his documentation would be a testament to the power of belief, the strength of the human spirit, and the profound impact of embracing higher states of consciousness. The stories he had gathered were not just personal anecdotes; they were a testament to the inherent capacity for growth and transformation that resides within each and every one of us.

As Marcus closed his journal and set down his camera, he felt a deep sense of fulfillment. He had played a small part in a much larger tapestry of human evolution, and he knew that the journey had only just begun.

With a renewed sense of purpose, Marcus joined hands with Shania, Natalia, and the growing community of individuals who had embraced 5D consciousness. Together, they would continue to illuminate the path, inspire others to awaken, and create a world where love, harmony, and interconnectedness reigned supreme.

The journey towards a higher consciousness was far from over, but Marcus was now an integral part of the transformational wave, riding it with unwavering conviction and an unyielding belief in the limitless potential of the human spirit.

CHAPTER 50

PERSONAL BATTLES

Shania found herself amid a whirlwind. As the public spotlight intensified and skepticism lingered, she faced exhaustion. The weight of responsibility, the scrutiny of skeptics, and the ongoing challenges were very demanding.

Amid the tumultuous changes in her life and her relentless commitment to assisting others, Shania found that she had inadvertently neglected her own self-care. Her empathic nature had, in essence, absorbed an array of energetic imprints from her surroundings, creating an unforeseen burden. Recognizing this, she understood it was imperative she immersed herself in Serena's Sacred teachings. This vital act would not only offer her respite, but also equip her with the spiritual tools necessary to maintain balance and not become overwhelmed amidst the dynamic energy currents swirling around her.

In her moments of vulnerability, Shania deliberately pivoted inward, finding comfort and solace in the serene sanctuary of her own soul. She dove deep into the sacred practices taught to her by

Serena. This included an energetic cleansing ritual that transmuted negative energy into positive, fostering equilibrium within her.

She devoted herself to meditative practices, creating a conduit for divine wisdom to flow through her, imbuing her being with a tranquility that transcended the physical realm. Supplementing her spiritual endeavors, she embraced the purifying ritual of taking sacred baths infused with frankincense and myrrh, oils known for their purifying and protective qualities.

Simultaneously, Shania nourished her physical vessel with clean, live foods and refreshing drinks, reinforcing her inner vitality. Amid the silence of her inner refuge, she discovered the resilience and courage required to continue her mission.

With each passing moment, she cleansed, re-energized, and fortified her empathic soul, preparing herself to face the world with renewed strength and compassion.

As Shania navigated her personal battles, an unexpected turn of events unfolded. Skeptics who had once criticized her work began experiencing their own personal transformations. They found themselves inexplicably drawn to the teachings of 5D consciousness, seeking solace and healing in the midst of their own challenges.

At first, Shania was surprised by this shift. The very individuals who had questioned the validity of her work were now seeking her guidance and support. She realized that their own skepticism had been born out of fear and resistance to change. But as they faced their own personal battles, their hearts began to open, and they were finally ready to embrace a new way of being.

Shania welcomed them with open arms, understanding the transformative power of compassion and forgiveness. She recognized that personal growth and healing were not limited to those who had already embarked on the journey of 5D consciousness. Everyone had the potential to awaken, and she was there to guide them along the way.

She witnessed skeptics rewire their brains, shedding their doubts, and releasing the limitations that had held them captive for so long. They experienced the profound shifts in perception and the awakening of their true selves. Their stories mirrored those she had documented throughout her career, further validating the process of transformation.

As the skeptics transformed into believers, their personal journeys became testaments to the power of resilience and the capacity for growth. Shania stood in awe, witnessing the profound impact of their personal battles on their own lives and the lives of those around them.

The ripple effect of their transformations began to spread, reaching beyond the boundaries of their individual experiences. Friends, family, and communities witnessed the profound changes in these skeptics and became curious about the path they had embarked upon.

Word of mouth carried the message far and wide, attracting new seekers and believers. Shania and Natalia's workshops, retreats, and teachings gained momentum, drawing more individuals from all walks of life who were eager to embrace the transformative power of 5D consciousness.

Amid societal turmoil and personal battles, Shania continued to find solace in the support of her community. They rallied behind her, sending waves of love, positive energy, and unwavering support. More meditation groups formed in different parts of the world, coming together to collectively uplift Shania and Natalia in their journey.

The energy of love and unity fueled Shania's resolve, reminding her of the profound impact she had made and the lives she had touched. She drew strength from their collective intentions, knowing that they were all co-creators of a new paradigm of consciousness.

With each passing day, Shania witnessed the transformative power of love and compassion in action. She saw individuals shed their old patterns, embrace their authenticity, and embody the essence of 5D consciousness. It was a testament to the resilience of the human spirit and the boundless potential for growth and evolution.

In the midst of personal battles, Shania emerged stronger and more rooted in her purpose than ever before. She understood that the challenges she faced were part of her own journey of growth and healing. As she continued to navigate the storm, she held onto the unwavering belief that the light within her and within each individual would guide them to a place of peace, love, and harmony.

The personal battles she encountered were not obstacles to overcome, but opportunities for deepening her own understanding and compassion. She knew that the path of transformation was not always smooth, but it was through these challenges that true growth and expansion occurred.

As the storm subsided, Shania stood on the precipice of a new chapter. She felt a renewed sense of purpose, ready to guide others through their personal battles and into the realm of 5D consciousness.

With each step forward, she carried the collective energy of her community, the unwavering support of those who had witnessed the power of transformation, and the profound wisdom that came from navigating her own personal storms.

The journey towards 5D consciousness continued, and Shania was determined to continue serving as a beacon of light, illuminating the path for others to follow. She knew that personal battles would arise, but she also knew that within each battle lay the seeds of growth, transformation, and the emergence of a higher state of being.

With gratitude in her heart and a deep sense of purpose, Shania embraced the challenges and triumphs that lay ahead. She was ready to continue riding the wave of transformation, knowing that together with her community, they would create a world where love, unity, and interconnectedness reigned supreme.

CHAPTER 51

A NEW HOPE

Natalia stood on the precipice of a new era, a future where the principles of 5D consciousness were embraced by a new generation. As she looked around, she saw young individuals awakening to their true potential, eager to create a world filled with love, unity, and harmony.

The impact of their work had resonated deeply, and the transformative power of 5D consciousness had spread far and wide. People from all corners of the world sought guidance and support, drawn to the teachings and experiences that Shania and Natalia had shared.

But it wasn't just the individuals seeking personal growth and transformation who were influenced by their work. The academic world began to take notice of Marcus's meticulous documentation of the phenomenon. His research and findings provided a scientific foundation for the spiritual concepts that Shania and Natalia had been sharing.

Marcus's work, showcasing the detailed descriptions of individuals transitioning to 5D consciousness, gained academic attention. His published papers, backed by empirical evidence and supported by the experiences of countless individuals, ignited a spark of curiosity within the scientific community.

As scholars delved into his work, they recognized the need to bridge the gap between science and spirituality. Marcus's research not only shed light on the phenomenon of transitioning consciousness but also opened the doors for further exploration and understanding.

Universities and research institutions around the world sought to collaborate with Marcus, eager to expand the frontiers of consciousness studies. The once-skeptical scientific community found itself on a new trajectory, embracing the possibilities that lay beyond the confines of traditional paradigms.

Natalia observed with a sense of hope and fulfillment as the world around her underwent a profound shift. The younger generation, empowered by the knowledge of 5D consciousness, began to create communities centered around love, compassion, and sustainable living.

It was as if a wave of transformation circled the globe, leaving no space untouched. People from diverse backgrounds and cultures united under a common vision, working together to build a world that honored the interconnectedness of all beings.

Natalia witnessed the birth of countless projects and initiatives, each fueled by the principles of 5D consciousness. Sustainable farming practices, renewable energy solutions, and collaborative efforts for social justice flourished. The spirit of unity and cooperation permeated every aspect of society.

The youth, inspired by the wisdom shared by Shania and Natalia, became the torchbearers of change. They organized gatherings, festivals, and conferences, creating spaces for like-minded individuals to come together, share knowledge, and support one another in their journey towards 5D consciousness.

A group of forward-thinking scientists embarked on a mission to revolutionize the healthcare system. Some of the scientists focused on advanced holographic healing techniques, and others on electromagnetic healing. They aspired to introduce a groundbreaking approach to medical treatment, veering away from traditional pharmaceuticals. These scientists were acutely aware of the potential side effects often associated with pharmaceutical treatments. They understood that these substances could negatively affect the physical body in various ways.

One group of scientists on the path of veering away from pharmaceuticals turned their attention towards an innovative approach involving the use of sound waves. They proposed the idea of creating medicine through the manipulation of these waves. The underlying concept was rooted in the understanding that everything in the universe is composed of energy vibrating at specific frequencies.

With this foundational concept in mind, they proposed that each disease also has its unique frequency. This understanding opened a new path for medical treatment. They aimed to develop technology capable of producing a frequency that counteracts the disease's vibration.

The vision was to create a frequency that represented the 'cure' for the disease. By introducing this counter-frequency into the body, they believed it could effectively neutralize the disease frequency, leading to a potential cure. This innovative approach held the promise of transforming the way we approach disease and healing in healthcare.

Amid all the transformations taking place, Natalia and Shania continued their sacred work, guiding and nurturing those who sought their wisdom. Their teachings resonated deeply with the new generation, providing them with the tools and insights needed to navigate the complexities of a changing world.

The impact of their efforts reached beyond personal transformation. The principles of love, compassion, and interconnectedness began to influence policies and systems on a global scale. As more and more people transitioned to higher states of being, governments and institutions felt the pressure to align their actions with the values of 5D consciousness, creating a more equitable and sustainable world for all.

As Natalia reflected on the journey they had undertaken, she couldn't help but feel a sense of gratitude. They had faced countless challenges and overcame personal battles, but it was all worth it. The world they had envisioned, a world where love and unity reigned, was becoming a reality.

With a renewed sense of purpose, Natalia and Shania continued to inspire and uplift those around them. They knew that their work was far from done, but they also recognized the power of the collective. The countless individuals who had embraced 5D consciousness were creating a ripple effect, spreading love and compassion to every corner of the Earth.

As the sun set on the horizon, Natalia looked towards the future with hope. The journey of transformation would continue, and together with the new generation, they would create a world where love, unity, and harmony prevailed. With each passing day, the vision of a peaceful and awakened society grew closer, fueled by the unwavering belief that a new dawn was on the horizon.

CHAPTER 52

EMBRACING CHANGE

Shania, Natalia, and Marcus found themselves in a whirlwind of profound changes that were sweeping the globe. As they grappled with the magnitude of the transformation taking place, they also came to accept their roles in this global shift.

The trio gathered in a cozy cabin nestled in the mountains, seeking solace and a moment of respite from the demands of their newfound responsibilities. They sat around a crackling fireplace, the warm glow casting flickering shadows on their faces as they contemplated the magnitude of the changes that were unfolding.

"It's hard to believe how far we've come," Shania mused, her voice tinged with a mix of awe and humility. "We were once on separate paths, searching for our own truths, and now, here we are, at the center of a global movement."

Natalia nodded, her eyes reflecting a profound sense of purpose. "The journey has been filled with challenges and uncertainties, but we have always trusted in the path laid before us. We are living embodiments of the transformation we sought."

Marcus, ever the scientist, spoke up. "It's remarkable to witness the tangible impact of transitioning consciousness. The evidence is undeniable, and yet, there is still so much we don't understand. We are witnessing the birth of a new era."

As they delved deeper into their discussion, the weight of their roles became palpable. They were no longer mere observers but catalysts for change, guides for those who sought a higher path. Their work inspired countless individuals to question their beliefs and seek a deeper connection with the world around them.

Despite the exhilaration surrounding their achievements, the scale of their undertaking occasionally filled them with apprehension. Shania voiced her concerns, saying, "We've initiated a phenomenon that is significantly larger than ourselves. With the rapid pace of change, how do we ensure that we are thoroughly prepared to tackle any unforeseen hurdles that may arise?"

Natalia placed a reassuring hand on Shania's shoulder. "We must trust in the wisdom that guides us, just as we have trusted all along. We are not alone in this journey. The Creator has chosen us for a reason, and we will be provided with what we need."

Marcus chimed in, his voice steady and determined. "We have seen the transformative power of transitioning consciousness firsthand. We have witnessed lives being changed and societies being reshaped. We must continue our path, staying in alignment with our purpose. We must embrace change with open hearts."

As they spoke, their words resonated deep within their beings, reaffirming their commitment to their mission. They had come this far by remaining open to the unknown, by embracing the convergence of science and spirituality, and they knew that their journey was far from over.

In the weeks that followed, Shania, Natalia, and Marcus continued to play their respective roles in the global shift. They traveled, spoke at conferences, and shared their experiences with eager audiences hungry for guidance and inspiration. They recognized the importance of their voices in a world thirsting for change.

Their work was met with a mix of admiration and skepticism. Critics questioned the validity of transitioning consciousness, dismissing it as nothing more than a passing trend. But Shania, Natalia, and Marcus remained steadfast in their belief, knowing that the transformations they had witnessed were real and profound.

The trio faced the challenges head-on, addressing the doubts and concerns that arose. They engaged in conversations with skeptics, patiently presenting their evidence and personal experiences. Their unwavering commitment to their path began to chip away at the walls of doubt, slowly opening minds to the possibilities of a higher consciousness.

As they continued to navigate the ever-changing landscape, they also found solace in the growing community of like-minded individuals who embraced the principles of 5D consciousness. Together, they formed a network of support, a web of connections that spanned the globe.

The movement gained momentum, with even more meditation groups, workshops, and spiritual retreats sprouting up in cities and towns worldwide. People from all walks of life sought refuge in these spaces, craving connection and a deeper understanding of their own spiritual journeys.

Amidst the tumultuous changes, Shania, Natalia, and Marcus found solace in the knowledge that they were not alone. They were part of a collective awakening, a worldwide shift in consciousness that promised a brighter and more harmonious future.

As they embraced change and faced the unknown, they knew that their journey was far from over. There were still depths to explore, new truths to uncover, and countless lives to touch. With hearts full of determination and compassion, they set forth, ready to continue their transformative work.

CHAPTER 53

THE NEW NORMAL

As the world continued to embrace the principles of 5D consciousness, Shania, Marcus, and Natalia found themselves reflecting on the incredible journey they had undertaken. They marveled at the personal transformations they had experienced and their work's impact on countless lives. But amidst the growing acceptance, a new challenge arose in the form of corporate interest.

Major companies began expressing a desire to invest in the technologies Natalia had developed. They saw the potential in Natalia's AI and VR technology, as well as the upgraded camera Shania had fine-tuned for aura photography.

Initially, the representatives of these companies approached Natalia and Shania with seemingly noble intentions. They spoke of helping people and improving lives.

One company approached Shania and Natalia with a groundbreaking proposal. The concept revolved around an individual's aura photograph. Once this photograph was taken, the data from it would be uploaded into either glasses or contact lenses. This advancement would let the wearer detect emotional triggers in real-time while navigating their daily life.

The technology would not only recognize these triggers but also suggest effective strategies for dealing with associated emotions. It also promised to offer a higher, more insightful perspective, enabling the individual to comprehend and react appropriately to any triggering events, thereby, over time, rewiring their brain so that the situation would no longer be a trigger.

Moreover, these glasses or contact lenses would be wirelessly linked to a quantum computer located in space. This advanced computational device would have the capability to analyze the current environment of the wearer. Furthermore, it could anticipate any potential situations the person might be heading towards, providing a proactive approach to their emotional well-being.

This presentation piqued Shania and Natalia's curiosity, and they agreed to further discussions. However, when they had a meeting with the chief technology officer, chief operating officer and the CEO of this company, their intuition revealed the true nature of their plans.

Sitting across from these individuals, Shania and Natalia could sense the inauthenticity in their words. The company's initial proposals were mere veils for their underlying agenda of control. It became clear that they were under the direction of the controlling Elite, and they sought to exploit the duo's work for their own gain. Their primary objective was to acquire the innovations and use them to manipulate and control the masses, rather than fostering personal growth and empowerment.

With a firm resolve, they said no to their proposal. Shania and Natalia knew that their path was not about surrendering to the allure of financial success or power. Their purpose was to empower individuals, to guide them on their own journeys of self-discovery and transformation, leading them back to The Creator. They could not compromise on that.

Despite all of the tempting offers that were presented by various companies, they chose to continue on their own path, remaining true to their values and the principles of 5D consciousness. Shania and Natalia knew that the road ahead would be challenging, but they were prepared to face whatever obstacles came their way.

In the wake of their decision, they found solace in the unwavering support of their growing community. People from all corners of the globe rallied around their cause, recognizing the importance of maintaining the integrity of their work.

As they navigated through this uncharted territory, they persistently honed their technological tools. Shania collaborated intensively with engineers to develop supplementary aura photography cameras for the 5D facilitators, simultaneously upgrading the performance of her personal aura photography camera, a trusted companion throughout her transformative journey.

Natalia, too, collaborated with experts to further develop and fine-tune her AI and VR technology, creating immersive experiences that facilitated profound shifts in consciousness. Natalia was also working with scientists and others to address the issues she faced in court relative to Insufficient Scientific Backing, The Unregulated Tech, and the Lack of Standardization. If the time had ever presented itself, she would be ready to implement the technology back into their program.

But their focus remained on the individuals they served. The countless lives that had been transformed by embracing the principles of 5D consciousness fueled their determination. They knew that the real power lay in empowering each person to discover their own inner truth, transcend the limitations of the 3D world, and step into a higher realm of existence.

As they forged ahead, the new normal began to take shape. The principles of 5D consciousness became widely accepted, permeating various aspects of society. Schools incorporated mindfulness practices, businesses embraced conscious leadership, and communities fostered a sense of interconnectedness and compassion.

The impact of their collective efforts extended far beyond what they could have imagined. It was a testament to the power of authenticity, love, and the unwavering belief in the potential for human transformation. The ripple effect of their work spread like wildfire, igniting a global movement that would shape the course of humanity.

In the midst of these profound changes, they remained grounded in the knowledge that their journey was far from over. The road ahead would undoubtedly present new challenges and opportunities. But armed with the wisdom gained from their experiences, their guidance from The Creator, the support of their community, and the unyielding belief in the power of human consciousness, they were ready to navigate whatever lay ahead.

Together, they would continue to inspire and guide others on their own paths of awakening, fostering a world where love, compassion, and connection flourished. The new normal was not just a destination; it was a constant state of evolution, a journey of personal growth and collective transformation.

As they embraced the winds of change, they knew that the real power resided within each individual, waiting to be unlocked and shared with the world. Shania and Natalia were merely facilitators and guides on this magnificent journey toward a brighter, more enlightened future.

CHAPTER 54

EVOLVING PERCEPTIONS

As Marcus reflected on the incredible journey he had embarked on, he couldn't help but marvel at the evolution he had undergone. From his initial skepticism to becoming an ally of Shania and Natalia, the transformation in his own consciousness had been profound.

He thought back to the early days when doubt and skepticism clouded his perception. But through his encounters with Shania and Natalia, the experiences he witnessed, and the knowledge he gained, his perception began to shift. The boundaries of his belief systems expanded, allowing him to embrace the possibility of a higher consciousness. It was a journey that challenged him intellectually and emotionally.

At this moment, Marcus found himself marveling at the extraordinary transformation unfolding around him, a remarkable shift in which he had a significant role. People from all walks of life were awakening to their true potential, shedding the limitations of the 3D world and embracing a higher state of being. It was a grand Global unfolding of transformation, with people transitioning to 5D consciousness.

But amidst the grandeur of this global shift, Marcus found himself drawn back to Shania, her presence lingering in his thoughts. It was more than just her physical beauty that captivated him. It was the depth of her being, her unwavering commitment to the path of transformation, and the radiant light that emanated from within.

A smile tugged at the corners of his lips as he recalled their journey together. They had shared moments of doubt, triumph, and everything in between. Their connection, unexpected and yet undeniably profound, had deepened as they walked various aspects of their path of transformation side by side.

Whenever his thoughts returned to Shania, Marcus couldn't help but be enchanted by her presence. She possessed a rare beauty that radiated from within. Her deeply bronzed caramel skin glowed with a permanent sun-kissed hue, complementing her hazel eyes with hints of green that sparkled with depth and wisdom. Her dark, curly hair cascaded in wild waves, echoing the untamed spirit within her. Her curvaceous body carried a magnetic allure, a testament to her femininity and the power and grace she embodied.

In the quiet moments of reflection, Marcus couldn't help but feel a sense of awe and wonder at the beauty that had unfolded in their shared journey.

As the chapters of their lives continued to unfold, Marcus knew that their paths were intertwined in ways he could not fully comprehend. There was a magnetic pull, a shared purpose that connected them on a level beyond the physical.

As he continued to evolve, Marcus understood that the path of transformation was not just about personal growth but also about cultivating deep connections with others. It was through these connections that the ripple effects of change spread, creating a tapestry of collective transformation that reverberated throughout the world.

In this moment of reflection, Marcus acknowledged the beauty that surrounded him, both in the external world and within the depths of his own being. The journey had taught him to see beyond the surface, to appreciate the intricate facets of existence and the profound connections that weave us all together.

So, with a renewed sense of purpose and gratitude, Marcus embraced the next phase of his journey. The world was evolving, perceptions were shifting, and he was honored to be a part of this beautiful tapestry of consciousness that was unfolding before his very eyes.

CHAPTER 55

A GUIDING LIGHT

As Shania reflected on her journey, she marveled at the profound acceptance of her spiritual mission. What had once been a calling cloaked in uncertainty had now become a guiding light that illuminated her path. She had embraced her role in facilitating the transition from 3D to 5D consciousness, and the impact of her work with Natalia and Marcus has reverberated across the globe.

The blooming of global 5D consciousness societies filled Shania with a sense of awe and gratitude. She witnessed the transformative power of awakened souls as they reclaimed their inherent divinity and connected with the universal flow of energy. People from all corners of the world were coming together, sharing their experiences, and supporting one another on this journey of expansion and awakening.

In a harmonious twist of fate, Natalia found her divine mate on the path of 5D consciousness during their journeys. Shania couldn't contain her joy for her friend. His supportive and resonant energy beautifully intertwined with Natalia's work, adding a layer of shared purpose to their bond.

A myriad of improvements were unfolding, bringing positive transformations. The societal shift was palpable, as old paradigms crumbled under the weight of newfound awareness. Institutions and systems that once thrived on control and separation were being challenged by the collective consciousness. Love, compassion, and unity emerged as the guiding principles, weaving a tapestry of interconnectedness that transcended borders and cultural divides.

But as her thoughts drifted to the incredible impact their work was having on the world, Shania found herself smiling at the memory of her journey with Marcus. There was something about Marcus that resonated with Shania on a profound level. Beyond his handsome appearance, she knew a sense of kinship in their connection. Whenever they were together, she felt at ease, as if their souls recognized each other from another time and place.

She admired the way Marcus communicated with her, always listening attentively and offering insightful perspectives. His authenticity touched her soul, and she cherished the moments they shared, delving into deep conversations about the mysteries of the universe and the interplay between science and spirituality.

Actually, the moment Shania met Marcus, there was an undeniable familiarity as she peered into his eyes. She knew that they shared numerous lifetimes together, brimming with love and connection. This intuitive understanding told her that Marcus, once again, had entered her life to accompany her on this unique journey, and it was only a matter of time before their paths intertwined fully.

However, before their souls could fully align, Marcus needed to evolve, raising his vibration to match hers. He had to experience an awakening, recognizing not just his identity but also understanding Shania's true essence. This awakening was not purely external; his commitment to research was driven by the stirrings of his Higher Self, pushing him towards ascension and enlightenment.

Deep within, Marcus felt an inkling that he was more than his present self, more than the confines of his known identity. His research was indeed a quest of self-discovery, an inward journey. It wasn't just about the transition from 3D to 5D consciousness, but a pursuit of profound self-understanding. Marcus was searching for answers within himself, yearning to unravel his own essence.

Empowered by her empathic gifts, Shania knew that she and Marcus were destined, once again, to become one, journeying together while guiding others in their transition to 5D consciousness.

But for now, Shania focused on the present moment, on the incredible shifts unfolding around them. The global awakening to 5D consciousness was a testament to the power of human potential and the infinite capacity for growth and transformation. She was grateful to be part of this pivotal time in history, where individuals were reclaiming their sovereignty and stepping into their true essence.

With each unfolding moment, Shania, deepening her conscious evolution, harmonized with her true essence and seamlessly integrated with Serena, her Higher Self. The distinctive whispers that had once guided her transitioned into a serene sense of knowing. Shania had achieved unity with Serena, hence embodying the most elevated and authentic version of herself.

So, as the guiding light of Shania's journey continued to shine, she held onto the knowing that the best was yet to come. The evolution of consciousness was an ever-unfolding process, and she and her companions stood at the forefront, ready to embrace whatever lay ahead.

With a renewed sense of purpose and a heart filled with love, Shania allowed herself to be carried forward by the waves of change. The world was awakening, perceptions were shifting, and together with Marcus and Natalia, she would continue to be a catalyst for transformation, igniting the flame of 5D consciousness and lighting the path for all those who were ready to embrace a new way of being.

APPENDIX

COMPANION GUIDE TO UNDERSTANDING 5TH-DIMENSIONAL CONSCIOUSNESS: A DEEP DIVE INTO "VIBRATIONAL SHIFT"

Welcome to this enriching companion guide tailored to enhance your journey through the realms of 5th-dimensional consciousness. As you've delved into the narrative of "Vibrational Shift," you've undoubtedly been introduced to the enthralling spiritual evolution of Shania and Natalia. Their experiences and the world they navigate provide readers with a glimpse into the transformative power of shifting consciousness, but there's so much more beneath the surface.

This guide aims to take you a step further by unpacking the profound concepts presented in "Vibrational Shift," providing a clearer, deeper, and more comprehensive understanding of 5th-dimensional consciousness. Through a combination of in-depth explanations, reflective takeaways, and supplementary content, this companion will bridge the gap between the story's narrative and real-world applications, making the profound wisdom of higher-dimensional consciousness accessible and practical for all.

Equally important, some of Shania and Natalia's experiences noted in this guide were "behind the scenes" of the pages in this novel so you will not find them in the story. But trust me, they did take place.

Whether you're a spiritual seeker, a curious reader, or someone eager to fully grasp the teachings nestled within the story of Shania and Natalia, this guide will serve as your beacon, illuminating the nuances and intricacies of 5th-dimensional consciousness. By the journey's end, you'll not only have a richer understanding of the "Vibrational Shift" narrative, but you'll also be equipped with tools and insights to foster your own spiritual evolution. Let's embark on this enlightening journey together!

A Journey Through Consciousness: From 3D to 5D

Understanding the Dimensions of Consciousness

As Shania and Natalia embarked on their journey through "Vibrational Shift", they navigated the complexities of 3D and 5D consciousness. Their experiences highlighted that in the realm of the spirit, 'dimensions' aren't alternate realities or parallel universes but distinct frequencies and energy patterns. Much like Marcus' evolving perceptions, each dimension has its own set of unique laws and principles, appearing different based on one's consciousness level. Think of dimensions as different radio frequencies: even though they coexist, you can only tune into one at a time.

3RD DIMENSIONAL CONSCIOUSNESS: A DIVE INTO THE PHYSICAL REALM

Characteristics

As Shania and Natalia navigated the intricate tapestry of their shared journey in "Vibrational Shift", they, as well as others grappled with the nuances of 3rd Dimensional Consciousness:

* **_Tangibility and Physicality_**: For the individuals that Shania and Natalia were assisting, much of their focus was on the material world. They focused on what was tangible and physical. Hence, those individuals lived their life with most of their focus on those things that they could see, touch, hear, taste and smell. In contrast, the individuals who attended the retreat were able to have experiences beyond what was tangible and physical. They had profound spiritual experiences that were life changing.

* **_Linear Time Perception_**: Throughout Shania and Natalia's journey, the duo often experienced time in a conventional sense, unfolding as past, present, and future in a linear sequence. However, when they and the participants began their upward journey to the top of the Enchanted Mountain, "time appeared to halt its march as they ascended." Their perception of time was no longer linear.

* **_Separation_**: In Shania's early years, she confronted moments where her profound sense of individuality and feeling misunderstood, created rifts, ushering in spells of solitude and isolation.

* **_Reactivity_**: The uncomfortable emotions that ebbed and flowed throughout society during the trial, were from believers

373

who clashed in a battle of ideologies. Each side fiercely defended their stance. They were *reacting and not responding* to what was occurring. This whirlwind of societal turmoil highlighted the reactive nature of their 3rd-dimensional experiences.

Constraints

* **_Limited Perspective_**: On their journey, Shania and Natalia met individuals trapped in a narrow viewpoint, unable to see beyond the boundaries of their own lives. Their mission was to broaden these horizons.

* **_Ego-driven Decisions_**: As they delved deeper, Shania and Natalia noticed a pattern - many were making choices based on ego, which fostered competition and prejudice, distancing them from their true selves and others.

Dualities

* **_Good vs. Bad_**: Shania and Natalia found that a common struggle among the ones they helped was this binary perception. People often trapped themselves in boxes, labeling experiences without truly seeking to understand them on a deeper level.

* **_Us vs. Them_**: In their quest to uplift, Shania and Natalia observed that emphasizing differences rather than embracing similarities was a recurring challenge, leading to unnecessary rifts and clashes.

Reflection Points for 3rd Dimensional Consciousness

1. **_Physical Reality Focus_:** As Shania and Natalia journeyed, they encountered many who based their entire understanding of existence on the tangible world. Do you, like them, prioritize only what you can see or touch, dismissing what lies beyond the physical realm?

2. **_Duality and Contrast_:** Throughout their adventures, Shania and Natalia observed people struggling with dichotomous thinking. Do you too find yourself trapped in a mindset of right/wrong or black/white, unable to see the interconnectedness of all?

3. **_Material Pursuits_:** Shania and Natalia met individuals whose happiness was linked to their material acquisitions. Do you measure your life's value by materialistic standards, like possessions or wealth?

4. **_Reactionary Living_:** The duo often comforted souls who felt victimized by their circumstances. Do you feel that life is something happening *to* you, rather than a tapestry you weave?

5. **_Linear Time Perception_:** Time and again, Shania and Natalia encountered those bound by the past or anxious about the future. Do you too perceive time as a straight path, with the past, present, and future as distinct segments?

6. **_External Validation_:** On their path, Shania and Natalia met many seeking approval from the world to feel worthy. Is your self-esteem also rooted in external recognition rather than inner acknowledgment?

7. **_Separateness_:** One of the most poignant observations for Shania and Natalia was the isolation many felt. Do you see yourself as separate from the cosmos, feeling alone in your journey, instead of part of a grander design?

UNDERSTANDING 4TH-DIMENSIONAL CONSCIOUSNESS: A REFLECTIVE GUIDE

As Shania and Natalia guided souls through their journeys, they often encountered individuals teetering on the brink of 4th-dimensional consciousness. This state served as a transformative bridge for many, leading them from the well-defined world of 3D towards the boundless realm of the 5th dimension. Throughout their endeavors, the duo realized that this corridor of awakening was instrumental in the evolution of many souls. So, if you ever feel like you're navigating between two realms, understanding, and reflecting on 4D consciousness can help pinpoint where you stand.

Purpose of 4D Consciousness

In their compassionate endeavors, Shania and Natalia frequently encountered souls in the midst of their 4th-dimensional transitions. The essence of this dimension, they observed, was transformational. Here, individuals started the process of shedding the rigid beliefs of the 3D world and began embracing the limitless vistas of the upcoming 5th dimension. Through Shania and Natalia's guidance, many recognized that they were no longer strictly tethered to a solely physical reality and dualistic thinking. Instead, they embarked on a journey of realizing the profound interconnectedness of all, began to perceive time beyond mere linearity, and started to tap into the boundless spiritual potential within themselves. Shania and Natalia were beacons of light, teaching individuals that the primary role of the 4th dimension is transitional. While 3D consciousness is anchored in physical reality and duality, 4D starts the process of understanding interconnectedness, realizing that time isn't just linear, and recognizing the vastness of one's own spiritual potential. *Some experiences presented are "behind the scenes" occurrences (not in the book) that Shania and Natalia encountered.

Characteristics of 4D Consciousness

1. **_Fluid Time Perception_**: Shania and Natalia observed many starting to view time as non-linear. They met individuals who shared experiences where the past, present, and future seemed to intertwine, offering profound insights.

2. **_Heightened Intuition_**: As they assisted, they noticed a surge in intuitive abilities among those they helped. Many reported heightened gut feelings, vivid dreams, and startlingly accurate premonitions.

3. **_Interconnectedness_**: The duo often heard tales of increasing synchronicities. The individuals they aided began recognizing the profound unity with all of existence, seeing patterns and connections in previously overlooked places.

4. **_Quest for Truth_**: Shania and Natalia provided resources and guidance to those hungry for universal truths. They saw an upswing in individuals voraciously diving into spiritual texts, spiritual practices, and introspective research.

5. **_Emotional Fluctuations_**: They comforted and supported many who faced rapid emotional changes—moments of ecstatic joy and profound clarity were often followed by intervals of doubt and introspective confusion.

Challenges of 4D Consciousness

1. **_Feeling 'Stuck'_**: Shania and Natalia met many who expressed feeling trapped between two worlds—the comfort and familiarity of the 3D realm and the vast, mysterious expanses of 5D. They worked to help these souls find balance and purpose amidst this uncertainty.

2. **_Increased Sensitivity_**: The duo frequently comforted individuals who, with their sharpening intuition, became more susceptible to the energies and emotions of those around them. These heightened sensitivities, while enlightening, often led to feelings of overwhelm.

3. **_Navigating Dreams_**: In their guidance sessions, Shania and Natalia would sometimes interpret profound, lucid dreams that their proteges experienced. These dreams, while offering insights, sometimes left the dreamer feeling unsettled, seeking clarity.

4. **_Letting Go_**: One of the most heart-wrenching tasks the pair undertook was assisting individuals in the process of shedding. As these individuals evolved, they often had to release deeply ingrained beliefs, habits, and occasionally, relationships that were no longer aligned with their higher purpose.

Reflection Points of 4th Dimensional Consciousness

- Before or after reading about Shania and Natalia's journey, have you felt moments where the past collides with the present, as if time is blurring?

- Before or after embarking on this journey with Shania and Natalia, have your dreams grown more lucid, or intuitions about events intensified?

- In line with the lessons from our duo, are you sensing a deeper connection with the environment, animals, or newfound acquaintances, or experiencing heightened empathy?

- Are you driven by a newfound curiosity to explore spiritual or metaphysical topics?

If you've found yourself nodding to these reflections, it's likely you're navigating the rich and transformative landscape of 4th-dimensional consciousness. Embrace the journey, as it's a significant steppingstone to the expansive universe of 5th-dimensional awareness.

UNVEILING THE 5TH DIMENSION: A REALM BEYOND THE PHYSICAL

Characteristics

 * **_Expansiveness_**: Through Shania and Natalia's guidance, many began to feel their individual boundaries fading, sensing a connection to everything and everyone.

 * **_Now-Moment Awareness_**: Embracing Shania and Natalia's teachings, individuals started perceiving time differently, with an emphasis on living in the 'now.'

 * **_Unity_**: With their help, a palpable feeling of unity and a deep bond with every living being emerged among those they assisted.

* ***Intuition Over Logic***: Guided by Shania and Natalia, many transitioned from over-analyzing to trusting their intuitive instincts in making decisions. Their decision-making came from a place of intuition and inner guidance rather than overthinking or external influence.

Understanding its Nature

* ***Beyond Physical Constraints***: With Shania and Natalia's insights, individuals began realizing that while they inhabited physical forms, they could sense energies, vibrations, and even realms beyond their usual experience.

* ***Heart-Centered Living***: Under Shania and Natalia's guidance, many shifted their decision-making, centering it on love, compassion, and a sense of unity instead of being driven by fear or feelings of separation.

* ***Manifestation***: As they journeyed with Shania and Natalia, individuals discovered that their thoughts and intentions began to materialize more swiftly, emphasizing the importance of a positive outlook and clear intentions.

Reflection Points for 5th Dimensional Consciousness

1. **Universal Connection:** Guided by Shania and Natalia's teachings, ask yourself: Do I sense an intricate bond with everything, feeling as if all life participates in a grand cosmic dance?

2. **Transcendence of Time:** In line with Shania and Natalia insights, do you see time as pliable, with instances where everything seems to unfold in an unending present?

3. **Intuitive Living:** Reflecting on Shania and Natalia's guidance, do you lean more towards decisions stemming from an inner knowing or intuition, even if it defies logic or reason?

4. **Heart-Centered Awareness:** Thinking of the lessons from Shania and Natalia, do you navigate life with a heart brimming with love, empathy, and discernment, especially during trials? Is your approach to life and others primarily rooted in love, compassion, and understanding, even in challenging situations?

5. **Abundance Mindset:** Inspired by Shania and Natalia's perspective, have you begun to view the universe as generous, holding a conviction that it provides plentifully and trusting that your needs will always be met?

6. **_Seeing Beyond Dualities_:** From the tales and lessons of Shania and Natalia, can you now embrace the harmony in opposites, seeing the ties that bind contrasting elements?

7. **_Co-creation with the Universe_:** Reflecting on Shania and Natalia's shared wisdom, do you feel that you're actively co-creating your reality with the universe, understanding that your thoughts, feelings, and intentions play a significant role in your experiences?

8. **_Cosmic Perspective_:** Recalling the broader vision Shania and Natalia introduced, can you often gaze upon situations from a vantage point, discerning the vast cosmic narrative and your chapter within, and spotting the deeper lessons or chances for growth in obstacles?

If you've resonated with several of the reflection points in any of these sections, it can offer insight into where you currently resonate in terms of your consciousness. This information can help you gain a clearer perspective on your personal spiritual journey, better recognizing where you currently resonate and where you aspire to be. Remember, transitioning between dimensions of consciousness is a fluid process, and it's perfectly natural to exhibit characteristics of multiple dimensions simultaneously. Your understanding serves as the foundation for further exploration into the world of 5th-dimensional consciousness, as depicted in the profound narratives of "Vibrational Shift."

NAVIGATING THE TRANSITION: BRIDGING 3D TO 5D

Understanding the Shift

Shania and Natalia's shared path illustrated beautifully that the voyage from 3D to 5D isn't a sudden change but a gradual elevation of awareness, vision, and realization. Guided by their wisdom, many came to understand the intermediary realm of the 4th Dimension (4D) as a foundational 'bridge' connecting these vast states of awareness. As they traveled this bridge, led by Shania and Natalia, many began to re-evaluate entrenched beliefs, confront the confines of the ego, and see the woven tapestry connecting all living beings.

Signposts of Transition

- **Awakening Intuition**: Alongside Shania and Natalia's mentorship, many discovered an emergent awareness, where one starts to sense things beyond the five physical senses.

- **_Increased Synchronicities_**: With Shania and Natalia's insights, individuals began discerning profound coincidences and sequences in their existence.

- **_Time Fluidity_**: In moments with Shania and Natalia, many expressed sensing time's ebb and flow, feeling it accelerate or stretch.

- **_Desire for Purpose_**: Under Shania and Natalia's gentle guidance, a strong pull emerged within many to decipher their grander role or mission in the vast dance of life.

Challenges in the Transition

Transitioning from a 3D to a 5D state is not without its challenges. As your frequency begins to rise, you may experience:

- **Physical Symptoms**: Which could include energy surges, fatigue, or unexpected aches.

- **Emotional Fluctuations**: This could include intense feelings, with episodes of sadness or elation that is unexplained.

- **Shifting Relationships**: As one grows, they might begin to feel distanced from those who are not on a similar spiritual path. This could lead to changes in friendships or family dynamics.

Guidance for the Journey

Shania's empathic abilities and Natalia's deep understanding of consciousness, as showcased in the story, act as lighthouses for those navigating these transformative waters. Their narratives, challenges, and triumphs provide:

- **_Validation_**: Assuring readers they're not alone in their experiences or feelings.

- **_Tools and Techniques_**: Offering meditation practices, energy-clearing methods, and mindfulness techniques to aid the journey.

- **_Perspective_**: Highlighting the beauty and purpose behind every challenge, reframing them as growth opportunities.

The Horizon: Embracing 5D Living

In their shared mission, Shania and Natalia envisioned guiding others towards a global transformation. As one progresses under their gentle guidance, the 5D state evolves beyond mere comprehension; it manifests as a lifestyle. In this world, love directs actions, unity triumphs over division, and the heart's wisdom takes precedence over the mind's distractions. Through Shania and Natalia's teachings, while the world remains constant, the way individuals perceive and engage with it undergoes a profound metamorphosis.

By walking alongside Shania and Natalia through their journeys in "Vibrational Shift", you not only gain a theoretical understanding of these dimensions but also practical insights, encouragement, and inspiration to embark on and embrace your unique path toward higher consciousness.

SIGNS OF 5TH-DIMENSIONAL CONSCIOUSNESS AWAKENING

Under the guidance of Shania and Natalia's insightful teachings, many began to comprehend the nuances of their transformation. As individuals transition to 5th-dimensional consciousness, the vibrational shift manifests in various physical, emotional, and spiritual ways. With the tools and knowledge provided by Shania and Natalia, recognizing these signs are instrumental in understanding one's progress on this profound journey of awakening.

Physical Signs

1. **_Energetic Sensitivity_**: An increased sensitivity to the energy of places, people, and even objects. Shania and Natalia emphasized how certain environments or individuals can either invigorate or drain one's energy.

2. **_Changes in Sleep Patterns_**: Experiencing interrupted sleep, vivid dreams, or waking up frequently during spiritual hours, especially between 3 to 5 AM. Shania and Natalia often discussed the significance of these spiritual hours in their teachings.

3. **_Alterations in Diet and Appetite_**: A shift towards intuitive eating, with natural inclinations towards more plant-based, organic foods and reduced cravings for processed or dense foods. In their sessions, both Shania and Natalia highlighted the connection between diet and vibrational frequency.

4. **_Sensory Enhancement_**: Heightened senses, particularly in terms of seeing auras or light frequencies, hearing beyond the usual range, or experiencing intensified touch, taste, and smell. Natalia and Shania offered exercises to harness and refine these enhanced perceptions.

5. **Physical Detoxification Symptoms**: This can include headaches, body aches, skin eruptions, or digestive issues as the body releases old energies and adapts to new frequencies. They assured many that these symptoms are temporary and are a part of the adjustment process.

6. **Increased Vitality**: At times, there might be bursts of energy, making you feel rejuvenated and younger. Through their teachings, Shania and Natalia helped others harness this newfound vitality.

7. **Sensations of Ascension**: Moments where you feel as if you're floating, buzzing, or vibrating at a different frequency. They emphasized the importance of grounding during these sensations in their workshops.

8. **Eye Changes**: An increase in light sensitivity, seeing brighter colors, or perceiving new shades. Natalia and Shania highlighted the beauty of these visual transitions in their guidance.

9. **Altered Heartbeat**: Occasional rapid heartbeats or palpitations as the heart chakra expands and adjusts. They often reminded individuals that this is a sign of the heart's alignment with higher frequencies.

Emotional Signs

1. **_Deep Empathy_**: Have you been feeling an overwhelming connection to others, often sensing their emotions as if they were your own? Shania and Natalia often mentioned how this heightened empathy is a beacon of higher consciousness.

2. **_Inner Peace_**: Do you find a consistent sense of serenity and calm within you, even when the world around seems chaotic? They believed that such inner tranquility is a signature of ascending souls.

3. **_Desire for Authenticity_**: Are you feeling a push towards genuine self-expression and an aversion to anything that feels inauthentic or superficial? Shania and Natalia encouraged embracing this authenticity as a true reflection of the soul.

4. **_Sense of Oneness_**: Have you started to feel deeply connected to everything and everyone, truly understanding the interconnected tapestry of existence? In their teachings, they spoke of this as a realization of universal unity.

5. **_Letting Go_**: Do you find it becoming easier to release old grudges, past traumas, and negative emotions? Natalia and Shania

highlighted the power of forgiveness and understanding on this journey.

6. **_Deep Inner Reflection_**: Is there a strong pull within you to understand yourself better, leading you towards practices of self-discovery and self-improvement? They believed that this internal quest was vital for spiritual elevation.

7. **_Joyful Moments_**: Have you experienced unexpected and profound moments of joy and euphoria without any apparent cause? They spoke of these spontaneous bursts of joy as touchpoints of the soul's evolution.

8. **_Shift in Relationships_**: Do you find yourself gravitating towards more meaningful, soulful relationships and distancing from those that no longer resonate? Shania and Natalia emphasized the importance of nurturing relationships that aid spiritual growth.

9. **_Desire for Solitude_**: Do you often feel the need for personal space and time to introspect, away from daily distractions? In their sessions, they discussed the sacredness of solitude in enhancing one's connection to the self.

10. **_Expanding Compassion_**: Have you felt an overwhelming sense of compassion not just for close ones, but even strangers or those you once saw as adversaries? They often highlighted this boundless compassion as a signpost of true spiritual ascension.

Spiritual Signs

1. **_Intuitive Amplification_**: Have you been trusting your intuition more and receiving clearer guidance? Shania and Natalia always emphasized the significance of honing this inner voice.

2. **_Time Perception Shift_**: Do you feel that time is blurring, where past, present, and future seem interconnected? Natalia often spoke of this as a marker of advancing consciousness.

3. **_Cosmic Awareness_**: Are you feeling a heightened interest in the cosmos and your place within it? Shania shared insights into how this cosmic curiosity aligns with 5D consciousness.

4. **_Meditative Depth_**: Do you find yourself diving deeper into meditation and receiving profound insights more quickly? They both believed that such depths offer glimpses into the soul's journey.

5. **_Encounters with Higher Beings_**: Have you had visions or sensations of high-frequency beings, like angels or spirit guides? Shania and Natalia taught that these encounters are affirmations of spiritual alignment.

6. **_Recognition of Life's Synchronicities_**: Are you noticing patterns or 'coincidences' that seem more than mere chance? Natalia often shared how these moments are signs of divine orchestration.

7. **_Heightened Creativity_**: Is there an overwhelming urge within you to create and express? Shania always highlighted that such creativity often stems from higher-dimensional inspirations.

8. **_Dream Lucidity_**: Have you been experiencing lucid dreams and gaining insights from them? Natalia often discussed the profound messages these dreams can convey.

9. **_Attraction to Crystals and Sacred Geometry_**: Do you feel drawn to the energy of crystals and sacred shapes? Shania taught about the vibrational resonance these elements hold.

10. **_Telepathic Abilities_**: Have you sensed a rise in unspoken communication, especially with close ones or spiritual guides? They both believed this to be a testament to evolving consciousness.

11. **_Enhanced Manifestation_**: Are you realizing that your intentions manifest quicker in reality? Shania and Natalia often taught the power of focused intent in the 5D realm.

12. **_Past Life Recollections_**: Have you had glimpses or dreams providing insights into past lives? Natalia emphasized how these memories offer lessons for our current journey.

13. **_Chakra Sensitivity_**: Do you have a heightened awareness of your chakras, sensing their activation during specific moments? Both Shania and Natalia imparted techniques to tune into and harmonize these energy centers.

Recognizing these signs in oneself can be both exhilarating and overwhelming. As showcased in the journey of Shania and Natalia, the emergence of 5D consciousness, while transformative, requires understanding, patience, and self-care. Embracing these symptoms as confirmations of one's spiritual evolution can provide reassurance and guidance as one continues this path of heightened awareness.

Additional Symptoms

1. **_Mental Expansion_**: Have you been feeling an insatiable thirst for knowledge, particularly about spirituality and the universe?

Shania often spoke of this as the soul's yearning for true understanding.

2. **Shift in Priorities**: Do you find that material desires are becoming less important compared to your spiritual and emotional well-being? Natalia highlighted how this shift is a natural progression in the 5D journey.

3. **Feeling 'Out of Place'**: Have you ever felt a deep sensation of not quite belonging here or a longing for a celestial 'home'? Shania and Natalia taught that this is a common sentiment for souls awakening to their cosmic origins.

4. **Auditory Shifts**: Are you sometimes hearing high-pitched tones, frequencies or ethereal music that seems out of place? Natalia described these as signals of alignment or communication with higher vibrational realms.

5. **Unified Consciousness**: Do you sense that your individual consciousness is interwoven with a grander, universal consciousness? Both Shania and Natalia emphasized the importance of recognizing and embracing this unity.

Everyone's journey is unique, and while these signs are common, one might experience them differently or in a varied sequence. As with Shania and Natalia's story, it's essential to approach these changes with an open heart, seeking understanding and grounding during this profound transition.

TOOLS FOR NAVIGATING THE 5ᵀᴴ DIMENSION

Meditation Techniques to Connect with Higher Consciousness

1. **Guided Visualization**: Drawing from Shania's teachings, one envisions a beam of light from the cosmos descending and permeating the entire body through the crown chakra.

2. **Heart-Centered Meditation**: Natalia passionately taught about focusing on the heart's expansion with every breath, fostering a deep connection to universal love.

3. **Pineal Gland Activation**: As embraced by both Shania and Natalia, concentrating on the brain's center can awaken the 'third eye', elevating one's intuition and spiritual connection.

4. **Galactic Meditation**: Natalia often encouraged the practice of visualizing ties to distant galaxies, bringing a surge of cosmic insights and wisdom.

5. **_Merkaba Activation_**: Envisioning a spinning light field around oneself, as Shania often illustrated, allows for profound spiritual explorations.

6. **_Sacred Geometry Focus_**: With patterns like the Flower of Life, Shania and Natalia conveyed that meditation can align practitioners with the universe's intrinsic energies.

7. **_Twin Flame Meditation_**: Natalia frequently spoke about forming a bond with one's twin flame, thereby amplifying one's vibrational resonance.

8. **_Sound Healing Meditation_**: As Shania highlighted, immersing oneself in specific frequencies like binaural beats can act as a bridge to elevated consciousness.

9. **_Akashic Records Journeying_**: Guided by the shared teachings of Shania and Natalia, journeying to the Akashic library can unveil ageless wisdom and insights.

10. **_Chakra Balancing and Activation_**: Inspired by Shania and Natalia's shared wisdom, progressing from the root to the crown chakra is essential for aligning and energizing one's spiritual core.

CRYSTALS FOR TRANSITIONING TO 5TH DIMENSIONAL CONSCIOUSNESS

1. **Moldavite**: Shania and Natalia utilized this stone for its transformative properties, accelerating their spiritual evolution.

2. **Selenite**: The duo harnessed the clarity it provided, enhancing their connection to the higher self and angelic realms.

3. **Lemurian Seed Crystals**: They turned to these crystals to access the ancient wisdom and memories from Lemurian times.

4. **Lapis Lazuli**: Both cherished this stone for its capacity to bolster intuition, spiritual insight, and deepen connections to spiritual guardians.

5. **Amethyst**: Shania and Natalia revered Amethyst as a powerful protector, using it to purify and connect with divine energies.

6. **Labradorite**: This magical stone was a favorite in their toolkit, awakening their psychic abilities and illuminating their inner spirit.

7. **Herkimer Diamond**: The pair often utilized this crystal to amplify spiritual energy, promoting dream recall and astral voyages.

8. **Clear Quartz**: Known to them as the master healer, they employed it to amplify energies, intentions, and to attune to their higher selves.

9. **Kyanite**: Essential in their meditative practices, this stone aligned all chakras and aided in attuning to higher dimensions.

10. **Azeztulite**: Shania and Natalia treasured Azeztulite for its high vibrational energy, utilizing it frequently in their quests for spiritual enlightenment.

Breathing Exercises and Grounding Techniques

1. **Root Breathing**: Shania and Natalia practiced drawing energy from the Earth through their feet, grounding themselves with every exhale.

2. **Four-Seven-Eight Breathing**: The duo inhaled for 4 counts, held for 7, and exhaled for 8, using this rhythm to calm their minds and stabilize energy.

3. **Cord Cutting Breath**: By envisioning the severance of unwanted energetic ties with each exhale, they both set firm energetic boundaries.

4. **Heart-Centered Breathing**: Shania and Natalia would breathe deeply into their heart spaces, fostering feelings of love and unity.

5. **Circular Breathing**: The pair utilized this continuous breathing loop to optimize energy flow and tap into altered states of consciousness.

6. **Tree Grounding**: They visualized themselves as mighty trees, pulling nurturing energy from deep earthly roots.

7. **Solar Plexus Power Breath**: With quick inhales and exhales at the solar plexus, both women amplified their personal energy and confidence.

8. **Mountain Meditation**: Shania and Natalia steadied their energies, standing as rooted and majestic as mountains.

9. **Waterfall Cleansing Breath**: They often imagined a luminous waterfall purifying their auras with each breathing cycle.

10. **Earth Embrace**: Lying upon the Earth, they would breathe in its vital energy, feeling a profound interconnectedness and support.

This guide provides a foundation to harness the expansive energies of 5th-dimensional consciousness, aiding in a smooth and enlightening transition.

Navigating the 5th dimension requires a diverse toolkit to ensure one's energy remains balanced and grounded while also making the most of the new experiences and perspectives. Here are additional tools that can assist you in your journey:

1. **Sacred Geometry Grids**: Shania and Natalia have meditated with patterns like the Flower of Life and Metatron's Cube, feeling a tangible alignment with 5th-dimensional energies.

2. **Oracle and Tarot Cards**: Through the purposeful use of these cards, both found clarity and received affirmations from beyond this realm.

3. **Essential Oils**: With oils like frankincense and rose, the pair elevated their vibrational state, enriching their meditative sessions.

4. **Tuning Forks & Singing Bowls**: By harnessing these sound tools, Shania and Natalia recalibrated their energies, feeling more attuned to higher dimensions.

5. **Sacred Texts and Channeled Materials**: They've delved into ancient scriptures and channeled messages, gaining deeper insights into navigating the higher dimensions.

6. **Energy Healing Modalities**: Engaging in Reiki and Theta Healing, both experienced refined energy alignments suitable for 5D explorations.

7. **Guided Journeys & Hypnosis**: Through guided sessions, Shania and Natalia unearthed past memories and high wisdom, equipping them better for their spiritual journey.

8. **Sacred Sites & Vortexes**: By visiting high-energy locales, their connections to the 5th dimension intensified, resulting in profound spiritual experiences.

9. **Light Language Activation**: Shania and Natalia have encountered light language, sensing a deeper connection and evoked memories from these higher-dimensional symbols.

10. **Journaling**: Chronicling their dreams and experiences, both could chart and reflect upon their evolving spiritual journey.

11. **Spiritual Retreats**: Participating in meditation retreats, they've deepened their understanding, feeling further equipped for the dimensional transition.

12. **Energetic Protection Tools**: With tools like smoky quartz and visualization techniques, they've successfully shielded themselves from unwanted energies.

13. **Dietary Adjustments**: Adopting diets rich in high-vibrational foods, they've felt a physical boost to match their energetic shifts.

14. **Digital Detox**: Shania and Natalia have minimized their screen time, realizing a clearer energetic space conducive to 5D immersion.

15. **Nature Immersion**: Regularly immersing themselves in nature, they've fortified both their physical and energetic ties during this transformative phase.

By integrating these tools and practices into one's daily life, individuals can better navigate the nuances and vibrancy of the 5th-dimensional consciousness.

CHALLENGES OF THE TRANSITION AND OVERCOMING THEM

Obstacles When Shifting to a Higher Consciousness

1. **_Emotional Overwhelm_:** Shania and Natalia taught that the spiritual journey often surfaces intense emotions, requiring deep introspection.

2. **_Physical Symptoms_:** They highlighted that as individuals evolve spiritually, they may experience physical discomforts like headaches or fatigue.

3. **_Relationship Strains_:** As Shania and Natalia elucidated, spiritual growth can reshape relationships, leading to potential misunderstandings.

4. **_Overstimulation_:** According to their teachings, heightened sensitivity can make navigating bustling environments a test of endurance.

5. **_Doubt and Confusion_:** Both have shared that questioning the reality of spiritual experiences is common, and one shouldn't feel isolated in their uncertainty.

6. **_Fear of the Unknown_:** They've emphasized that delving into new consciousness realms can be overwhelming, but the journey is worth the challenges.

7. **_Time Disorientation_:** Shania and Natalia discussed the fluid perception of time as a notable signpost on the spiritual path.

8. **_Isolation_:** They've expressed that feeling isolated is a common challenge, as one's evolving perspective may differ from the majority.

9. **_Mental Clutter_:** The duo taught that past traumas need addressing, as they can be barriers to spiritual advancement.

10. **_Attachment_:** Holding onto the past, as they've shared, can stall one's progress in their spiritual journey.

11. **_Distractions_:** Shania and Natalia cautioned that modern distractions can deviate one from their spiritual trajectory.

12. **_Spiritual Ego_:** They've addressed the pitfall of spiritual arrogance, warning against considering oneself superior due to spiritual insights.

13. **_Misinformation_:** The two emphasized discernment in spiritual teachings, as not all information resonates with truth.

14. **_Impatience_:** They reminded their students that the spiritual journey is individualistic, and comparing progress can lead to undue frustration.

15. **_Overdependence_:** Shania and Natalia stressed the importance of having a relationship with The Creator and warned against excessive reliance on spiritual tools, gurus and other external spiritual aids that could lead to the loss of personal empowerment.

By recognizing potential obstacles and arming oneself with strategies, the journey from 3rd-dimensional to 5th-dimensional consciousness can be navigated with greater grace, understanding, and balance.

Equally important for the transition from 3D to 5D

Because we all operate, most of our day from habits (which is how our brain is programmed/wired), practicing strategies to rewire your brain will also be extremely beneficial in making the transition from 3rd-dimensional consciousness to 5th-dimensional consciousness. A good resource to assist you in this process is the book, 'I Rewired My Brain; My Journey to Freedom', and the workbook, 'I'm Rewiring My Brain; My Journey to Freedom'. It is recommended to have both the book and the workbook. They are available on Amazon.

GLOSSARY OF TERMS RELATED TO 5TH-DIMENSIONAL CONSCIOUSNESS, INCORPORATING CONCEPTS FROM THE STORY ABOUT SHANIA AND NATALIA

avigating the world of 5D consciousness and spiritual ascension can be complex. While these definitions provide a foundation, the depth and nuances of these concepts can be explored further within the narrative of Shania and Natalia's story and in teachings on 5th-dimensional consciousness. As you dive deeper, you will uncover layers of understanding and insights that resonate with your own spiritual experiences.

1. **3D Consciousness:** Through Shania and Natalia's teachings, 3D consciousness is described as a state grounded in the physical realm, marked by perceived separateness and duality.

2. **4D Consciousness:** Shania and Natalia define 4D consciousness as a bridge between 3D's tangible reality and 5D's spiritual vastness, emphasizing unity and a fluid understanding of time.

3. **5D Consciousness:** In their lessons, Shania and Natalia portray 5D consciousness as an elevated awareness that transcends limitations, recognizing the interconnectedness of all existence.

4. **Ascended Masters:** Through Shania and Natalia's teachings, Ascended Masters are understood as enlightened beings who, having walked the Earth, now provide wisdom to those ascending spiritually.

5. **Ascension:** Shania and Natalia teach that ascension is the journey of spiritual growth, transitioning from states like 3D to higher vibrational consciousness such as 5D.

6. **Aura:** In their lessons, the aura is explained as an individual's energy field, influenced by various factors; notably, Shania has a special aptitude to discern and interpret them.

7. **Awakening:** Shania and Natalia describe awakening as a profound inner realization that often sparks a transformative shift in one's consciousness.

8. **Chakras:** Through their guidance, chakras are understood as the body's energy hubs, with each relating to specific functions, and their balance being essential for spiritual progression.

9. **Clairvoyance:** Natalia and Shania teach that clairvoyance is a psychic gift, allowing a person to see beyond the tangible into spiritual realms, revealing insights across time.

10. **Cosmic Consciousness:** In Shania and Natalia's teachings, cosmic consciousness is the realization of the universe's interconnectedness, feeling a profound bond with all existence.

11. **Dimension:** Shania and Natalia describe dimensions not as places but as states of consciousness or vibrational levels.

12. **Dimensional Overlap:** Through their insights, moments or locales where various dimensional energies converge are recognized, enabling a clearer perception of the intangible.

13. **Divine Timing:** Natalia and Shania emphasize the idea that events unfold perfectly for soul development, even if not immediately apparent.

14. **Ego Death:** They teach that ego death is the transformative process of relinquishing the restrictive self-identity to embrace one's authentic spiritual essence.

15. **Empath:** Shania, as conveyed in their teachings, epitomizes an empath—someone deeply attuned to others' emotions and

energies, granting a unique perspective on emotional interconnectivity.

16. **Energy Frequency:** Shania and Natalia teach that energy frequency is the oscillation rate of energy, with heightened consciousness states like 5D aligning with superior frequencies.

17. **Enlightenment:** Through their guidance, enlightenment is depicted as the profound understanding of universal truths, bringing forth a sense of unity and serenity.

18. **Etheric Body:** In their teachings, the etheric body is a companion to the physical, capturing the essence of our emotions, intellect, and spiritual journeys.

19. **Frequency Holders:** Shania and Natalia highlight frequency holders as souls who ground high-energy vibrations to Earth, elevating its collective resonance.

20. **Global Elite:** As portrayed in their shared narrative, the global elite are those aiming to dominate the majority, often entrapping them in lower states of consciousness like 3D.

21. **Grounding:** They emphasize grounding as the harmonization of ethereal and earthly energies, especially pivotal for those delving into high-vibrational realms.

22. **Heart Chakra:** Natalia and Shania focus on the heart chakra, the fourth energy nexus symbolizing love and unity, as central in the journey toward 5D consciousness.

23. **Heart Chakra Activation:** In their wisdom, this activation signifies an energetic breakthrough, fostering boundless love and deeper bonds with fellow beings.

24. **Higher Self:** They illuminate the higher self as an enlightened facet of an individual, existing dimensionally above, offering insights and direction.

25. **Intuition:** Through their lens, intuition in 5D consciousness emerges as an innate comprehension, transcending logical thought processes.

26. **Lightworker:** Drawing from Shania and Natalia's teachings, a lightworker is a beacon, incarnated with a purpose, guiding the collective toward higher awareness and planetary healing.

27. **Manifestation:** They elucidate manifestation as the alchemy of translating thoughts and feelings into tangible reality, intensified in states like 5D consciousness.

28. **Meditation:** As they advocate, meditation is the art of inner silence, fostering communion with the inner essence and elevating one's awareness.

29. **Merkaba:** In their guidance, the merkaba is everyone's enveloping whirl of light energy, aiding in spiritual evolution and interdimensional awareness when activated.

30. **Multidimensionality:** They expound on multidimensionality as the existence of one's essence across manifold dimensions and timelines simultaneously.

31. **New Earth:** Shania and Natalia visualize the New Earth as the evolving blueprint of existence, where higher vibrational states and 5D consciousness will be prevalent.

32. **Portal Opening:** They describe portal openings as temporal or locational junctures with augmented cosmic energy influxes, optimal for spiritual endeavors.

33. **Psychic Shield:** In their wisdom, this is an energetic safeguard, defending against harmful energies or psychic disruptions.

34. **Quantum Field:** Drawing from their teachings, the quantum field is the bedrock of existence, where infinite possibilities reside, enabling powerful manifestations with intent.

35. **Quantum Leap:** They define a quantum leap as an expansive, swift transition in consciousness, analogous to the leap from 3D to 5D states.

36. **Resonance:** Drawing from Shania and Natalia's insights, resonance is the alignment of one's vibration with higher frequencies, allowing them to attune to those elevated states of consciousness.

37. **Shadow Work:** As taught by Shania and Natalia, shadow work involves confronting and integrating one's hidden or repressed aspects, fostering comprehensive healing and spiritual elevation.

38. **Soul Contract:** In their teachings, a soul contract is a pre-birth pact outlining life's lessons and experiences, directing an individual's spiritual path.

39. **Soul Tribe:** Shania and Natalia describe a soul tribe as a cluster of interconnected souls, bound by past life ties and shared objectives, whose collective presence uplifts global consciousness.

40. **Synchronicity:** As illuminated by them, synchronicity denotes purposeful coincidences that reveal the universe's intricate interconnectedness and its subtle ways of communicating.

41. **Third Eye:** Through Shania and Natalia's teachings, the third eye, or the sixth chakra, stands as a symbol of intuition, psychic prowess, and elevated wisdom.

42. **Twin Flame:** They explain twin flames as two manifestations of a single soul, whose union in a lifetime fosters profound spiritual growth and transformation.

43. **Unity Consciousness:** In their wisdom, unity consciousness epitomizes the realization and embodiment of universal oneness, characteristic of 5D awareness, promoting empathy, compassion, and collective endeavors.

44. **Vibration:** Echoing Shania and Natalia's teachings, vibration signifies the unique frequency at which all existence oscillates, reflecting one's consciousness and overall state.

45. **Vibrational Alignment:** They emphasize the act of synchronizing one's vibrational frequency with their aspirations, convictions, and higher essence.

46. **Vortex:** As described by them, vortexes are energetic Earthly zones where the interdimensional veil is thin, enhancing spiritual experiences and being ideal spots for meditative and transformative practices.

47. **Wave of Ascension:** Shania and Natalia identify waves of ascension as temporal bursts of high-frequency energies that prompt profound shifts in the collective consciousness.

48. **Zero Point Energy:** Drawing from their insights, zero point energy is the essence of limitless potential and creativity, symbolizing the very origin of all creation.

Here's a continuation of the glossary, providing even more terms and concepts related to 5th-dimensional consciousness. These additional terms and concepts offer layers of depth and wisdom. They serve as a gateway to a world of expanded awareness, inviting you to explore, question, and evolve.

49. **Akashic Records:** Shania and Natalia's teachings highlight the Akashic Records as a universal database, capturing every

experience and emotion, which can be tapped into for insights on past lives and broader cosmic knowledge.

50. **Channeling:** As expounded by Shania and Natalia, channeling involves relaying messages from higher-dimensional entities, delivering wisdom and guidance from realms beyond our own.

51. **Crystal Children:** According to their teachings, Crystal Children possess a pristine aura, representing their innate purity and serenity, and they've incarnated to guide humanity towards a harmonious future.

52. **Dark Night of the Soul:** In the context of Shania and Natalia's teachings, the Dark Night of the Soul is a profound spiritual crisis leading to deeper awakening, self-realization, and transformation.

53. **Decalcifying the Pineal Gland:** Shania and Natalia emphasize practices that awaken the third eye, notably by detoxifying the pineal gland through specific diets and meditative techniques.

54. **DNA Activation:** They teach that hidden strands within our DNA can be triggered to unveil psychic skills, profound wisdom, and innate healing potential.

55. **Downloads/Spiritual Downloads:** Shania and Natalia describe these as spontaneous influxes of wisdom from the spiritual realm, often resulting in transformative realizations or heightened guidance.

56. **Energetic Grids:** Through their teachings, these are seen as intangible webs enveloping our planet, linking power spots and encapsulating specific energies. Some are called to rejuvenate or energize these grids to bolster global ascension.

57. **Indigo/Crystal Children:** As explained by Shania and Natalia, these souls, brimming with psychic abilities and a profound mission, incarnate to uplift the collective consciousness of the world.

58. **Light Codes:** In their lessons, light codes are energetic imprints acquired during spiritual practices, awakening latent knowledge and capabilities.

59. **Orion Wars:** Shania and Natalia touch upon these as ancient cosmic confrontations, potentially shaping current spiritual dynamics on Earth.

60. **Pineal Gland:** Their teachings identify the pineal gland as a vital organ, akin to the third eye, pivotal in unlocking elevated states of consciousness.

61. **Sacred Geometry:** Drawing from their teachings, sacred geometry depicts the universe's foundational patterns, like the Flower of Life, symbolizing the cosmic design.

62. **Starseed:** As taught by Shania and Natalia, starseeds are souls hailing from far-flung cosmic locales, incarnating on Earth to expedite its spiritual evolution.

3D Earth   ## 5D Earth

Fear   LOVE

Separation   Unity

Attachment   Transcendence

Denial  Recognition

Unawareness  Awakening

Unawareness

In the context of 3D consciousness, "unawareness" refers to a lack of recognition or understanding of one's greater potential, interconnectedness, and the deeper spiritual dimensions of existence.

Characteristics of unawareness in 3D consciousness include:

1. **Limited Perspective**: Shania and Natalia taught that this is a focus solely on immediate physical experiences, often overlooking deeper truths.

2. **Reactive Living**: According to Shania and Natalia, this is a state of functioning on autopilot, responding impulsively to life's events without conscious intention.

3. **Disconnection**: Shania and Natalia described this as a mindset where one feels isolated from others and the environment, ignoring the intrinsic interconnectedness of all beings.

4. **Missed Synchronicities**: As introduced by Shania and Natalia, these are significant coincidences or patterns in life that often go unnoticed or are disregarded.

5. **Surface-level Existence**: Shania and Natalia emphasized that this pertains to a life centered predominantly on external approval and superficial achievements, neglecting profound emotional or spiritual exploration.

Unawareness in 3D consciousness is essentially about being engrossed in the immediate, tangible aspects of life without recognizing or seeking deeper understanding or connections.

Denial

In the context of 3D vs. 5D consciousness, the term "denial" in 3D consciousness refers to a resistance or unwillingness to accept, recognize, or understand deeper spiritual truths, realities, or potentials beyond the material world. This can manifest as:

1. **Material Fixation**: Shania and Natalia taught that this is an excessive reliance on the tangible world, valuing only what is directly perceivable or scientifically verifiable.

2. **Ego-Centric Thinking**: As explained by Shania and Natalia, this is an approach dominated by personal wants, anxieties, and aspirations, frequently overlooking broader insights or empathy for others.

3. **Resistance to Change**: Shania and Natalia conveyed that this involves clinging to set convictions, habits, or behaviors, even if they are detrimental or restrictive.

4. **Disconnection**: According to Shania and Natalia, this is the sensation of being isolated from others, the environment, or the cosmos, neglecting the inherent unity of everything.

5. **Spiritual Bypassing**: Shania and Natalia emphasized that this entails evading one's emotional or mental issues by superficially embracing spiritual rituals or ideologies without genuine comprehension or assimilation.

In essence, denial in 3D consciousness is about being entrenched in a more limited perspective and not recognizing or embracing the broader, interconnected, and spiritual aspects of existence.

Attachment

In the context of 3D consciousness, "attachment" refers to the clinging or holding onto people, beliefs, objects, experiences, identities, or outcomes in a manner that can inhibit growth, freedom, and a broader understanding of existence. Attachment in 3D consciousness can manifest in various ways:

1. **Material Attachment**: As Shania and Natalia highlighted, overvaluing material belongings can lead to basing one's self-worth on possessions, creating a hollow sense of fulfillment.

2. **Emotional Attachment**: Shania and Natalia pointed out the danger of persistently holding onto past experiences, as it hinders healing and personal growth.

3. **Ego Attachment**: Shania and Natalia discussed the peril of overly associating with specific roles or titles, which can cause defensiveness and limit personal evolution.

4. **Relational Attachment**: Depending excessively on others for contentment, as Shania and Natalia noted, fosters unhealthy relationships characterized by possessiveness or dependency.

5. **Outcome Attachment**: Shania and Natalia emphasized the pitfalls of obsessing over desired results, leading to disappointment and a lack of appreciation for the journey itself.

6. **Belief Attachment**: As taught by Shania and Natalia, an inflexible attachment to beliefs obstructs personal growth and curbs openness to new insights or perspectives.

Attachment, in this sense, is grounded in a perception of scarcity, fear, or the need for external validation. It contrasts with higher dimensional consciousness concepts, which emphasize detachment, fluidity, intrinsic worth, and interconnectedness.

Separation

In the context of 3D consciousness, "separation" refers to the perception and belief that individuals are distinct and isolated entities, separate from each other, nature, and the broader universe. Key aspects of separation in 3D consciousness include:

1. **Individualism**: Shania and Natalia cautioned against prioritizing personal needs to the detriment of the collective, leading to a fragmented society and reduced collaboration.

2. **Duality**: Shania and Natalia highlighted the limitations of binary thinking, emphasizing that it often oversimplifies complex situations and prevents holistic understanding.

3. **Isolation**: As Shania and Natalia observed, feeling isolated can hinder personal growth and prevent one from benefiting from the strength of community and shared experiences.

4. **Lack of Universal Connection**: Shania and Natalia stressed the significance of recognizing a connection to a grander existence, noting that its absence can lead to feelings of purposelessness and disconnection.

5. **Competitiveness**: Through their teachings, Shania and Natalia illuminated the drawbacks of a competitive mindset, indicating that it can stifle collaboration and breed unnecessary conflict.

Separation in 3D consciousness is characterized by a limited perspective that emphasizes individuality and distinction over unity and interconnectedness. It contrasts with higher dimensional consciousness, which often focuses on the inherent unity and oneness of all existence.

Fear

In the context of 3D consciousness, "fear" denotes the emotional and psychological response to perceived threats or uncertainties, rooted in survival instincts and often magnified by a limited perspective of one's place in the universe. Key facets of fear in 3D consciousness include:

1. **Survival Instinct**: Basic primal fears, Shania and Natalia explained, are rooted in the need for safety, sustenance, and security. Operating in survival mode, can lead to a perpetual state of fear and hinder personal growth.

2. **Fear of the Unknown**: Shania and Natalia taught that resisting or fearing change, new experiences, or anything unfamiliar, restricts personal exploration and can block new opportunities.

3. **Ego-based Fears**: Worries related to self-worth, social standing, and external validation, such as fear of failure, rejection, or judgment can cause a life dominated by superficial approvals and inauthenticity.

4. **Attachment-related Fears**: According to Shania and Natalia, fears of losing what one has, be it relationships, possessions, status, or health, can entrap individuals in constant worry, detaching them from the present and resisting change.

5. **Existential Fear**: Shania and Natalia asserted that anxieties about death, meaninglessness, or the nature of existence, are often due to a disconnection from broader spiritual or universal perspectives. This fear can overshadow the joy of existence, leading

individuals to neglect the profound interconnectedness and purpose of life.

In 3D consciousness, fear often dominates decision-making and perception, inhibiting growth, connection, and exploration. This contrasts with higher dimensional consciousness, where love, unity, and understanding typically diminish the grip of fear.

5D EARTH

Awakening

In the context of 5D consciousness, "awakening" denotes the initial realization or awareness of a broader, interconnected, and more profound reality beyond the limitations of the 3D physical and ego-bound world. Key aspects of awakening in 5D consciousness include:

1. **Expanded Awareness**: Recognizing the interconnectedness of all things and sensing a deeper layer of reality beyond the tangible.

2. **Dissolution of Ego**: Beginning to see beyond personal identities, roles, and ego-driven desires, realizing there's more to oneself than previously believed.

3. **Synchronicity**: Noticing meaningful coincidences and patterns in life, suggesting a harmonious universal design.

4. **Innate Oneness**: Feeling an intrinsic connection with others, nature, and the universe, diminishing feelings of isolation or separation.

5. **Seeking Deeper Truths**: An innate drive to understand higher truths, leading to explorations in spirituality, metaphysics, or other esoteric fields.

Awakening in 5D consciousness is akin to a shift in perception, where one starts to perceive and interact with the world in a more holistic, unified, and spiritually attuned manner.

Recognition

In the context of 5D consciousness, "recognition" refers to the deep acknowledgment and understanding of the truths and insights glimpsed during the initial "awakening" phase. This stage involves actively perceiving and resonating with the interconnectedness and spiritual essence of existence. Key facets of recognition in 5D consciousness include:

1. **Affirmation of Truths**: Shania and Natalia taught the importance of internalizing and validating the broader realities and spiritual insights encountered during one's awakening journey.

2. **Seeing Beyond Illusions**: Through the teachings of Shania and Natalia, individuals learn to recognize the fleeting nature of 3D constructs like materialism and societal expectations.

3. **Empathic Resonance**: Shania and Natalia emphasized the profound ability to deeply feel and understand the emotions of others, highlighting the shared essence among beings.

4. **Heightened Intuition**: Trusting in one's inner compass and insights beyond logic is a key concept taught by Shania and Natalia.

5. **Embracing Unity**: Shania and Natalia advocate for a life that mirrors the interconnectedness of everything, promoting harmonious relationships and understanding.

In 5D consciousness, "recognition" is about not just passively understanding these higher truths, but actively resonating with, embodying, and reflecting them in one's daily existence.

Transcendence

In the context of 5D consciousness, "transcendence" pertains to the active process of moving beyond or rising above the limitations, duality, and constraints of the 3D experience. This phase is characterized by profound inner transformations and elevated states of being. Key aspects of transcendence in 5D consciousness include:

1. **Overcoming Duality**: Shania and Natalia taught that moving beyond binary thinking, such as good/bad or right/wrong, allows for a more holistic perspective.

2. **Elevated States of Being**: Shania and Natalia believed in experiencing moments of bliss and heightened consciousness independent of external situations.

3. **Release of Attachments**: Shania and Natalia emphasized letting go of strong attachments to outcomes and possessions as a pathway to inner freedom.

4. **Inner Alchemy**: Shania and Natalia advocated for consciously transmuting lower energies like fear into higher states such as love.

5. **Connecting to Higher Self**: Shania and Natalia taught that by aligning with or channeling guidance from one's higher self, decisions and actions can be rooted in profound wisdom.

Transcendence in 5D consciousness is about actively navigating and rising above the challenges of the 3D world, anchoring oneself in higher vibrational states, and aligning with the soul's purpose and universal truths.

Unity

In the context of 5D consciousness, "unity" denotes the profound understanding and embodiment of the interconnectedness and oneness of all existence. It's a state where perceived boundaries between self and others, humans and nature, or the individual and the cosmos dissolve. Key aspects of unity in 5D consciousness include:

1. **Universal Oneness**: A deep realization that at the fundamental level, everything is interconnected and part of a singular, divine source.

2. **Harmonious Interactions**: Interacting with others and the environment from a place of love, compassion, and mutual respect, recognizing the shared essence.

3. **Dissolution of Separateness**: Moving beyond the ego-driven perception of "I" and "other," embracing a collective consciousness.

4. **Holistic Perspective**: Seeing the bigger picture in situations, understanding the intricate web of cause and effect, and the balance in the universe.

5. **Heart-Centered Living**: Making decisions and taking actions that are rooted in love, compassion, and the greater good, rather than individual gain.

Unity in 5D consciousness is the embodiment of holistic oneness, where individual actions and thoughts are aligned with the collective well-being, and one operates from a place of love, recognizing the divine in all.

Love

In the context of 5D consciousness, "love" represents a universal, unconditional, and boundless energy that transcends the limited, often conditional expressions of love found in 3D consciousness. In 5D, love is the foundational essence from which all creation emanates and the force that binds everything together. The Creator is love. Key aspects of love in 5D consciousness include:

1. **Unconditional Love**: A profound acceptance and appreciation for all beings and situations without judgment, conditions, or expectations.

2. **Universal Connection**: Recognizing and feeling the inherent love and divine essence in everyone and everything.

3. **Energetic Harmony**: Resonating with the high-frequency vibration of pure love, which fosters healing, balance, and well-being.

4. **Self-Love**: Understanding and embracing one's own divine nature, which in turn amplifies the capacity to love others unconditionally.

5. **Love as Creation**: Recognizing love as the primary creative force behind existence and using it to manifest and co-create with the universe.

In 5D consciousness, love is not merely an emotion but a state of being. It's an intrinsic quality of existence that one aligns with, channels, and radiates, fostering unity, understanding, and the highest potential in all interactions.

Rewiring the Brain

Rewiring the brain is a critical component in the transition from 3D to 5D consciousness. The brain serves as a mediator between our conscious experiences and our external realities. By modifying how the brain processes information, we can fundamentally alter our perception, beliefs, and experiences.

Here's why rewiring the brain is important in the context of transitioning between these states of consciousness:

1. **Neuroplasticity**: The brain's ability to form and reorganize synaptic connections, known as neuroplasticity, implies that our thought patterns, beliefs, and behaviors can be reshaped. This adaptability is crucial for moving from a 3D consciousness (rooted in duality, materialism, and ego) to a 5D consciousness (characterized by unity, spiritual understanding, and heart-centered living).

2. **Breaking Limiting Beliefs**: 3D consciousness often harbors limiting beliefs, formed due to past traumas, societal conditioning, or negative experiences. Rewiring the brain helps in replacing these limiting beliefs with expansive, positive ones that align with 5D principles.

435

3. **Emotional Regulation**: The way our brain processes emotions significantly affect our vibrational frequency. By rewiring our brain to handle emotions like fear, anger, or jealousy more healthily, we can maintain a higher vibrational state, resonant with 5D consciousness.

4. **Enhanced Mindfulness**: Rewiring facilitates greater mindfulness, allowing individuals to be more present, observant, and connected to their surroundings. This presence is vital for recognizing and embracing the interconnectedness inherent in 5D consciousness.

5. **Manifestation**: Our reality is shaped by our beliefs and thoughts. Rewiring the brain to align with 5D principles enhances our ability to manifest realities rooted in unity, love, and abundance.

6. **Deepening Spiritual Practices**: Altered brain states, such as those achieved through meditation, can facilitate profound spiritual experiences. Consistently engaging in these practices can rewire the brain, making it more attuned to higher-dimensional experiences.

7. **Intuition & Higher Guidance**: A brain attuned to 5D consciousness is more receptive to intuition and guidance from higher self or other spiritual entities. This guidance can serve as a compass during the transition process.

It's essential to understand that while rewiring the brain is a vital component of the transition, it is just one part of a multifaceted journey. The heart, soul, body, and mind all play interdependent roles in this evolutionary process. Nonetheless, given the central role of the brain in processing and mediating our experiences, its rewiring is undoubtedly of paramount importance in the shift from 3D to 5D consciousness.

*Remember this author's book on Rewiring the brain: '*I Rewired My Brain: My Journey to Freedom*'. Also, the workbook is very important: '*I'm Rewiring My Brain: My Journey to Freedom*'.

The Interdependent Roles of the Heart, Soul, Body, Mind and Rewiring the Brain when Transitioning from 3D to 5D

Transitioning from 3D to 5D consciousness is a holistic journey that encompasses various facets of our being. Each component—the heart, soul, body, mind, and the process of rewiring the brain— plays a crucial and interdependent role in this evolutionary process:

437

1. **Heart**:

   - **Role**: The heart is the center of our emotional experiences, unconditional love, and compassion.

   - **Contribution**: By activating and engaging the heart center, one can access higher frequencies of love and unity, fundamental aspects of 5D consciousness. A heart-centered approach fosters deep connections, understanding, and genuine interactions with all forms of life.

2. **Soul**:

   - **Role**: The soul carries our higher purpose, past life memories, karmic lessons, and is the eternal essence of our being.

   - **Contribution**: By aligning with the soul's wisdom and purpose, one can access a more profound understanding of existence beyond the physical realm. This alignment facilitates the shedding of ego-driven desires and the embrace of one's divine nature, aiding the transition to 5D consciousness.

3. **Body**:

  - **Role**: The physical vessel that allows us to experience the material world. It's also a conduit for energy and spiritual experiences.

  - **Contribution**: Honoring, nourishing, and maintaining the body ensures it's a conducive vessel for higher vibrational frequencies. Practices like yoga, conscious eating, and energy work help align the body with 5D principles, making it more receptive to higher-dimensional experiences.

4. **Mind**:

  - **Role**: Responsible for our thoughts, beliefs, perceptions, and cognitive processes. The mind mediates our interactions with the external world.

  - **Contribution**: Cultivating a disciplined and focused mind, free from limiting beliefs and patterns, is essential for grasping the expansive concepts of 5D consciousness. Practices like meditation, affirmations, and mindfulness can help in this alignment.

5. **Rewiring the Brain**:

  - **Role**: The brain is the central processing unit for our experiences, emotions, and perceptions. Its wiring determines how we respond to stimuli, process emotions, and form beliefs.

  - **Contribution**: By actively rewiring the brain through neuroplasticity, one can shift from 3D patterns (rooted in fear, duality, and reactivity) to 5D patterns (rooted in unity, love, and proactivity). This rewiring facilitates a more direct experience and understanding of 5D principles, making the transition smoother.

These components are deeply interwoven:

- The **mind** shapes beliefs and thoughts, which, when repeated, influence the **brain's** wiring.

- The **heart** influences the emotions and feelings we process within the **mind** and **brain**.

- The **soul** provides guidance and purpose, influencing the heart's desires and the mind's pursuits.

- The **body** serves as the vessel for all these experiences, influenced by the heart's emotions, the mind's beliefs, and the brain's wiring.

For a seamless transition to 5D consciousness, it's vital to recognize and nurture each component's role, understanding their intricate interdependence.

What is Meant by the "Heart" in the 3D to 5D Transition?

In the journey from 3D to 5D consciousness, when we refer to the "heart," we are not primarily speaking about the physical organ that pumps blood throughout the body. Instead, we are referencing the "heart center" or "heart chakra," which is an energetic and symbolic representation of love, compassion, empathy, and connection. This concept of the heart goes beyond the tangible and enters the realm of the spiritual and energetic.

Here's a detailed and clear breakdown of what is meant by the "heart" in this context:

1. **Energetic Center**:

 - In various spiritual traditions, the body is believed to have several energy centers or "chakras." The heart chakra, located in the center of the chest, is one of these main energy centers.

- It resonates with the emotions of love, compassion, and joy and is considered the bridge between the lower (more physical) chakras and the higher (more spiritual) chakras.

2. **Emotional Core**:

   - The heart is often seen as the center of our emotional experiences. When people speak of feeling "heartbroken" or having a "heart full of joy," they are referencing this emotional core, even if they're not consciously speaking in spiritual terms.

3. **Universal Love and Unity**:

   - In 5D consciousness, the heart represents the understanding and experience of universal love and interconnectedness. It's the space from which unconditional love flows, connecting us to all beings and the universe.

4. **Intuition and Inner Knowing**:

   - Many believe that the heart center is a source of intuitive wisdom, a kind of inner knowing that goes beyond logic and reason. This "heart's intuition" can guide us in our journey, especially when navigating the realms of higher consciousness.

5. **Balancing Point**:

 - The heart center is seen as the balancing point between the physical and spiritual realms. As we shift into 5D consciousness, it's the heart that often leads the way, guiding us toward unity, compassion, and understanding.

In essence, when we speak of the "heart" in the journey from 3D to 5D consciousness, we are talking about a multi-faceted concept that encompasses energetic, emotional, intuitive, and spiritual dimensions. It's a symbolic and energetic representation of the core of our being, from which love, compassion, and higher wisdom emanate.

WHICH PATH DO YOU CHOOSE?

The Choice Between 3D and 5D Consciousness: A Transformative Journey Awaits

In the boundless tapestry of human experience, each of us stands at a crossroads—a choice between remaining in the familiarity of 3rd-dimensional consciousness or embracing the expansive journey towards 5th-dimensional consciousness. While both paths have their experiences, the latter holds the promise of a life enriched with profound connection, unconditional love, and heightened awareness.

Remaining in 3D Consciousness:

Staying in 3rd-dimensional consciousness often feels like wading through a world defined by duality: right and wrong, good and evil, us and them. Here, the lens of perception is often clouded by ego-driven desires, material pursuits, and the insatiable hunger for external validation. The emotional landscape can be tumultuous, with joy, anger, sadness, and envy changing like the unpredictable weather. There's a persistent feeling of separation—a yearning for something more, something deeper. Relationships might be anchored in conditions, expectations, and transactional

444

interactions. While there's comfort in the known, this realm can sometimes feel limiting, like wearing a pair of shoes that no longer fit.

Embarking on the 5D Consciousness Journey:

Transitioning to 5th-dimensional consciousness is akin to stepping into a vast, boundless ocean, where every drop of water is connected, and the horizon stretches infinitely. This realm is characterized by unity, where the illusion of separation dissolves and all of life is interconnected. You begin to experience love—not the conditional kind, but a profound, universal love that embraces every being, every experience. The noise of the ego quiets, and in its place emerges a symphony of peace, understanding, and harmony.

Doing this inner work isn't a walk in the park—it's a transformative journey. Like a caterpillar metamorphosing into a butterfly, there might be moments of darkness, like 'The Dark Night of the Soul', uncertainty, and solitude. But remember, it's within these cocoons that the most profound transformations occur. The inner work will challenge you, push you, and sometimes even break you, but it's all in service of molding you into your most authentic, radiant self.

And as you tread this path, know that you're not walking alone. Having a relationship with The Creator—whatever that means for you, be it God, Universe, Source, or another term—is like having a guiding star in the darkest night. This divine relationship offers solace, guidance, and an ever-present reminder of your sacred purpose and the love that permeates all existence.

Why Should You Consider This Journey?

Because you deserve more than a life of fleeting pleasures and temporary solaces. You deserve to experience the boundlessness of your true nature, to feel the interconnectedness of all life, and to bask in the perpetual glow of universal love. By embracing 5D consciousness, you're not just elevating yourself; you become a beacon of light, guiding and inspiring others.

In the grand tapestry of existence, the threads of our choices weave the stories of our lives. So, consider this: do you want a narrative limited by constraints, or one that soars through boundless skies? The journey to 5D consciousness awaits. Though the path may be steeped in challenges, the view from the summit—a world radiant with love, unity, and understanding—is worth every step.

The full Companion Guide and more can be found on my website:

Drkayspeaks.com

www.ingramcontent.com/pod-product-compliance
Lightning Source LLC
Chambersburg PA
CBHW032047020426
42335CB00011B/222